TRAVELING WOMEN

SUSAN CLAIR IMBARRATO

Traveling Women

Narrative Visions of Early America

Ohio University Press   Athens

Ohio University Press, Athens, Ohio 45701
www.ohio.edu/oupress
© 2006 by Ohio University Press

Ohio University Press books are printed on acid-free paper ∞ ™

14 13 12 11 10 09 08 07 06   5 4 3 2 1

Library of Congress Cataloging-in-Publication Data

Imbarrato, Susan Clair.
  Traveling women : narrative visions of early America / Susan Clair Imbarrato.
    p. cm.
  Includes bibliographical references and index.
  ISBN-13: 978-0-8214-1674-7 (alk. paper)
  ISBN-10: 0-8214-1674-X (alk. paper)
  1. Travelers' writings, American—History and criticism. 2. American prose
literature—Women authors—History and criticism. 3. Travel writing—History—
18th century. 4. Travel writing—History—19th century. 5. Women travelers—
United States—History. 6. United States—Description and travel—History. I.
Title.
  PS366.T73I43 2006
  810.9'320922—dc22
                                    2006000708

CONTENTS

ILLUSTRATIONS

ACKNOWLEDGMENTS

Drawn into the world of early American women travelers by students' questions about the "ordinary" in the Sarah Kemble Knight *Journal*, I subsequently discovered a rich source of women's experiences that led me on an eight-year journey of my own. I am grateful to my students as well as to the *many* scholars whose meticulous archival research provided invaluable models and whose works offered inspired guides for navigating women's travel narratives.

I would like to thank the Ohio University Press for its great care and attention to detail in bringing this manuscript into print. David Sanders, the director, has been a steadfast, thoughtful supporter and an impeccable guide throughout this process. I also thank Nancy Basmajian for her generous assistance and discerning editorial eye; Beth Pratt for her skilled design assistance; and Jean Cunningham and the marketing staff for promotional assistance. I appreciate the anonymous reader's helpful comments and good suggestions. I am especially grateful to Carla Mulford for her expertise in reading my work with precision, insight, and honesty—one could not ask for a better reader.

To the many librarians, archivists, and curators who assisted in locating materials for this book and granting permissions, I extend my appreciation: Jackie Donovan, American Antiquarian Society; Julia Gardner and Judith Dartt, Chicago University Library; Barbara Austen, Ruth Blair, Judith E. Johnson, Richard C. Malley, and Susan P. Schoelwer, Connecticut Historical Society; Ronald F. Frazier, Dedham Historical Society; Constance Cooper, Historical Society of Delaware; David A. Cobb, Harvard College Map Library; Jody Bendel, Art Director, Minnesota State University Moorhead; Dianne Schmidt and Larry Schwartz and the staff at Livingston Lord Library, Minnesota State University Moorhead; Martha Briggs, Jill Gage, and John Powell, Newberry Library; Vicky Wells, University of North

Carolina Press; Elizabeth L. Plummer, Ohio Historical Society; Jennifer Betts and Meredith Paine Sorozan, Rhode Island Historical Society; Margaret Downs Hrabe, Jeanne C. Pardee, and Michael Plunkett, University of Virginia Library; and Laurie Klein and George Miles, Beinecke Rare Book and Manuscript Library, Yale University.

Regarding previously addressed materials, I thank the University of Tennessee Press for permission to adapt materials from a previous discussion of Elizabeth Ashbridge's *Some Account of the Fore Part of the Life of Elizabeth Ashbridge* and the Elizabeth House Trist correspondence with Thomas Jefferson that appeared in a different form in Susan Clair Imbarrato, *Declarations of Independency in Eighteenth-Century American Autobiography* (1998). I also thank *Women's Studies: An Interdisciplinary Journal* for permission to adapt materials in chapter 2 from "Ordinary Travel: Tavern Life and Female Accommodation in Early America and the New Republic," *Women's Studies: An Interdisciplinary Journal* 28 (1998): 29–57.

Throughout the researching and writing of this book, I have benefited greatly from the generous administrative support provided by the Minnesota State University Moorhead faculty grants that helped fund research and travel related to this project. I have also been fortunate to have the support of my good colleagues in the English Department. Special thanks go to James Bense and Marie Tarsitano for their encouragement and for the many and lively conversations.

The Society of Early Americanists (SEA) has been especially nurturing throughout my study of women travelers in early America. I appreciate having had the opportunity to deliver papers at their biennial conferences and to benefit from hearing about the work of many fine scholars. I have been inspired by their thoughtful interaction with primary sources that has given voice to the woman's perspective in early America.

I would especially like to thank and acknowledge William L. Andrews, Mary McAleer Balkun, Sargent Bush Jr., Michael P. Clark, Pattie Cowell, Elizabeth Maddox Dillon, Emory Elliott, Sharon M. Harris, Annette Kolodny, J. A. Leo Lemay, Lisa Logan, Carla Mulford, Jeffrey Richards, David S. Shields, Frank Shuffleton, Susan Stabile, Zabelle Stodola, and Edward Watts for their good humor, keen criticism, and warm collegiality that has buoyed and inspired this work over these many years. Warm and grateful thanks go to Timothy Steele for his patient and thorough explanations of matters metrical and for his kind encouragement as this work made its way to press. Joyous thanks go to Wendy Martin for her longtime support and her shared enthusiasm for women travelers.

Finally, I thank my brothers, Allen and Tony, and my father for their sustaining and unconditional support.

NOTE ON THE TEXTS

Throughout the eighteenth century and into the early nineteenth, no standardization of spelling, capitalization, and punctuation was imposed on the printed word or on handwritten journals and epistles. In transcribing these journals and letters, I worked from original manuscripts when available either in manuscript or on microfilm, and otherwise from printed copy. For these transcriptions, I have adopted the following conventions regarding abbreviations, punctuation, and spelling. The long ſ has been changed to s. Paragraph breaks have been sparingly inserted in letters in which few or none exist and are used to indicate a change of subject matter. Most but not all abbreviations have been retained, so that "Septr" stands for "September"; "tho" stands for "though"; but "affecnt" has been changed to "affectionate." The ampersand for "and" and the form "&c." for "etc." have been retained. Punctuation has been lightly imposed, with full stops, commas, and semicolons added silently. Capitalization has been slightly modified, so that sentences begin with capital letters, while capitalization for emphasis and for nouns has been retained. When the source is an original manuscript, as with Sarah Beavis, Eliza Williams Bridgham, Mary Coburn Dewees, Elizabeth Gilpin, Susan Edwards Johnson, Lucy Newton, and Maria Sophia Quincy, handwritten emphasis is indicated by underline; otherwise, when working from previously printed materials, italics have been retained to signal emphasis.

Introduction

Travelers' accounts of early America depict a dynamic, ethnically diverse society shaped by an incessant mobility. Whether eager to trade goods or to share news from a nearby town, the traveler served as an information conduit. In a time when travel twenty to fifty miles from home brought contact with distinct differences, the traveler remarked upon architecture, plants, foods, and customs that went otherwise unnoted by the local populations. With senses heightened and habits disturbed, the traveler provided a keen, eyewitness view of early American society and recorded his or her findings in great detail and often with lively characterizations. For both men and women, travel offered opportunity for adventure and advancement. Families relocated with great dreams for their future, and for single, unmarried travelers, the new towns of the West promised new legacies. Migration signaled the possibility of a better life as courageous immigrants and brave pioneers headed into the wilderness and onto the frontier with ax and gun, on horse and in covered wagon. From such images, a powerful mythology developed of the inspired traveler settling the western frontier. And while Plymouth Plantation and the Oregon Trail remain important to our cultural history, there is another story to tell, another version of migration and travel in early America. Counter to the developing mythos of the pioneer who embraced the unknown and sought the uninhabited, the genteel female traveler often faced the frontier with a certain ambivalence. For this traveler, the benefits of migration did not initially outweigh the losses, and departing from familiar social networks—family, friends, church, and community—was cause more for anxiety than for celebration. As a result, the woman's narrative honestly conveys the difficulty of exchanging what was known and comfortable for what was unknown and unfamiliar, and thus portrays travel in all its frustrating glory. Notable for the accomplishments they record and the hardships they enumerate, women marshaled their resources and exerted admirable strength. With particular attention paid to how people interacted and how regions differed, women's travel narratives are a valuable source for understanding the process by which cultural values were transferred and transformed across the new nation. Determined and adventurous, women played a key role in this culture building and were quite simply integral to the settling of early America and the New Republic.

Women's travel narratives illustrate a range of responses from conventional genteel protests over rustic conditions to a genuine engagement and curiosity about their surroundings. The women who traveled west seeking new homes pragmatically scrutinized the frontier landscape, and the women who embarked on more leisurely journeys critically evaluated the social landscape. In each case, travel was a transformative experience for both travelers and the local inhabitants with whom they came in contact. From these encounters, we learn of gender and class distinctions and witness early American culture defined primarily by change and interaction rather than by a set of static ideologies. This dynamic quality underlay each journey as women reacted to these exchanges and negotiated new terrain. Accordingly, I have organized the following discussion to include women's commentary on the physical and the social aspects of travel and to address their concerns for civility and decorum.

This study covers the years from 1700 to 1830, a period framed by travel on horseback and travel by stage, with journeys north and south along the Atlantic seaboard and west onto the Ohio frontier. From the approximately fifty extant women's travel narratives from this period, published and in manuscript, this study closely examines more than twenty-five journals representing varied geographical and social perspectives.[1] These include the well-known 1704 journey of Sarah Kemble Knight[2] from Boston to New York and the lesser-known accounts of Sarah Beavis's 1779 journey to Ohio via Kentucky; Elizabeth House Trist's 1783–84 jour-

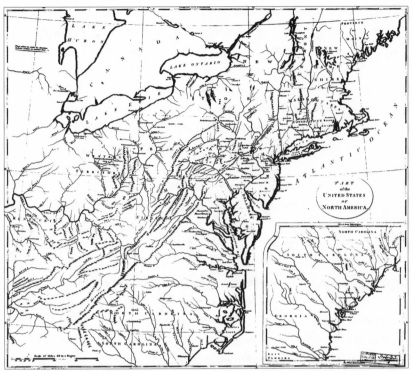

OVERVIEW MAP OF EARLY AMERICA. John Stockdale's 1798 map of the newly
formed United States makes clear the vast spaces and formidable mountainous
barriers that women faced as they traveled west onto the Ohio Frontier. John
Stockdale, *Part of the United States of North America* (London: J. Stockdale, ca. 1798).
Harvard College Library, Map Coll. (Pusey), MAP-LC, G3700 1798.S7.

ney from Philadelphia to Natchez;[3] Mary Coburn Dewees' 1788 journey
from Philadelphia to Lexington in Kentucky;[4] Susan Edwards Johnson's
1801–2 journey from New Haven, Connecticut, to Fayetteville, North
Carolina;[5] Margaret Van Horn Dwight's 1810 journey from New Haven to
Warren, Ohio;[6] Eliza Williams Bridgham's 1818 travels through New England and New York; and Elizabeth Gilpin's 1830 round-trip journey from
Wilmington, Delaware, to Johnstown, New York. By collecting these narratives into one study and drawing on primary materials so extensively,
I am making them more accessible to students, scholars, and the general
public. The detailed, energetic records of these early American women
may surprise readers unfamiliar with this literary and cultural period.
Scholars more familiar with the field will have a chance to consider a

greater sample of women's travel narratives. In each case, the traveler's tale is set within a larger, more complicated context, one that bridges the explorer's promotion of America and the pioneer's appropriation of the West. In these narratives, readers will find bravado mixed with hesitation, as these women journeyed forth—for business, relocation, and pleasure—and told compelling stories about fording rivers, riding across mountains, facing hunger, encountering Native Americans, sleeping in taverns, and confronting slavery. I examine these narratives from a New Historicist perspective that considers gender, class, ethnicity, and social and political events, while also appreciating them as historical records, personal narratives, and literary texts that elucidate the transference of custom and the construction of gender in early America.

Despite the hundred-year gap between the time of composition and the date of publication for many of these narratives—Knight written in 1704 and published in 1825; Trist written in 1783–84 and published in 1990; Dwight written in 1810 and published in 1912—keeping a travel journal was itself significant. For as women took on the chronicler's role, they challenged gender assumptions and provided role models. Had they been published for a contemporary audience, moreover, these narratives would have challenged some authors' fictional portraits of women as either passive figures or as overtly civilizing agents. Instead, these women diarists and letter writers actively confronted new situations and negotiated unfamiliar social scenarios. The delay in publication may be explained by a changing appreciation of the travel narrative for its historical value and subsequent recovery efforts. Theodore Dwight's 1825 publication of Sarah Kemble Knight's 1704 journal resulted from his desire to celebrate an "American" literature and to remind the public that "documents, even as unpretending as the following, may possess a real value, if they contain facts which will be hereafter sought for to illustrate interesting periods in our history" (qtd. in Bush, 85). Moreover, only journals of renowned figures or commissioned reports would have been printed in these women's own time. Noting these gaps between writing and publication does not diminish the value of women's texts, but marks a change in viewing the historical record, with a more recent interest in reading a more inclusive, textured, and diverse account of early America. As these narratives bear out, a woman's observations held merit, no matter the delays in publication or the limitations of her audience.

That women traveled at all is significant, for travelers were largely a male contingent in early America, as women were more closely bound to the domestic arena, raising children and managing households. From 1750 to 1800, life expectancy ranged from thirty-four to thirty-eight years, as Stephane Elise Booth explains, so that during "twenty years of married life, the number of pregnancies a woman could expect ran into double digits" (7). Two-year birth cycles did provide a few windows for travel. Laurel Thatcher Ulrich reports that pregnant women who did travel were most likely to do so during the second trimester, when it was considered safest, and that by far the most excursions were taken during an "interim" period between the tenth and fifteenth month after birth. Ulrich speculates on the potential effects of these "weaning journeys" on both mother and infant, considering them "abrupt and traumatic" or "simply the ritual termination of an already waning stage" (*Good Wives*, 140–43). In many instances, weaning journeys provided women an important chance to renew connections with relatives and friends. Though travel while pregnant may have not have been comfortable, it was possible, as Nathalie Sumter, who was seven months pregnant with her third child, explained to her friend Mrs. Heron Hooper on July 22, 1809: "12 miles from Fredericksburgh. I never was so large with my other children the day before lying in as I am now, & the jolting of the carriage has given me pains which are very troublesome. . . . I think that when I get to Washington I will get myself Bled as a precaution, my size really alarms me" (34–35). Despite her fears, Sumter arrived safely, and her pregnancy was without complications. However infrequent or difficult, travel provided a worthy challenge for women, and a woman's narrative, especially one as detailed as Sumter's, brings a distinctive perspective to travel in early America. Sumter's account lends support to what William C. Spengemann identifies as a key attribute of the eighteenth-century travel narrative: it provided "Americans the meaning of their unique historical situation" (38–39). Women thus took up this role of historian as they reported on town or tavern, filling pages about how they found them alternately entertaining and wanting.

In seeking extant women's travel narratives, moreover, one finds a scenario that is the exact opposite of Reuben Gold Thwaites's dilemma in his 1966 preface to volume 1 of his thirty-two-volume *Early Western Travels, 1748–1846*: "In planning for this series of reprints of Early Western Travels, we were confronted by an embarrassment of riches. To reissue all of the many excellent works of travel originally published during the formative period of Western settlement, would obviously be impossible. A selection had therefore to be made, both as to period and material" (11). More frequently, one identifies with Mary M. Crawford, who notes in her 1944 preface to "Mrs. Lydia B. Bacon's Journal, 1811–1812," "Practically all of the contemporary accounts of travel between the eastern seaboard and the West in the early nineteenth century were written by men. For this reason, it is interesting to find letters and a journal written by a woman at that time" (367).[7] As Crawford acknowledges, women's travel narratives offer a valuable perspective. Historians and scholars have done a great service by recovering these accounts. For doing so allows gender roles perpetuated by a literary canon once dominated by male authors to be reconsidered. Along these lines, Sharon M. Harris addresses issues of canon development and gender: "Those of us today who teach an expanded canon are familiar with the numerous and varied ways in which gender roles were inscribed in early America." Harris then underscores the importance of including early American women's writings: "But we cannot fully understand the *influence* of these structures without the inclusion of a variety of women's writings; only then will we begin to understand how women also abetted or challenged these gender inscriptions. Without women's opinions, we have only a partial picture of early America and, more dangerously, we run the risk of perpetuating our new but still partial picture as a universal one" ("Early," 225). Following this sentiment, by recovering and studying the woman's travel narratives, we see more clearly that early America was explored and settled by women, as well as by men, and that women's travel narratives warrant recognition for how they uniquely document the frontier experience and complete the historical record.

Journeying to America: Motives and Perceptions

While travel itself has long been equated with opportunity, travel to the New World promised wealth and assured heroism, as adventurers conquered nature and subdued native peoples. In 1616, for example, Capt. John Smith enticed his audience in *A Description of New England* with the possibilities of "crossing the sweet air from isle to isle, over the silent streams of a calm sea, wherein the most curious may find pleasure, profit, and content." In 1637, Thomas Morton described the bounties of New England in *New English Canaan* as "so many goodly groves of trees, dainty fine round rising hillocks, delicate fair large plains, sweet crystal fountains, and clear running streams that twine in fine meanders through the meads, making a sweet a murmuring noise." By such accounts, the New World was embellished as a fertile land, unspoiled and pure, and available for acquisition and ready for settlement. These promotional tracts, often written as official reports, became a key voice for expressing curiosity with new lands. When Meriwether Lewis explored the Missouri River on June 8, 1805, he wrote elegantly of the surrounding landscape, "a rich, fertile, and one of the most beautifully picturesque countries that I ever beheld, through the wide expanse of which innumerable herds of living animals are seen, its borders garnished with one continued garden of roses, while its lofty and open forests are the habitation of myriads of the feathered tribes who salute the air of the passing traveler with their wild and simple yet sweet and cheerful melody" (170). For the explorer, such accounts, however exaggerated or embellished, sustained interest and encouraged funding. From the military records of Zebulon Pike, who charted the Mississippi River, Louisiana, and New Spain (1805–7), we learn about advantageous fort locations, diverse tribal populations, indigenous food sources, and other matters necessary for expansion and dominance. On October 5, 1805, after passing the Crow River, he recorded: "Had hard water and ripples all day; passed by some old Sioux encampments, all fortified. . . . At this place a hard battle was fought between the Sioux and the Sauteurs in the year 1800: killed one goose; distance advanced, eleven miles" (61). With these exploratory and military objectives, travelers sought valuable resources, new trade routes, and secure military posts. Largely commissioned reports, these accounts presented a yet unsettled frontier awaiting adventure.

Sharing a common intent to transform the frontier, men and women recorded their journeys with confidence inspired by discovery. Whereas men might have been motivated by dreams of glory, women often imagined the social complexities of settlement. In this regard, Annette Kolodny compares the woman's urge to cultivate the landscape with the man's

desire to conquer it, so that "women claimed the frontiers as a potential sanctuary for an idealized domesticity" (*Land Before*, xiii). Karen R.
Lawrence agrees: "Women writers of travel have tended to mistrust the
rhetoric of mastery, conquest, and quest" (20). Brigitte Georgi-Findlay
elaborates by addressing connections between women and travel writing: "Within the discursive frameworks of westward expansion, women
were not only objects of representation and control but also participants
in the exercise of control" (17). As women sought their own relationship
to the frontier, therefore, they too altered their surroundings, both physically and socially. Less invested in aggrandizing their exploits than many
of their male counterparts, women were nonetheless resolute and adventurous. Women did not necessarily rehearse exploration narratives bent
on acquisition; instead they presented more nuanced reactions to the frontier by remarking on both the physical world and the intricacies of social interaction with an eye for custom and gender.

By contrast to travel narratives as empire-building texts, travelers interested in more pacific, scientific findings wrote about travel from a
naturalist perspective largely inspired by Carl Linné's *The System of Nature*
(1755). Mary Louise Pratt notes that the Linnaean system significantly
changed travel and travel writing with its "descriptive system designed
to classify all the plants on the earth, known and unknown, according to
the characteristics of their reproductive parts" (24). Consequently, travel
writing began to include more extensive natural descriptions. From the
pen of Harvard educated botanist François André Michaux, for example,
we read of medicinal herbs, beautiful trees, and fertile soil, as on July 4,
1802, just outside of Greensburgh, Pennsylvania: "I had an opportunity
of remarking several parts of the woods exclusively composed of white
oak, or *quercus alba*, the foliage of which being a lightish green, formed a
beautiful contrast with the trees of a deeper colour. . . . The soil of the
environs is fertile; the inhabitants, who are of German origin, cultivate
wheat, rye, and oats with great success" (153). Throughout his *Travels to
the West of the Alleghany Mountains . . . 1801–1803* (1805), Michaux provides
similarly precise descriptions, often depicting a lush landscape, with an
occasional mention of other travelers and towns. This narrative style exemplifies Pratt's observation that "travel narratives of all kinds began to
develop leisurely pauses filled with gentlemanly 'naturalizing'" that "could

form the main storyline of an entire account" (27–28). Combining description and data represented a deliberate shift toward a more didactic text, as Joyce E. Chaplin explains: "The impetus to make travel narratives into scientific writings composed in descriptive language was a reaction against earlier accounts that were quite the opposite" (72). Whereas earlier accounts insisted that travel be part of a "pilgrimage or crusade" to avoid being "unworthy" or merely an "aimless secularity," as Chaplin elaborates, New World explorers set tangible, material goals and provided specific, empirical descriptions.

In addition to the explorer and naturalist, the leisured and migrating traveler alike recorded findings and provided information on the developing social and civic infrastructures as they passed through towns and cities, traveling on regular postal and trade routes along the eastern seaboard. Generally less proprietary, these travelers often expressed curiosity and delight as they described new locales, frequently combining description with advice to show how the travel narrative can both entertain and instruct, a valued eighteenth-century attribute. Scottish traveler Janet Schaw, for one, found travel quite stimulating, as on March 22, 1775, when she visited her brother in North Carolina: "I think I have read all the descriptions that have been published of America, yet meet every moment with something I never read or heard of" (151). On June 6, 1744, Dr. Alexander Hamilton recorded this entry about Philadelphia: "Att my entering the city, I observed the regularity of the streets. . . . The State House, Assembly House, the great church in Second street, and Whitefield's church are good buildings" (189). By describing the "regularity of the streets" and the "good buildings," Hamilton gives Philadelphia an ordered, well-mannered mien. Following the Treaty of Paris (1783) and the Louisiana Purchase (1803), travelers ventured west in increasing numbers and evaluated their surroundings with an eye for development. On January 9, 1784, Elizabeth House Trist assessed Pittsburgh's locale: "The land is exceeding rich and abounds with an abundance of maple trees, from which they make quantitys of sugar. . . . There are several wild vegetables that I wou'd give the preference to those that are cultivated: Wild Asparagus, Indian hemp, shepherd sprouts, lambs quarters, &cc—besides great abundance of Ginsang, Gentian and many other aromatick" (212).[8] Similar to writers of earlier exploration literature filled with botanical descriptions, Trist indicates her increased appreciation for and familiarity with indigenous plants. As both settler and explorer, Trist evaluates the landscape for its agricultural promise and social possibilities, as when she describes standing on Grants Hill overlooking Pittsburgh and notes that "if the country which is mountanous was cleard, it wou'd be beyond description beautifull . . . and, was there good Society, I shou'd be contented to end my days in the Western country" (213). In its present state, Pittsburgh lacked a civic core, what Trist calls "Society," and so she qualifies her approval and notes her desire for social engagement. For Elizabeth Gilpin, a visit to New York drew contrasts to Philadelphia, as on September 22, 1830: "I was very much struck with noise and bustle and business like air of the streets, very different from the quietude and stillness of Philadelphia, and it appears to me much more like an European city than any place I have seen in America" (6).[9] Travelers such as Hamilton, Trist, and Gilpin thus exemplify again and again what Joyce E. Chaplin identifies as "fixed portraits," wherein the travel narrative provides "description of character and social customs" (77). In noting regional differences and offering advice, travelers engaged in a type of cultural commerce by suggesting "improvements" and pronouncing judgments as they recorded their observations of early America.

Considering this range of a traveler's motives—from the overtly imperialistic to the empathic observer—women offered yet another perspective, one that often fostered community and guided social discourse. In their role as cultural purveyors and shapers, women assessed and evaluated while modeling appropriate behaviors. So guided, they could endure rustic conditions and limited social contact. Charged with this moral imperative, women's confident proclamations mixed with moments of discomfort and uncertainty, reactions that complicated notions of a unified, orchestrated westward movement. For though economic possibility spurred them as it had previous generations who crossed the Atlantic, Elizabeth House Trist, Sarah Beavis, Margaret Van Horn Dwight, and Elizabeth Van Horne, among others, hesitated before the open spaces and sparsely populated landscape to question just how they would adapt to their new surroundings. Travel west of the Ohio River proved especially challenging, as women struggled against the particularly fluid boundaries between settlement and frontier. Annette Kolodny has in fact called for a

reformulation of the term "frontier" to mean a borderlands, "that limi-
nal landscape of changing meanings on which distinct human cultures
first encounter one another's 'otherness' and appropriate, accommodate,
or domesticate it through language" ("Letting Go," 9). For many travelers, this contact was initially disorienting, and they used the travel narrative to process their reactions in narratives entitled "A Journal of a
Trip" or "Travel Diary," wherein they wrote as much about their feelings
of displacement as their wonder for the landscape and the natural beauty
of mountains and valleys. Women thus viewed the western territories
with an idealism tempered by pragmatism. Margaret Van Horn Dwight,
for one, was clearly unimpressed when she surmised halfway along her
journey, "We have concluded the reason so few are willing to return
from the Western country, is not that the country is so good, but because
the journey is so bad" (36–37).[10] Travelers were often not fully prepared
for the physical hardships, let alone the social deprivation, yet as the
woman's travel narrative makes clear, perseverance and determination
prevailed.

Women's accounts, in turn, often reflect an anxious impatience for familiarity. Without the conventional layout of a town, distinctions blurred.
There could be no "good part of town" or "best room" without the civic
structure to reinforce hierarchy. The woman's journal, in this respect,
countered assumptions that migration guaranteed a movement toward a
better life. Stephane Elise Booth addresses similar concerns and finds that
"many women who came to the Ohio frontier complained of the isolation and the breakdown of the social network that had given them needed
support in their previous situations" (188). Rather than representing an
idealized freedom, therefore, relocation meant social restriction and intensified domestic labor. Instead of immediately embracing the frontier
for its anticipated rewards, these women resisted the conditions that
seemed to threaten their identity. Fondness for the wilds of the West developed gradually. For these earlier travelers, it was often not their first
impulse nor inclination to abandon their urban, genteel preferences. To
their credit, women's travel narratives honestly express conflicted responses of both the presumed colonizer and the reluctant pioneer. Desire to recreate a familiar world thus clashed with the realities of a wholly
new social and physical landscape.

Whether venturing north and south along the eastern seaboard or westward into the frontier, women imagined new identities within different social orders. Elizabeth Bohls, in fact, finds that travel for women can be "destabilizing in ways that generate both anxiety and, at times, exhilaration. Geographic displacement seems to loosen the grip of familiar cultural orderings just enough to let them glimpse alternatives" (17). In this regard, travelers wrote about their experiences as an act of preservation, to set their journeys on paper; and, to various degrees, they found the landscape both inspiring and cumbersome, so that compromise and adjustment were often given space equal to that of observation and speculation. Bruce Greenfield elaborates on the relationship between traveler and text: "By means of his journal, the traveler writes himself into and out of the unknown country; by means of his narrative, he makes his journey a significant event" (19). Travel narratives thus help travelers place their experiences within a larger cultural and historical context. For the early American female traveler, the narrative may have initially been more reporter's log than reflective journal, but the very act of keeping a record represents a significant entry into the larger discourse of travel exploration.

As women began to contribute to travel literature, moreover, they faced barriers more literary than physical. Even if women could envision themselves in new roles as settlers and explorers, they were stymied by presumptions of authorship and literary domain. In Amanda Gilroy's discussion of women's travel writing in England (1775–1844), she notes that even as the number of women travelers increased and they "produced some of the most significant travel texts of the period, they had to negotiate with the normative assumption that the travel writer was male and with the symbolic association of women and home" (5). Mary Suzanne Schriber reminds us that "gender is always in play in women's accounts of travel" and is in fact a "matter of performance" (6). Sara Mills elaborates on the relationship between gender and land: "There is not such clear-cut division between male and female writers, but . . . socially-determined spatial relations are negotiated with differently because of class, race, and gender and one's access to certain discursive structures" (20). The very mobility of women moreover counters Jürgen Habermas's strict delineation of public and private spheres as gender allocated. Instead, women travelers illustrate what Elizabeth Maddock Dillon observes in relation to her larger study of gender and liberalism: "Women are not in the least absent from the public sphere of desire: rather, their presence there is significant in both cultural and political terms" (7). Shirley Foster and Sara Mills, in turn, find women travelers often stereotyped as "eccentric and adventurous." Consequently, such images contributed to a "standard against which many women travelers measure themselves and it has set the discursive boundaries for women writing about their travels" (3). To correct this perception, Foster and Mills explain that women's narratives are informative in other areas and describe proper traveling clothes and "problems relating to physicality," such as "how to walk in soaking wet skirts, or how best to keep cool in high temperatures" (9). Notably, the early narratives are bereft of such personal descriptions, focusing instead on external conditions. Gender thus figures into these narratives in terms of style and content. Interestingly, women both adhere to and reject these strictures, for though they may be writing in the style of the travel narrative, their assertive voices and adventurous contents suggest new identities.

By contrast, nineteenth-century travelers often used the travel narrative for self-reflection. In this sense, as Rebecca Hogan notes, journals and diaries "may be exemplars for others, give the diarist a sense of the shape and contour of his or her life and self, set the record straight or give a perspective on a period of history. The important idea here is that a diary embodies both self-creation and self-discovery" ("Diarists," 11). Sharon M. Harris marks another key aspect of women's writings: "One of the most significant and necessary ways of approaching early American women's writings is to understand the production of these texts as self-creating acts" ("Early," 225). So engaged, the female traveler constructed her narrative and modeled her adventures, which contributed to cultural change. For Janis P. Stout, modern travelers express a distinct confidence: "In making their departures, women assume the role of subjects in their own stories rather than objects sought and exchanged by men" (3). Travel as a means of self-assertion is a layered affair, as Marilyn Wesley suggests: "The trope of women's travel is an innovative, contradictive, and dynamic response to the recurring tension between imposed ideological stasis and gendered freedoms" (xiv). Following these sentiments, travel is associated with freedom, with the open road serving as a metaphor for personal transformation. Certainly, for women who traveled for relocation onto the Ohio frontier, the journey was often a test. Success depended on their willingness to adapt in these dynamic territories. For them, the frontier was a fluid boundary, one that absorbed disparate projections, and the travel narrative was well suited to portray such transitory states.

Although the frontier appeared open for settlement, the territory had long been contested. Decades before these women arrived, the Seven Years' War (1754–63) created conflicts among tribes, including the Miamis, Delaware, Wyandots, Shawnees, and Mingos, as they each attempted to ward off the European invaders. Following the Revolutionary War, the Northwest Ordinance of 1787 established the framework, as Emily Foster explains, for the "governance of the territory," with each "six-mile-square township made up of thirty-six sections of 640 acres each" (68). In addition, W. Stitt Robinson provides this definition of frontier: "areas of limited population, containing approximately from two to six persons per square mile . . . a geographic setting near unoccupied regions, usually endowed with available land and other natural resources capable of prosperous development" (xiii). The frontier thus appears as both a physical and an ideological construct. It was, moreover, fast becoming a commodity; Douglas R. Hunt describes the Harrison Frontier Land Act of May 10, 1800, which allowed settlers "to purchase public lands on credit" at the cost of two dollars per acre. By 1805, lands along the Great Miami River were being sold by private dealers for $6.50 per acre, but credit was required (173–74). Native Americans were systematically displaced as waves of emigrants moved in, so that by 1800, Ohio had an Anglo population of approximately 42,000, and by 1810, it was 231,000 (Hunt, 375). Generally speaking, migrating travelers expressed a sense of entitlement to these lands, evident in their assumptions of ownership and in their lack of concern for indigenous peoples. Despite providing details about accommodations and travel conditions, for example, travel accounts virtually ignore the Native American's plight. For that matter, women's narratives rarely explain why the women were heading west, except for the general purpose of setting up a new home, and they do not go into detail about real estate ventures, land rights, or financial issues. Men more often handled these affairs, but the women's lack of reference is notable. Such omissions also underscore the travel narrative as a log of progress that marks a journey between familiar and imagined landscapes. The traveler's values are often driven by what has been left behind rather than by an appreciation for what lies ahead. Inadvertently, it communicates the emotional tensions that accompany anticipation, but foremost, the travel narrative testifies to the frontier as opportunity.

Key legislation reinforced this perception. Edward Watts marks Thomas Jefferson's *Report of a Plan of Government for the Western Territory* (1784), the Land Ordinance of 1785, and the Northwest Ordinance of 1787 as collectively revealing "the development of a progressive imperialistic agenda: a plan for erasing, appropriating, classifying, and rebuilding the region in a way that could not and would not challenge Eastern control of the nation" (10). More specifically, the *Report on Government for Western Territory* (March 1, 1784) reads in part: "Resolved that the territory ceded or to be ceded by Individual States to the United States whensoever the same shall have been purchased of the Indian Inhabitants & offered for sale by the U. S. shall be formed into distinct States bounded in the following manner as nearly as such cessions will admit. . . . That such temporary government shall only continue in force in any state until it shall have acquired 20,000 free inhabitants, when, giving due proof thereof to Congress, they shall receive from them authority with appointments of time." Passed on July 13, 1787, the Northwest Ordinance, or "An Ordinance for the Government of the Territory of the United States, North-West of the River Ohio," claims: "Be it ordained by the United States in Congress assembled, That the said territory, for the purposes of temporary government, be one district, subject, however, to be divided into two districts, as future circumstances may, in the opinion of Congress, make it expedient." With their confident, almost doctrinal language, these legislative acts forthrightly present the land for sale, in definite parcels and under specific conditions. Given these larger political intentions, the eastern traveler was a type of missionary, bearing civilization to the frontier. True, the travelers' journals reveal only initial reactions, laden as travelers were with disorientation, but travelers' assumptions also bear out Watts's observation of a desire to "build an empire which would expand the nation yet preserve the supremacy of the coastal metropolis" (10). In addition, L. Scott

Philyaw finds that "the simple legislation of the Ordinance of 1784 proved inadequate to solve the nation's problems in the northwestern territories" (101). And like Watts, Philyaw finds a distinct prejudice on the part of "most congressional delegates" in their "attitude that the underdeveloped West should be kept in a state of dependence, similar to what the thirteen states had recently escaped" (96–97). The women in this study followed suit when they criticized frontier life as substandard, physically and socially, even as they steadfastly pursued a westward direction that would radically change their lives.

Writing themselves into the frontier thus proved challenging, and their records underscore the difficulty of their journeys while highlighting the spiritedness of their attitudes. For many, keeping a journal was as much for documentation as for solace. As such, the travel narrative captures an interesting intersection between assumptions about women's behaviors and women's actual responses. Counter to stereotypical, often fictionalized images of passive women, their resourcefulness testifies to their adaptability and strength. Admirably so, their fortitude and stamina sustained them. It is interesting in these accounts how often the "travel" frame is disregarded, or at least deviated from, in order to discuss social behaviors—but then travel has never been just about marking distance. It involves experiencing, comparing, and contemplating. One of the most striking features about women's travel narratives is their immediacy. Reactions are not necessarily crafted to promote exploration or expansion but are instead realistic about the trials and rewards of travel. Rather than simply arrive and clear ground, women evaluated potential for sociability and speculated on compatibility. Could they transport familiar, genteel ways to a new location? Would doing so require radical readjustment, for them and the frontier? The woman's travel narrative acts as a sounding board for such speculations, whereby cultural expectations inform the woman's commentary on frontier conditions, regional differences, and social institutions. Travel allows for such perspectives and subsequent pronouncements, and the narratives bring the woman's voice more fully into the historical, national record.

In addition to marking physical spaces, therefore, the woman's travel narrative illustrates how cultural values were transferred across the new nation. The weight of this transfer is especially apparent regarding gender, for even while women were expected to act from principles of virtue and generosity, they often ventured into areas where genteel codes were strained if not made irrelevant by struggles for survival and rudimentary conditions. Travelers such as Trist, Bacon, and Dwight thus served as ambassadors of sorts, expected to bear the mantle of "American virtue," a role they found burdensome at times. Still, in this New Republic founded on republican values tempered by sympathy, women were expected to preserve and to promote these values. In their discomfort with the crude and rustic and in their preference for the refined and the graceful, these women impressively negotiated rugged land and restrictive cultural expectations to voice their concerns and to mark their journeys.

Virtue, Politics, and Gender in the New Republic

Gender identity was, moreover, significantly shaped by the politicizing events of the eighteenth century. The Revolutionary War, for example, inspired women to act outside of their accepted gender roles by boycotting British goods, attending spinning bees, and sheltering patriots. Women who had been accustomed to subordinate roles suddenly found themselves commanding households and aggressively protecting home and family in the guise of both Columbia and Minerva. Although most early American women would not have considered themselves political figures, especially if "political" is defined by public actions, their lives exemplified significant change. Sara M. Evans observes: "Women who perceived themselves as uninterested in politics were quickly caught up in political thought and conversation" (48). Rosemarie Zagarri agrees that the "events of the day eroded the strict separation between public and private spheres. Because politics so directly affected their fates, women could be excused for probing into a traditionally male realm" (Woman's Dilemma, 85). Moreover, as Carla Mulford observes: "The writing of history might have been considered anti-authoritarian and 'masculine,' but, because of their newly acquired roles as cultural monitors, women could appropriate the tradition of history writing to themselves" (Dictionary, xxiii). In this spirit, Abigail Adams, Esther Edwards Burr, Hannah Mather Crocker, Judith Sargent Murray, and Mercy Otis Waren, among others, engaged in the public debate over this New Republic with intelligence and passion.

Two seminal collections, *American Women Writers to 1800* (1996), edited by Sharon M. Harris, and the *Dictionary of Literary Biography: American Women Prose Writers to 1820* (1999), edited by Carla Mulford, testify to the woman's avid interest in social, literary, and political issues. With over ninety entries in the Harris volume and fifty-nine in the Mulford edition, it is clear that women's active involvement was elaborate and expansive. Harris notes, for example, that women were significantly engaged "with the philosophical issues of the era, including the appropriate political order for a new nation" (*American*, 17). These writings and profiles are also important reminders that reading women's narratives requires an appreciation for what women valued rather than what might have been expressed. To do so avoids what Frank Shuffleton calls "mindlessly presentist impositions upon the past" (96). Despite women's keen interest, they were not always a welcomed party; as Linda Kerber points out, "The newly created republic made little room for [women] as political beings" (*Women*, 11). Still, women who may have resisted Mary Wollstonecraft's manifesto *A Vindication of the Rights of Woman* (1792) found themselves stepping outside of gender specific roles within this revolutionary political and social climate. In this regard, their perspective is especially valuable, for, as Kerber finds, "the early Republic does look different when seen through women's eyes" (xi). If there was a gendered view, what did these women see, and how did they approach travel and migration differently? How if at all was their perception different based on gender, religion, class, region, or ethnicity? Would they favor virtue over pleasure as they refigured the manners and civility of the new nation? How would a generation of women taught to honor patriarchal power vested in monarchy situate themselves within this new civic structure? And, how would they transfer these values onto the frontier? As the following chapters bear out, women experienced the frontier and wrote about their travels quite differently than men and with a particular eye for relationships between social classes.

Virtue was, moreover, central to these values, as it encouraged a benevolent attitude, especially toward subordinates. Within a democracy, virtuous actions seemed particularly noble, as they arose from a natural sense of the good. Mary Kelley finds, "*Virtue* was defined most broadly as a selflessness in which individual desires and interests were secondary to the welfare of the body politic. It was made the linchpin for social and political institutions" (60). Virtue was thus posited as both a moral and a civil code, serving as a guide for personal behavior and patriotic action, especially in contrast to corrupt British mores and actions. For Lester H. Cohen virtue was, in fact, the "genius" of republicanism, "a quality of human character and conduct that manifested the confluence of personality and public behavior" (481). This emphasis on public behaviors as a reflection of virtue weighed especially heavily on the female traveler, who found herself in situations in which there was little context for civility. Nevertheless, women were considered "better equipped than men to withstand moral corruption and promote virtue," as Richard Godbeer explains, which cast them "as guardians of public as well as private virtue" (295). Ennobled, and so pressured, women were elevated and yet judged by these expectations.

As genteel women, they sought to create social structures built on virtuous intentions and decorous behavior, a desire with both philosophical and social ramifications. These intentions were complex, for, as Philip Gould points out, the "republican language of 'virtue' was layered densely with gendered meanings during the transitional era of the early republic. 'Virtue' signified not only the tenets of classical republicanism and liberal individualism but also the precepts of affect, benevolence, and pious, universal love that descended in large part from eighteenth-century Scottish Common Sense philosophy" (*Covenant and Republic*, 62). Displays of virtue thus reflected class, gender, and education. Joyce Appleby, in turn, describes a distinctly American sensibility in that "republican polarities of virtue and corruption, disinterest and interestedness, public spirit and private ambition, participation and passivity, structured the world of politics [and] provided a language for discussing all actions in the public realm" (22). The term "virtue" also carried economic and political implications; Carla Mulford distinguishes between virtue "aligned with broad political and mercantile goals of sincerity and honesty in politics and business" and that which "signaled specific behaviors of citizens, women in particular, whose personal relations should be unquestionably pure in motive and free of lasciviousness" (Introduction, xiv). Virtuous actions thus permeated social codes, and virtuous sentiments appeared key to American democracy, for they allowed differences between class, religion, and gender to be suspended for the common goal of independence. Andrew Burstein offers yet another component: "Sensibility was a critical device in the promotion of patriotic sentiment and in the idealized conception of republican politics" (*Sentimental*, 288). Sentiment, sympathy, and virtue thus guided republican action, and for women to act otherwise would have been deemed unpatriotic. The Revolution, in turn, aggrandized the woman's role as a noble representation of the republic. Building on what David S. Shields calls the "hallmarks of the bluestocking world," women of the New Republic elevated "feminine sympathy into a political principle" (*Civil*, 120). In fact, for Elizabeth Barnes, "sympathy was to be the building block of a democratic nation" (x). Women were inspired by these democratic impulses to settle new lands and travel to new sights, while at the same time cautioned to remain within certain boundaries.

Clearly, education would become essential to elevating a woman's status and allowing her to participate in this virtuous campaign. Nina Baym elaborates: "Manifestly, ignorant women could not instruct others; hence the need to educate them" (23). Regarding nineteenth-century print culture, Sharon M. Harris notes, "Essays advocating female education were always welcome at the *New-York Magazine*, as was true for most early periodicals" ("*New-York Magazine*," 347). Charged with moral and civic edification, women took on active roles as educators, challenging male-centered academe. Even so, Mary Kelley describes the lag in education, whereby "New England's public schools generally excluded girls until the latter half of the eighteenth century, and even then offered them only a separate and lesser education" (57). Evidence of female education was thus noted with interest, as when Elizabeth Gilpin wrote from Troy, New York, on October 21, 1830: "We then visited Mrs. Whilhard's School or Academy for Young Ladies, which is in great repute as a place of education. They have a number of professors or teachers, and once a year a grand public examination" (30).[11] Such educational opportunities encouraged female participation in the larger political debates, while promoting women's role as moral instructors.

Understandably, the dramatic events of the war evoked impassioned responses, and women reacted with sentimental and sympathetic language. Concerns over family safety paralleled those for national security, for, as Shirley Samuels points out, "An anxiety about disorder within the family is often exhibited in the early sentimental or domestic novel," and the "family as a model for the nation [becomes] an instrument of social control" (17). Jay Fliegelman also remarks on these connections: "The problems of family government addressed in the fiction and pedagogy of the period—of balancing authority with liberty, of maintaining a social order while encouraging individual growth—were the larger political problems of the age translated into terms of daily life" (5). When Lydia Minturn Post wrote to her husband on October 3, 1776, about the "sorrowful" and "dreadful" fate of Nathan Hale, her patriotic sentiments illustrated this New Republican discourse: "I cannot write this without weeping. . . . So likely, so young, so brave" (qtd. in Harris, *American*, 296). In Mercy Otis Warren's *History of the Rise, Progress and Termination of the American Revolution*, she dramatizes the "outrage of innocence in instances too numerous to be recorded" and relates a particularly gruesome act of "wanton barbarity of the soldiers of the King of England, as they patrolled the defenceless villages of America" (327). Warren then narrates a tale of tragic circumstance about a woman from Elizabethtown, New Jersey, who, "sitting in her own house with her little domestic circle around her and her infant in her arms . . . shrouded by the consciousness of her own innocence and virtue," was suddenly "shot through the lungs" by a "British barbarian." The violence continued in a blatant display of disregard for person and home: "A hole was dug, the body thrown in, and the house of this excellent lady set on fire and consumed with all the property it contained" (327–28). Not only was this act cruel, but, as Warren explains, there were political undertones, for the absent husband, Mr. Caldwell, was apparently being persecuted for his "zeal for the rights, and his attachment of his native land" (351). Warren's tale shows the struggle between British exploitation and American virtue. This lady's innocence and the unsolicited nature of the attack, in turn, exemplify an attribute of sympathy that for Julia A. Stern gives "expression to the latent, reprobated social and political impulses of those Americans who do not 'count' in the language of the Founding." According to Stern, "such literature emanates from a feminized zone of imagination highly critical of republican 'disinterest'" (*Plight*, 6). The Caldwell murders underscore British cruelty, and Warren's account emphasizes the emotional loss by evoking the sentimental voice. Thus, while Lydia Minturn Post laments that "war is a weariness," she finds the struggle "a noble endeavor . . . the cry of humanity against oppression, usurped power, insolence, and rapacity" (qtd. in Harris, *American*, 298). For Post and Warren, virtue, democracy, and sympathy are essential components for imagining this new nation, as they respond passionately to the political and social upheavals of the time.

Virtue could also be used as a pretense for asserting superiority, whereby travelers espoused a proprietary, somewhat condescending attitude submerged in virtuous sentiment. In Mary Louise Pratt's discussion of travel literature in the 1780s and 1790s, she notes sentimentality as "a powerful mode for representing colonial relations and the imperial frontier." Travelers who adopted this mode would have seemed patronizing. This attitude, Pratt adds, sparked debates over the very style of travel writing: "the two main tensions being between 'naïve' (popular) and lettered writing, and between informational and experiential writing. Stylistic debates as to relative values of 'embellishment' and 'naked truth' often reflected tensions between the man of science and the man of sensibility, or between the lettered and popular writer" (87). Women's travel narratives exemplify these tensions, as they can be both didactic and embellished, informational and imperialistic. A woman's reactions to her surroundings and to the underprivileged thus reflected both how she was expected to respond and the cause of her basic discomfort. Sharp criticism might cause others to fault her benevolence. Indifference to the less fortunate might signal an uncharitable spirit. Virtuous reactions were tested when fundamental comforts were not met and safety not secured; as with explorers before them, disorientation often provoked these women. Still, as genteel women, they were expected to act accordingly. Unlike the sentimental novel or the public essay, which simply reinforce genteel values, women's travel narratives describe the clash between ideology and reality, one of their most interesting qualities. Adaptation was not instantaneous. Instead, women resisted what was unfamiliar. They did not always romanticize the wilderness, or rhapsodize over open spaces, but reacted to the uncertainty of the frontier with the animated, at times cantankerous testimonials of easterners transplanted to a new land. Despite their complaints, these determined women were strong enough to prevail over rough territory and in crude conditions. They did not back away from their opinions or falter in their visions of a new home in a transformed wilderness, and in doing so they exemplified patience and endurance, two virtues that signal strength.

Charged with concern for the greater good and expected to act with virtuous intent, genteel women travelers were at times stymied by the rustic incivility they encountered. Some tried to explain the lapse as a problem of religious training, while others saw it as an economic failing or even simply a lack of taste. This incivility challenged the women's ability to be generous and sympathetic. While the end to colonial rule suggested a more egalitarian social structure, it did not prove a seamless transition for the genteel traveler, who recoiled at the crude manners and impoverished conditions found on the frontier. David S. Shields elaborates on this incongruity: "Though the American Revolution dissolved the legal ties binding the colonies to England, it did not break their dependence upon metropolitan manners or insulate them from the international market in fashionable goods" (Civil, 308). Bridging these gaps in manner and style would require more than a treaty, as the simplicity associated with republican values attempted to gain favor over more elaborate, decadent, Anglo-European taste. Even so, women were expected to take on the role of "Republican Motherhood," which Linda Kerber finds "altered the female domain [and] justified an extension of women's absorption and participation in the civic culture" (Toward, 61). The genteel female traveler who fretted about a lack of social boundaries was caught between acting as a gracious, maternal figure and expressing her honest preference for propriety. Genteel women were supposed to act from principles of virtue and sympathy, and yet when they were faced with uncomfortable situations, their graciousness was strained. In dealing with these moments when expectations meet realities, women's travel narratives are surprisingly revealing; they show the limitations of virtue that affirms class status rather than expressing benevolent intentions.

—꙳

The traveler's tale is indeed a rich source for understanding early American customs and manners. As travelers exchanged goods along with information, their records focus attention on the everyday transactions of early American life. To understand how early Americans lived on a daily basis, the travel narrative is essential. For unlike the history, tract, or sermon, the travel narrative does not aim to espouse a particular message, but offers a collection of entries that in the end describe a journey, and that may or may not convey a coherent, overall meaning. To focus specifically on women's travel narratives shows how the very act of travel or migration appeared from a domestic and gendered point of view. As their accounts attest, women often found travel in this five-mile-an-hour world enlivening—if also, at times, exasperating. And as I had been accustomed to reading the nineteenth-century pioneer's journal against a larger nationalist backdrop that depicted a rugged individualism, I was initially uncertain how to read an early American woman's travel narrative filled with repetitive details about road conditions, accommodations, food, and other travelers that seemed to undercut this grand westward movement. Gradually, as I began to see the world through these female travelers' eyes, I understood a different narrative—relocation, while it eventually may have had benefits, initially meant a loss of social connections and urban pleasures that the journey over rugged terrain with nights spent in rustic taverns only exacerbated. The frontier was foreign territory both geographically and socially. From women's records, a complicated view of travel emerges that challenges prevailing assumptions that migration was predominately male driven and fundamentally rewarding. Instead, we learn that women were integral to settlement and that migration, while potentially satisfying, was fraught with mixed emotions.

The following discussion addresses the physical, discursive, and social aspects of women and travel in early America. Chapter 1 situates the woman's travel narrative within the larger genre of exploration literature and discusses the influence of aesthetic theories on travel writing. Chapter 2 builds on this discussion by providing the physical context of travel itself by discussing the public house and travel conditions. Chapter 3 focuses on the woman's travel narrative as a record of class encounters by looking at journeys along the eastern seaboard and onto the Ohio frontier. Chapter 4 examines the relationship between women's travel narratives and other early American literary genres, such as the novel and poetry, and explores how these genres influence each other in the telling of travel stories. Chapter 5 concludes this study by looking at how women captured their experiences differently in letters and travel narratives. The rich epistolary archives from this period complement the woman's travel record and show how place and perspective can significantly alter how experience is represented. Inserting the primary source prominently into this investigation gives the woman's travel narrative additional value as historical artifact and social document. Altogether, this book argues that women and their travel narratives made a significant, vital contribution to the migration and settlement of early America and the New Republic.

1

The Language of Travel

THE PRACTICAL AND THE PICTURESQUE

With a documentary sensibility for the details of daily life, the travel narrative provides a valuable window into the physical, social, and cultural worlds of early America. From these texts, life appears animated and social interactions diverse. Given the stops and starts of travel, with public houses situated approximately every twenty miles along the more popular routes, and the range in accommodations, each account is made unique by circumstance and made more interesting by point of view. To build on the introduction, this chapter focuses on the woman's literary vehicle, the travel narrative itself, and examines its unique capacity to serve as a most appropriate genre for her experiences. Filled with detailed data and pointed opinions, the travel narrative draws on several different genres—journal, letter, history, and promotional tract—resulting in a first-person narrative that is episodic, informative, and descriptive. Following the rhythms of travel, these accounts include notes on daily progress, road conditions, and accommodations. The actual construction of the narrative varied, as it was either composed from travel notes and later recopied or drafted without any editing. Physically, the travel narrative resembles other record-keeping texts, such as diaries or commonplace books, that could be easily transported. Regarding style, authors usually adopt a comparative mode that measures new surroundings against a familiar one. The traveler's own tastes then come to bear, as we learn of the various failings or benefits of a certain town or city.

Rather than offer exaggerated visions of the landscape or imperialistic designs of conquering a land, the unedited, unassuming travel narrative functions as a narrative map, from a time when maps were both hard to come by and constantly changing. In these prose maps, an important human voice emerges that enriches the historical and literary record, so that we learn not only how Anglo-European migrations altered the North American landscape but the perspective from which this settlement took place. Into the grandiose world of exploration literature, women confidently entered and wrote about custom, sociability, and accommodations, expressing themselves with a sensibility different from that of male explorers and travelers. The goal of this chapter is to create an appreciation for how the woman's travel narrative contributed to exploration literature. It surveys the characteristics and developments of this genre that women travelers took it upon themselves to transform.

Rarely printed but circulated in manuscript form instead, travel narratives were intended for a small, outside audience; they were shared with family and friends and, like a letter, read aloud, becoming part of a larger oral culture. Circulation figures for early America are thus difficult to determine, for, as with the novel, tracing a travel narrative's provenance proves complicated. But a general comparison to the letter suggests that twenty to thirty people, or the size of an extended family, may have either read a traveler's journal or heard about its contents. Ever wider circles of readers are attributed to ministers' travel journals, as Karin A. Wulf explains: "Ministers' accounts of their travels often circulated in manuscript. . . . Letters were read over and over to groups large and small" (23). Given its semipublic nature, the travel narrative can be grander than an individual letter and yet charmingly unassuming. Indeed, the travel narrative in the hands of Knight, Trist, Dewees, Johnson, and Dwight became far more than a vade mecum for travelers; it was an entertaining, customized guide with astute social commentary. The travel accounts of nineteenth-century pioneers took on even larger audiences, aided by print technology and a flood of migrants heading west along the Overland Trail from the Missouri River to the Oregon Territory. Noting the existence of over eight hundred published and archived diaries and day journals, Lillian Schlissel describes these texts as "something like a family history, a souvenir meant to be shared like a Bible, handed down through generations, to be viewed not as an individual's story but as the history of a family's growth and course through time" (11). She then distinguishes the overland diary as a "special kind of diary, often meant to be published in county newspapers or sent to relatives intending to make the same journey the following season" (11). As such, it is filled with information that was appropriately helpful. The travel narrative is thus an enduring, highly adaptable text, influenced by changing cultural and literary conventions.

In some cases, the travel narrative was written to a specific person and served as an extended letter addressed to a highly interested audience. With anticipatory, somewhat tentative beginnings, women directed their narratives accordingly. On November 9, 1795, for example, eighteen-year-old Mary Bishop Cushman left Coventry, Connecticut, with her family for the frontier settlement of Exeter, New York, where she would teach school and help with the family business. Cushman's two-year journal is addressed to her friend Laura (surname possibly Strong), and so begins: "Dear Laura you will not be much pleased I fear in reading this journal, for so slim and cheap is the part alloted me to *act* that it is seldom I shall have anything sufficiently interesting to entertain you, but however I shall be more than rewarded for my trouble in the idea I am obligeing the good hearted Laura" (268).[1] Although Cushman initially doubted her ability to relay an exciting missive, she would, as indicated, faithfully record her travels, which ultimately prove quite entertaining. According to Elizabeth Collette, in her preface to the Elizabeth Van Horne narrative, this journal was directed to members of Van Horne's "father's Baptist congregation" in Scotch Plains, New Jersey (4). On October 4, 1807, Van Horne, addressing her "valued friends," began her journal of her trip from New Jersey to Ohio: "Agreeable to request, I have commenced my Journal to be directed to Mr. Osborn, our friend and their families; we have received kindness & attentions that will long live in our memories" (9).[2] Mrs. Lydia B. Bacon's journal, composed in 1811–12, was reconstructed twenty years later at the "oft repeated request" of her nephew James J. Jarves. It begins on May 9, 1811, with the salutation "My dear James," followed by an explanation that the following narrative was a compilation of "extracts from letters" and "from a journal keep [sic] some part of the time." Margaret Van Horn Dwight directed *A Journey to Ohio in 1810* to her cousin Elizabeth Woolsey, to whom it was promptly sent upon Dwight's arrival in Warren: "Shall I commence my journal, my dear Elizabeth, with a description of the pain I felt at taking leave of all my friends, or shall I leave you to imagine?" (1). Eliza Williams Bridgham dedicated her "Diary of a Journey through New England and New York 1818" in this manner: "To Her Royal Highness the Lady Abigail of Providence, this Journal is most respectfully dedicated, By her affectionate Sister—Eliza." On July 16, 1818, Bridgham began her journal: "As it was your wish, dear Abby, that this famous journal should be dedicated to you, I have thus complied with it— & anticipate with pleasure many a hearty laugh over it, on my return" (5–6).[3] Thus personalized and directed as if an extended letter, the travel narrative afforded these women a singular venue for writing about their experiences, often bearing witness to strange and unusual sights. Though beholden to audiences back home, women were not bound by expectations of publication, allowing them to write candidly and with unaffected enthusiasm as they sorted out their reactions to new surroundings.

Within the comparative mode of assessment, travelers invariably passed judgment while also communicating standards of taste. Comments were part observation, part social critique. The language of comparison is evident even in the earliest travelers' accounts and proves a key characteristic. On November 16, 1679, Jasper Danckaerts and Peter Sluyter, newly arrived from Amsterdam, passed the night at Mr. Greenland's tavern on the Millstone River in the New Jersey Colony and noted: "We were better lodged and entertained here, for we slept upon a good bed, and strengthened ourselves against the future" (170). On November 5, 1781, the Marquis de Chastellux was "neatly lodged" at Chandler's Tavern in North Carolina, which was "one of the best" in America (2:215). On December 5, he revisited an inn where he had stayed two years earlier: "[T]he house was changed for the better, and we made a very good supper" (2:300). Travelers included such information with the understanding that those who followed would be less interested in conquering a land than in finding hospitable lodging and a comfortable place to rest for the night. In this manner, as Robert Micklus explains, the travel narrative "naturally appealed to an age that stressed sociability as a key—if not the key—to happiness" (78). For the early American traveler, such insights, along with a good map, proved indispensable.

The genteel traveler thus documented for other likeminded travelers the comfort they could expect and the places to avoid. For example, Susan Edwards Johnson noted on November 14, 1801: "[W]e dined this day, at a small town call'd Elkton, the best publick house we were in on the road; had an elegant dinner; the house kept with peculiar neatness, the furnature very good, & every accommodation to render it agreeable— kept by one Richardson" (6).[4] After several disappointing days, Johnson was especially pleased to find such agreeable lodgings. In February 1807, Fortescue Cuming had letters to post while in Harrisburg, Pennsylvania, and described this scene: "The office being shut, the postmaster very civilly invited me into his parlour, to settle for the postage, where seeing a large map of Pennsylvania, I took the opportunity of tracing my journey, which the postmaster observing, he politely assisted me in it, pointing out the most proper route. There were some ladies in the room, apparently on a visit, and there was an air of sociality and refinement throughout, which was very pleasing" (39). Cuming appreciated the women's socializing and the postmaster's respectful, polite attentions as reassuring demonstrations of genteel behaviors. For those heading west, comparisons based on the more developed, eastern cities were inevitable. On December 27, 1783, Elizabeth House Trist made these observations of Carlisle, Pennsylvania: "After breakfast we left Capt. Simpson and cross'd a very pretty creek call'd Yellow Breeches. . . . The town much larger than I expected to see at such a distance from navigation. . . . I was surprised on entering the town to see such fine buildings" (203). Trist assertively draws these comparisons between Carlisle and her hometown of Philadelphia, following other travelers in a mutual sharing of information about geography and towns and concerns for good food and clean, comfortable lodgings.

The Traveler's Guide: Women's Travel Writings and the American Grand Tour

Travel in early America was by and large a practical matter. One ventured away from home to trade, relocate, minister, and, occasionally, visit. Few traveled solely for pleasure, as Barbara G. Carson confirms regarding Dr. Alexander Hamilton's 1744 journey from Annapolis, Maryland, to York, Maine, wherein he "did not mention meeting a single individual or family group traveling, like himself, purely for health and recreation" (368). Travel for pleasure and even health were, in fact, rare enough to be noted as slightly odd. More unusual still was the traveler who sought edification and cultural refinement. As travel culture developed throughout the eighteenth and nineteenth centuries, travel literature provided increasingly specific information about routes and accommodations. James Buzard attributes this urge to travel to larger philosophical tenets, such as that found in John Locke's *Essay Concerning Human Understanding* (1690): "If knowledge is rooted in experience and nowhere else, travel instantly gains in importance and desirability" (37). Whereas earlier travelers focused on the availability of shelter and the rigors of the road, later travelers expanded on the quality of accommodations and the beauty of the landscape. Leisured travelers drew on new criteria altogether by comparing their excursions with the descriptions available in popular guidebooks. Pragmatism, though not altogether absent from travel, gave way in the early 1800s to a more pleasurable attitude that coincided with the rise of a tourist industry and the advent of an "American Grand Tour" to showcase a distinctly American landscape. Main stops along the northern tourist route included New York City; the Hudson River Valley & The Catskills; the Springs (Ballston, Saratoga, and New Lebanon); Niagara Falls & the Erie Canal; the Connecticut River Valley & the White Mountains. Tours south and west included Charleston and St. Louis as key destinations.

As women embraced travel as a leisured activity in addition to traveling for relocation, not only did travel conditions change but so did the record of travel itself. To read Elizabeth House Trist (1783–84), Mary Coburn Dewees (1788), or Margaret Van Horn Dwight (1810), for example, is to learn about routes, accommodations, and incidents presented episodically without extensive commentary or elaborate personal narrative. But to read Lydia Bacon (1811), Eliza Williams Bridgham (1818), Sophia Quincy (1829), or Elizabeth Gilpin (1830) is to discover the best time of day to view Niagara Falls, where to encounter the fashionable and the literati, and how to capture picturesque lighting. While migrating travelers focused on the availability of shelter and documented the rigors of the road, "tourists"—the new name for travelers—simply followed the itineraries available in popular guidebooks. As a result, the travel journal changed from a hurriedly written, somewhat fragmented account of places, routes, and conditions to a more stylized text with composed passages of scenes recollected and revised in the manner of a memoir and travelogue, or what is often referred to as travel writing. Two broad developments brought about these distinct changes in style and content: the establishing of a New Republic that inspired a fervent nationalism and a developing tourist "industry" that promoted travel as a cultural, picturesque adventure.

Touring had long been considered the privilege of the educated and the elite, who sought the European mountains and countryside in search of inspiration and experience. James Buzard describes the typical one- to five-year European Grand Tour as a "social ritual" and "an ideological exercise" intended to "round out the education of young men of the ruling classes by exposing them to the treasured artifacts and ennobling society of the Continent" and thus prepare them to "assume leadership positions preordained for them at home" (38–39). John Towner agrees and calls the Grand Tour "that circuit of western Europe undertaken by the wealthy in society for culture, education, health, and pleasure" (96). In keeping with this tradition, Americans initially flocked to Europe to tour and join in the fashionable scene. Mary Suzanne Schriber explains that for nineteenth-century American women going abroad, travel was "a ritual, a 'cultural performance' to which importance, respectability, and meaning attached. Itineraries and routes were not original. Rather, they were prescribed in guidebooks such as Murray and Baedeker and Knox, making the traveler's choices clear and providing itineraries and routes to sacralized sites" (16). To mark their adventures, as Jeffrey Alan Melton notes, "nineteenth-century Americans searching for their cultural identity increasingly turned to travel writing, which served a vital aesthetic and practical purpose by helping readers to understand themselves as they encountered a variety of cultural behaviors and assumptions foreign to their own" (18). The notion of a European Grand Tour adapted to American soil, therefore, confirmed America as its own entity, one worthy of a tour that would signal refinement, while providing adventure and improving health for a more inclusive clientele.

The Americanization of the tour had social and gender implications. James Buzard expands on class issues: "'Grand Tour' began as a French phrase—le grand tour—but it was appropriated by Britons of the late seven-

teenth and early eighteenth centuries," who represented a new class that
was weathy enough to travel for leisure (38–39). Beth L. Lueck elaborates
on the connections between patriotism and travel writing: the "American
travelers' passion for picturesque beauty was fostered by various accounts of landscapes worth viewing, by artists' rendering of scenery that
appeared in periodicals . . . and by the nationalist fervor following the
War of 1812" (4). To institute an American Grand Tour thus brought together issues of class, gender, aesthetics, and nationalism. Less pretentious
still was the "fashionable tour," which Dona Brown describes as a "string
of attractions that brought travelers from New York City up the Hudson
River to Albany and 'the Springs,' then west by way of the Erie Canal to
Niagara Falls" (16). The timely intention of these tours, grand and fashionable, as Henry Dilworth Gilpin explains in his introduction to *A Northern
Tour* (1825), was to show Americans the value of their own locales: "The
idea which so long prevailed, of making European countries the only field
for observation and amusement, has passed away; and while a few are led
across the Atlantic by a more ardent curiosity, the great majority of our
countrymen are content to gratify it amid congenial manners and institutions in their native land" (1). Travel was, no less, an affirmation of patriotic pride. Given this patriotism, women were more welcomed on this
American version than on the more elite European tour.

Travel guides responded to these developments by including notable
destinations, establishing them as "tourist spots," and providing colorful
descriptions to foreground travelers' experiences. In this regard, as Gilpin
notes, the guide was meant "to accompany [travelers] in some of their
excursions, to point out to them those scenes which are worthy of their
notice, to revive those recollections on which it is useful and pleasant to
dwell, and to afford them at once a memorandum and a guide" (2). In
addition to Gilpin's *A Northern Tour* (1825), the more popular tourist guides
of the early 1800s include Moore's *The Traveller's Directory* (1804); Henry S.
Tanner's *The Traveller's Guide* (1825); and Theodore Dwight's *The Northern Traveller* (1831). Other guides include Theodore Dwight's *Things as They Are*
(1834) and *The Tourist; or, Pocket Manual for Travellers on the Hudson* (ninth edition
by 1841).[5]

Travel guides were indeed quite helpful, offering information on hotels,
inns, and boardinghouses; steamboats, stages, ferries, and trains; churches

and shops; vistas and resorts; natural wonders and forts; maps and routes. For example, the combined volume of Dwight's *The Northern Traveller* and Gilpin's *A Northern Tour*, which catered to the tourist and migrant alike, provides this information about New York: "*Principal objects of interest in New York* . . . On the west side of the Park is Paff's exhibition of Pictures; and in Barclay-street the Exhibition of the *American Academy of Fine Arts*, and the painting room of John Trumbull Esq" (10–11); this note on education for Boston: "Schools have existed in New England from early times, being supported by law and free to all classes. . . . The public schools of Boston are in some respects the best in the Union" (277); and for the westward traveler, this advice: "*Farmers* going to settle in the West, had better travel with their horses and wagons if they have them, and take their clothing, tools, kitchen utensils, and in general all lighter and more valuable moveables. The heavier may in some cases be advantageously sent by water, but can generally be purchased in the West at a saving" (381). Estimated costs for migration in 1834 are quoted as 4 1/2 to 6 cents per mile by stage; and by steamboat from New Orleans to St. Louis, $25; from Boston to Pittsburgh, "less than $50 for an emigrant and his wife, without any freight" (381–82).

These guides influenced not only travelers' routes but travel writing itself as travelers modeled their own entries after the descriptions intended to attract them. For example, Eliza Williams Bridgham recorded this entry from Saratoga Springs on July 29, 1818: "We arrived here safely this morning, dear sister, & have found in one house quite a little world. . . . [T]his house which is called 'Congress Hall,' accommodates 150, at this present time. It is 197 feet in length & three stories in height, & kept by S P. Schoonhoven, a Dutchman, don't you think it quite an establishment?" (22). Notably, the names of accommodations reflect the flair of the tour, for, as Dona Brown points out, "inns were customarily referred to by the landlord's name, such as 'Mr. Whitney's, at the sign of the Eagle,' or simply 'Mr. Putnam's House.' Hotels were given high-sounding names with no personal reference: 'Congress Hall' or 'Cataract House'" (26). Moreover, compare Bridgham's entry with the "Saratoga Springs" section of *The Northern Traveller*: "On reaching the foot of the hill, the Congress Spring, the great attraction of the place is seen at a short distance on the right, usually surrounded by a throng of people. Congress Hall is 196 feet long

on the street, with two wings of 60 feet running back, and contains lodging for 150. . . . The price of board is $10 per week" (121–22). Bridgham's
description and subsequent delight are mirrored in the guide's account,
each writer adopting a language of measurement and assessment. Such
passages, in turn, commodify America by offering its landscape and towns
and its people and habits as notable entities worthy of a stop on the tour.
"Religion" constituted its own category in these guides, as here in the
"Shaker Village" section of The Northern Traveller: "[T]heir worship consists
principally of a strange and disagreeable kind of dancing, whence they
have their name, accompanied with a monotonous song" (41). Travelers
were compelled to visit certain places dictated by the guides as a sign of
status and prestige for having the leisure and the means to venture and
record. These informative descriptions also explain the standardization
and formulaic style in the later journals. The narratives in this study thus
represent a range from records kept before such standardization to those
influenced by an established travel industry. And while early American
travel writing and tourism are most often located in the nineteenth century and associated with writers such as Mark Twain and Washington Irving, female travelers of the eighteenth century were already writing about
lodging, roads, and social events, often including their own humorous
anecdotes. Women thus absorbed and responded to their contemporary
culture with an interesting interplay between material culture, travel, and
literary production.

Observing Nature: The Sublime and the Picturesque

The travel narrative is also a record of natural phenomena, as travelers
note indigenous plants and document resources. The traveler's relationship to nature, in turn, distinguishes the type of journey and subsequent
narrative style. While the seventeenth- and eighteenth-century narrative
reflects a preference for a tamed, cultivated natural world, later nineteenth-
century accounts express appreciation for a wilder, unspoiled landscape.
For women such as Knight, Trist, and Dwight, the regularity of towns, the
potential for crops, the intricacy of gardens, and the variety of architecture were more likely to elicit admiration than were open spaces and un-
cultivated lands. Leisured travelers such as Bridgham, Laurens, and Gilpin,

who were influenced by a romantic sensibility, looked to nature for inspiration, often embellishing their accounts with extended passages on nature's beauty. These distinctions situate the early American woman's travel narrative in its appropriate context; later, more stylized narratives should be understood as responding to a very different set of aesthetics. Earlier travelers recorded first impressions without overdone reflection or literary artifice, writing the narrative in transit and not necessarily editing it afterward. Later travelers wrote more self-consciously and often recopied their accounts from travel notes, which resulted in a more polished, literary text. Whereas the earlier texts appear as eyewitness accounts, the later ones read more as travelogues and memoirs. From the grandeur of exploration rhetoric, to data-rich accounts, to romantic images, travel narratives express attitudes toward nature manifest in aggressive appropriation, scientific discovery, and pleasurable observation.

As travel writing developed throughout the eighteenth century, it derived inspiration from aesthetic theories, such as "the sublime and the beautiful" and "the picturesque." Edmund Burke's *A Philosophical Inquiry into the Origin of Our Ideas of the Sublime and the Beautiful* (1757) describes sublime sources as producing the "strongest emotion which the mind is capable of feeling." Such powerful sources must be viewed from a safe distance; otherwise, as Burke explains, "they are incapable of giving any delight, and are simply terrible; but at certain distances, and with certain modifications, they may be, and they are delightful, as we every day experience" (58–60). Following Burke, William Gilpin's essay "On Picturesque Travel" (1794) charges travelers to seek more than mere amusement by traveling "for more important purposes," such as the pursuit of picturesque objects, which share some characteristics of the sublime and the beautiful. The infinite variety of these objects inspires the traveler to revisit nature in pursuit of inspiration and beauty, as Gilpin explains: "This great object we pursue through the scenery of nature. We seek it among all the ingredients of landscape—trees—rocks—broken-grounds—woods—rivers—lakes—plains—vallies—mountains—and distances. These objects in *themselves* produce infinite variety. No two rocks, or trees are exactly the same. They are varied, a second time, by *combination*; and almost as much, a third time, by different *lights*, and *shades*, and other aerial effects. Sometimes we find among them the exhibition of a *whole*; but oftener we find

only beautiful *parts*" (42). In such pursuits, travelers recorded the grand
and the simple with the understanding that their records would be sus-
ceptible to time and other "aerial effects."

Sidney K. Robinson cites Lord Kames's *Elements of Criticism* (1762) for its
recognition of mixture as a "source of the greatest aesthetic satisfaction"
and explains that the "intermixture of grandeur with neatness, regularity with wildness, and gaiety with melancholy" is key to a successful composition (7). From this perspective, the traveler gazing on a certain scene
in nature evaluated its layered composition and marveled at its magnifi-
cence. David Marshall, in fact, notes that while William Gilpin "used the
term *picturesque* for the most part to appreciate those accidental scenes that
might be encountered by the traveler—and increasingly the tourist—
passing through the landscape, others were concerned with designing
landscape as well as appreciating it" (415). Shirley Foster and Sara Mills
agree that for many nineteenth-century women travel writers "drawing
on the picturesque involved describing the landscape in terms of its
compositional elements" (92). In this manner, as Robinson explains, "the
Picturesque shifts attention away from individual elements to the relation
between them" (5). Viewing the landscape as a composition, in turn,
suggests a desire for more control over the scene as the traveler framed
the moment.

This search for the sublime and the picturesque in nature further inspired the promotion of an American Grand Tour to showcase an American landscape distinct from those of Europe and England and encouraged
travelers to travel in search of landscape beauty. Citing William Gilpin,
Beth Lueck explains the general aesthetic theory behind these expedi-
tions: "The pleasures of the tour centered on the anticipation and discovery of picturesque beauty, as well as the later recollection of the scenery
by sketching or writing about it" (11). In "On the Art of Sketching Landscape" (1792), Gilpin foregrounds these points: "The art of *sketching* is to
the picturesque traveler, what the art of writing is to the scholar. Each is
equally necessary to fix and *communicate* it's [sic] respective ideas" (61). Visual and written responses serve the traveler's desire to commemorate
experience. In some cases, immediate reaction to nature was suspended
so that intellectual responses could develop and later be refined. In Caroline Olivia Laurens's "Journal of a Visit to Greenville from Charleston in

the Summer of 1825," she demonstrates this process: "June 5th, In the evening we took a walk round the village, and admired it very much. It is situated on a pretty hill, which is most improved by two or three large brick buildings. Walking up and down the main street, one may have a tolerable good view of the Blue Ridge. We again visited the falls, and viewed them from a rock which is of some height, and almost opposite to the larger falls. We saw them to great advantage and were highly pleased. Eleanor and I proposed to each other, to go one day in the week, purposely to try and sketch a view of it." Two days later, the women fulfilled this promise: "Went immediately after breakfast to sketch a view of the falls, and succeeded tolerably well" (167). By sketching the scene, Laurens could document it and appreciate it after the fact. Savoring the images was also linked to the picturesque, for according to David Marshall the "picturesque represents a point of view that frames the world and turns nature into a series of living tableaux. It begins as an appreciation of natural beauty, but it ends by turning people into figures in a landscape or figures in a painting" (414). Laurens thus recorded her impressions of the landscape and drew on the picturesque to guide her composition. Reaching a destination was only part of the journey, for anticipating the experience enhanced its pleasures.

Mary Coburn Dewees combines realistic details with a sense of the sublime while describing her surroundings, as on October 12, 1788: "It was really awful pleasing to behold the clouds arising between the mountains at a distance"; October 13: "Proceeded to Larel Creek and ascended the hill. I think this and many more of the scenes we have passed through we have seen Nature display'd in her greatest undress; at other times, we have seen her dress'd Beautiful beyond expression" (12–13).[6] In keeping with Dewees' overall optimism, the inspired scenes testify to nature's glory. At times, she adopts an archaic poetic style, as on November 22: "pass'd Fish Creek, being the largest one we have passed. There is a beautifull level Bottom on each side which, with the hills on hills, which seem to surround it, must render it truly delightfull in the summer season, when the woods are cloathed in their freshest Verdure" (38). With trees bereft of leaves, Dewees projects a lush summer scene, making the location more inviting, if not familiar. She was truly taken by this picturesque landscape with its variety of textures, depths, and typology, as she continues, "The diversity of Mountains & Vallys, and the Creeks that empty into the Ohio on both sides, with a variety of Beautifull Islands in the river, renders it one of the most Beautifull rivers in the World" (40). De-wees promotes the landscape as if she were echoing land development advertisements. Indeed, she was so enthralled with nature that she laments missing anything, even for sleep. On November 25 she wrote: "You can't imagine how much I regret the time lost in sleep, it deprives me of see-ing so many of the Beauties of nature" (46). To this Philadelphian, natu-ral beauty was intoxicating, as she praises rivers, mountains, and valleys and found the landscape welcoming. Elizabeth Van Horne considered her journey to the Ohio frontier inspiring, if also arduous, as she recorded on October 19, 1807: "The views from the *mountains* of the surrounding *Hills & Mountains* were really charming—such prospects I never beheld, all the tops of the surrounding Hills covered with lofty Pines intersperced with Chestnut and Oak. The chilling blasts of Autumn cause them to look variegated Picturesque and grand" (13–14). A willing, enthusiastic trav-eler, Van Horne marks the charming view and the grand pines, as if cap-turing images for later reference or future audiences as she headed into relatively unknown territory. It is interesting to see how quickly the American landscape is traversed and consequently integrated into a na-tional discourse. While Trist ponders the isolation of Pittsburgh in 1784, Mary Coburn Dewees rhapsodizes over the beauties of western Pennsyl-vania in 1788. Simultaneously, the scene appears inhospitable and wel-coming. Notably, the woman's travel narrative offers diverse reactions to a varied landscape.

This impulse to observe and to frame nature in aesthetic terms, in turn, gentrifies the travel experience. For example, in Madame de La Tour du Pin's account of her journey from Boston to Albany via Lebanon in mid-June 1794, nature appears animated and sympathetic: "The remarkable fertility of this virgin land had encouraged the growth of an enormous number of parasitic plants, wild vines and lianas which wound them-selves from one tree to the next. In the more open areas, there were thick-ets of flowering rhododendrons, some of them purple, others pale lilac, and roses of every kind." Wild exotic vines thus contrast with delicate flowering roses in her depiction of upstate New York. La Tour du Pin, who wrote her journal after the fact, more as memoir than travel diary,

frames the scene as if it were a painting, carefully composed and designed:
"The flowers made a vivid splash of colour against the grassland, which
was itself studded with mosses and flowering plants, while in the low-
lying parts which were furrowed, and watered by small streams or creeks,
as they are called, every kind of water plant was in full flower. This unspoiled nature enchanted me to such an extent that I spent the entire day
in ecstasy" (234–35). As La Tour du Pin remembered the scene, it was obviously a source of delight, providing a day of "ecstasy," in fact. Given that
this picturesque portrait was reconstructed after the journey and not
sketched at the moment of viewing, it is not clear if these impressions
were also present in her first encounter, or if they were embellished as her
memory came to imagine them. Composing the scene, rather than recording it as she initially experienced it, results in a more deliberately constructed, literary narrative, one that may not necessarily be invested in du-
plicating reality. In this regard, W. M. Verhoeven rightly acknowledges
"distortion, or misrepresentation of the object" as an "inherent aspect of
the travel narrative," and credits this very quality "with having given the
genre its vitality and diversity," in that there are as many textual formats
as motives (187). For La Tour du Pin, nature appears animated yet enchant-
ing, as a traveler's "distortion" becomes the privilege of the observer.

William Bartram's *Travels* (1791) offers another example in which a
traveler draws on different styles while recounting a journey, in his case
one through the Carolinas, Georgia, and Florida from 1773 to 1778. Into
an otherwise meticulous rendering of scientific data, he occasionally interjects fanciful, descriptive passages, as here while traveling down the
Alatamaha River in Savanna, Georgia: "Thus secure and tranquil, and
meditating on the marvellous scenes of primitive nature, as yet unmodi-
fied by the hand of man, I gently descended the peaceful stream, on whose
polished surface were depicted the mutable shadows from its pensile
banks; whilst myriads of finny inhabitants sported in its pellucid floods.
The glorious sovereign of day, clothed in light refulgent, rolling on his
gilded chariot, hastened to revisit the western realms" (64). Adapting archaic language ("finny inhabitants" for fish) and employing metaphor
and allusion ("glorious sovereign of day, clothed in light refulgent, rolling
on his gilded chariot" for the sun), Bartram casts this beautiful scene as
art. In this unspoiled landscape, Bartram was struck by the picturesque

qualities of the changing light and derived pleasure from the "marvel-lous scenes." Such elaborate and sensitively drawn portraits enhance Bartram's scientific, botanical text. Traveling through Cherokee country in Georgia, Bartram paused to include another vivid sketch: "I approached a charming vale, amidst sublimely high forests, awful shades! Darkness gathers around; far distant thunder rolls over the trembling hills: the black clouds with august majesty and power, move slowly forwards, shading regions of towering hills, and threatening all the destruction of a thunder storm" (281). With slowed motion, Bartram re-creates the approaching storm as an impending danger in romantic, almost gothic, imagery. *Travels* is hardly a straightforward botanical text at this moment; the passage is a testament to nature's powerful beauty. Bartram continues with a dramatic description of the storm's fury, with images alternately romantic and biblical. With his measured prose, Bartram appears the gentleman traveler eager to note his impressions and to play the role of nature's interpreter, all the while aware of the transience of his visit. Given its wide coverage and five-year composition, moreover, *Travels* has less of the urgency of a travel narrative and more of the grand scope of a history. As with other writers who composed after the fact, Bartram tends toward a more literary narrative. Traveling for pleasure allowed even more time for such contemplations and composed renderings.

In keeping with this appreciation for the sublime, the lure and popularity of Niagara Falls increased, and travel guides reinforced its reputation. John F. Sears identifies Niagara Falls as "the preeminent American tourist attraction in the nineteenth century, [one that] had absolutely no counterpart in the Old World. . . . Its height and breadth, and its inexhaustible volume of water flowing over it made it an apt emblem for the resources of the new nation" (12). *The Northern Traveller* refers to the falls as a "sublime scene" and offers specific suggestions for viewing from the American side: "It may be recommended to the traveler to visit this place as often as he can, and to view it from every neighboring point; as every change of light exhibits it under a different and interesting aspect. The rainbows are to be seen, from this side, only in the afternoon; but at that time the clouds of mist, which are continually rising from the gulf below, often present them in the utmost beauty" (74). Following William Gilpin, this scene could be experienced repeatedly "from every neighboring point" in order to capture the changing light and different perspectives. Because nature was so varied, it invited repeated visits and renewed connections, as the traveler sought new perspectives.

Along the tour, a stop to Niagara Falls appeared mandatory, especially as the falls took on mythic qualities. John F. Sears elaborates: "Niagara embodied both the values and the contradictions of the society for which it served as the principal shrine. . . . The manner in which the sacred and profane, the mythic and the trivial, the solemn and the irreverent were mixed at Niagara Falls is a common feature of tourist attractions" (29). Lydia B. Bacon echoed this enthusiasm as she anticipated viewing Niagara Falls in August 1812: "These Falls, of which, I had heard so much, I had a great desire to see, & oft times had said when speaking of returning home, we must see Niagra falls before we return, & now I could be gratified." Moreover, Bacon's opportunity to see them was, as she put it, "strangely brought about": she and her husband were being escorted as British prisoners following their capture within eighteen miles of Detroit as they returned with the troops from the Tippecanoe campaign. Apparently, a prisoner's request to view the falls was considered reasonable: "[I]mmediately after dinner General, & Capt H, Husband, & myself escorted by the *Guards*, proceeded, to the falls, which answered our expectations, as far as we had time to examine them . . . but since then, under more *propitious circumstances*, we have been astonished and delighted with the stupendous & sublime work of nature" (74). Despite the prisoners' status, the guards honored their wish, as if the beauty and power of the falls transcended the restraints of law. Bacon's return to the falls and subsequent pleasure testify to the falls' power to inspire.

Mary Lyon also notes the lure of Niagara.[7] And yet after she had "heard so many things said by one and another who visited the Falls," she was uncertain whether she might be disappointed or delighted. In a letter from Buffalo to her friend and colleague Zilpah Polly Grant, written on August 31, 1833, Lyon elaborates: "I feared that I should be unable to feel the soul-moving power, and I had an ardent desire that I might not acknowledge, even to myself, any second-hand emotions, any influence which did not affect my own heart. But I have been to see for myself, and I am glad I have been. I want to go again; I shall love to dwell on the most distant remembrance" (121). For Lyon, the falls have taken on a spiritual force, influenced by her romantic notions of the landscape and given shape in her travel journal. The power of the scene increases through recollection of one's initial responses to nature. Tourism counts on such desires and repeat visits, and travel writing consequently reflects a kind of anxiety different from that found in the frontier journal. Anticipation, observation, and recollection all contributed to the pleasures of the picturesque traveler.

For the leisured traveler, the travel record affirms the destination almost as if a commodity; for the frontier traveler, the record testifies to survival and accomplishment. Anxiety of class is evident in each account, with varying degrees of sensitivity to being the outsider. This desire to dwell on remembrance appears in the search both for the sublime and for the picturesque, while travel for pleasure encouraged gentrified reactions to nature. John Whale, in fact, describes William Gilpin's picturesque traveler as a "surrogate explorer" who dwells in a "safe middle ground . . . happily mediating the dangerous Burkean opposites of the Sublime and the Beautiful" (176). For travelers who sought this mediated space, as Lyon suggests, the landscape often served as a backdrop to self-discovery, and travel writing became a vehicle for personal reflection.

This interplay between traveler, travel guide, and travel writing is also evident in Maria Sophia Quincy's 1829 journal of a three-week journey from Cambridge, Massachusetts, to Malta, New York, wherein she illustrates a romantic style of travel writing influenced by a tourist sensibility. This was the twenty-four-year-old's first visit to New York, and she was accompanied by her mother, Mrs. Josiah Quincy (Eliza Susan Morton), and her sister, Anna Quincy. They were to visit Mrs. Quincy's sister Margaret, Mrs. David Ritzemer Bogert, in Malta and the nearby Ballston Spa, a fashionable health resort. In this passage from August 12, Quincy describes Saratoga Lake: "Beautiful views of distant mountains, & rivers, the course of which was distinctly marked by the mist hanging above them in the morning air. If the scenery in the Green Mountains would have afforded subjects for a Salvator Rosa, the pencil of a Claude could alone do justice to the exquisite landscape we have seen since we left them" (27).[8] Quincy frames the scene with key elements of the picturesque: the perspective brought on by distance, mountains, and a romantic mood suggested by morning mists. She also alludes to two landscape artists: Italian baroque painter, etcher, and poet Salvator Rosa (1615–73); and the French painter Claude Lorrain (1600–82), considered one of the foremost landscape painters of his day. A naturally beautiful scene is thus refined and complicated through description and allusion. Shirley Foster and Sara Mills note that these artists, along with French baroque painter Nicolas Poussin (1594–1665), were "taken as a standard of evaluation," and including them, as Quincy does, allowed a woman to "claim a certain discursive authority" (92). In addition to these references, Quincy incorporates elements of danger, rendering scenes closer to the sublime. An entry written on the Mohawk Trail, August 15, reads: "We proceeded slowly along a most picturesque road on the high bank above Deerfield River for seven or eight miles, & in my opinion parts of the way were more dangerous than even the mountain road. The woods were very thick almost all the way, & we travelled on till after the moon rose in clouded majesty above the mountains." Quincy dramatizes the scene with imminent harm diffused by the majesty of the moonrise above the mountains. After sustaining the suspense, Quincy adds: "The feeling of danger escaped is certainly one of the pleasantest in the world, & we had bought it dearly" (38–39). As befits a romantic sensibility, Quincy concludes her sublime, romantic experience with triumph. Storytelling and travel narrative thus combine in Quincy's account to reveal her cultural and social influences. As Quincy reminds us, travel is not just about reaching a destination but about having an adventure, and thus the American road narrative begins. To travel is to discover new sights but also to learn about one's preferences through one's reactions to those sights. Quincy anticipates Henry David Thoreau and Mark Twain in this passage as she marvels at nature's beauty and finds pleasure in escaping danger while "on the road."

Increased leisured travel further inspired tours both grand and fashionable, and travel records reflect an interesting familiarity with certain locations, such as Ballston Spa and Saratoga Springs. On September 23, 1830, Elizabeth Gilpin, for example, reflected on her day's travels by the steamboat North America, headed for Albany: "We retired to bed pretty well tired particularly with looking, as I did all day through my glass. For every moment new beauties presented themselves before me and I feared to miss any of the pleasure I had so long anticipated from a sail up the far-famed Hudson. Nor was I in the least disappointed; for however great were my expectations, they were fully realized and seldom if ever have I passed a day of more gratification" (10). Travel is thus richly contextualized by anticipation and reflection, as the now famous Hudson River fortunately lived up to Gilpin's expectations. Throughout her thirty-seven-day, seven-hundred-mile journey, Gilpin expressed similar enthusiasm for sightseeing, noting social aspects as well as natural phenomena, as on October 13, when she arrived at Trenton Falls "just at dark, and found the hotel there, the 'Rural Resort,' an excellent one, and the people most attentive and civil" (19). Though the next day was rainy, they ventured out, and she was quite pleased with views of Conrad's Mills Fall and Sherman's Falls: "On turning a corner, we come in sight of the first falls, a broad sheet of water rushing over an immense ledge of rocks, which extends across the river, and on the left hand the water having worn a deep niche or hollow in the rock, rushes over with great violence and noise and causes a great spray, which covers you and the path on which you walk" (20–21). Delighted by the power and beauty, Gilpin then relates a story about "Mr. Bill" who "slipped into the torrent and was carried down the fall this summer," and then resumes her descriptions: "The next fall or falls, for it consists of two separate falls one above the other, is by far the most beautiful and grand. It is really beyond my powers of description, for I never saw any thing equal to it. It is called the Amber fall from the color of the water in one part which is a rich amber, until it unites in one mass of foam with the rest below" (21). The sights and the scramble up a narrow path to view yet another fall were accompanied by several harrowing stories of walkers who had slipped into the river, the terror heightening the pleasure. Before departing the next day, Gilpin "rejoiced to behol[d] the sun," which prompted a quick return to the falls: "The scene was far more beautiful than the day before, as the rain of the two days had increased the water very much, and the bright sun formed a most beautiful rainbow over the falls" (24). In these passages, Gilpin conveys a tourist's excitement for the new adventure and the exciting vista, and her narrative style reflects the subsequent control of a leisured traveler, pressed neither for time nor resources.

Elizabeth Gilpin seems to have drawn from two guidebooks here. Her brother, Henry Dilworth Gilpin, in his *A Northern Tour*, describes Trenton

Falls as "a beautiful cataract of great elevation, immediately below which is a bridge of ninety feet span. This fall is a mass of cascades, of unequal height; and all combined form one of the most picturesque views that can be imagined" (97). *The Northern Traveller* includes this passage describing Trenton Falls: "This most interesting vicinity is well worthy the attention of every person of taste, being justly considered one of the finest natural scenes in this part of the country" (55). It also warns of "dangerous" places along the paths, recounting a "melancholy accident" in 1827 in which "a lady from New-York was drowned by slipping from a low bank; unseen, although her friends and parents were near her" (56). Such parallels give documentation new meaning, as the traveler follows the travel guide's recommendations and the later account verifies that the traveler has indeed visited the right spots and followed the appropriate routes marking the tour. Beauty and potential terror combine to create a sublime adventure. The similarities between Elizabeth Gilpin's entries and the guides' recommendations demonstrate the infusion of status into the act of travel. In Marjorie McNinch's preface to the Gilpin journal, she reinforces the connections between traveler and travel guide: "Remarks about fashion, architecture, music, and art, as well as descriptions of towns and cities, are sometimes remarkably similar to travel-guide passages" (228). Though Elizabeth Gilpin never mentions her brother's guide, these parallels do hint at shared knowledge, and perhaps collaboration at some level. Clearly, the travel guide imposes a sense of control on the landscape, while the American Grand Tour confirmed settlement, nationalism, and social identity, prompting women to view the landscape as a composition on which they could improve and that they could recollect in their travel accounts. By contrast to the explorer, who sought unfamiliar territory, the eastern traveler set off for destinations that had gained a sublime reputation. These are perspectives that Elizabeth House Trist, for one, could not have imagined because of her concerns for survival, let alone her sense of the travel diary and its overall intention. The traveler in pursuit of transcendent states was probably not worried about the rigors of homesteading. A versatile genre, travel writing can thus range from adventure and conquest to contemplation and discovery. Showing great flexibility, the travel narrative can accommodate travelers who infuse the text with moments of beauty and those who write tentatively about an unfamiliar land.

From the Grand Tour to the Westward Journey

How quaint the picturesque view appears when compared to Margaret Van Horn Dwight's comments on October 27, 1810, from Mansfield, New Jersey: "We yesterday travell'd the worst road you can imagine—over mountains & thro' vallies—We have not I believe, had 20 rods of level ground the whole day . . . so rocky & so gullied, as to be almost impass-able" (13). Focused on details, Dwight highlights the frustrations of day-to-day conditions and shows no interest in contextualizing her experience. Such descriptions give chase to the idea of travel as a sublime experience. In Dwight's report, the very congestion of westward travel is more likely to elicit complaints than inspired meditations on national progress, as in this remark Dwight made while crossing the Allegheny Mountains on November 17: "From what I have seen and heard, I think the State of Ohio will be well fill'd before winter,—Waggons without number, every-day go on—One went on containing forty people—We almost every day, see them with 18 or 20—one stopt here to night with 21—We are at a baker's, near a tavern which is fill'd with movers & waggoners" (47). Many taverners, overwhelmed by this volume, grew wary and indiffer-ent and felt no inclination to provide more than the most basic services. On November 5, West of Carlisle, Pennsylvania, Dwight recorded, "The man says he has been so bother'd with movers, that he has taken down his sign, for he does not need his tavern to live" (30). This was not the leisure travel market, but a determined group of emigrants. According to Dwight's unflattering account, migration was a haphazard, congested affair. Possibly as a coping strategy, Dwight maintained a sense that she could always return, although the route was daunting. Only one week into the journey, Dwight wrote to her cousin: "I wish I could fly back to you a few minutes while we are waiting" (13). At this point, travel occa-sioned more homesickness than adulation. Dwight often plays down the advantages of migration and remains intent on evaluating her journey for its potential for sociability. This reluctance to portray her experience as particularly grand or unique further distinguishes the travel narrative from travel writing. While such responses undercut an explorer's bravado, they are realistic and commendable in their own right. Dwight never backed down from the challenge, nor does she gloss over the difficulties.

Women who traveled for relocation communicate a sensibility altogether different from that communicated by women who traveled for pleasure. Pontification and contemplation require less urgent circumstances. For this initial wave of westward travelers, diary keeping was valued more as a historical record of a singular event, of an unparalleled journey in a woman's life, than as an opportunity to experience nature as sublime. Consequently, these earlier travelers often describe a radical reorientation process while writing about the land, as they were alternately emboldened and frustrated, with nature a certain challenge.

Women's relationship to nature is distinguished and varied. In Susan Scott Parrish's discussion of early American women naturalists, she identifies a "complex female connection with American nature" (197). Colonial women were curious observers and, according to Parrish, active collectors who were occupied by "digging up flowering plants, [and who] squelched along the shore in search of bivalves, drew outlines of hundreds of leaves, carefully packed butterflies to reach cataloguers in Europe, filled silk bags with quantities of seeds, or rose early to measure comets" (206). Women thus meticulously explored and investigated their surroundings. It follows, then, as Glenda Riley asserts, that "in large part, the idea of female fear of nature is a myth. A significant proportion of American women loved nature. They drew upon a longstanding tradition of outdoor activity established by generations of European, especially English, women predecessors" (xii–xiii). Although Riley's observations may better suit women who lived in more urban settings, the desire among pioneer women to cultivate flower gardens echoes these sensibilities. Their candid reactions to a new landscape and their realistic descriptions, furthermore, countered both land-development promotions of the prairies and tourist-oriented advertisements to offer a view that was less easily packaged. Eighteenth-century women may not have embraced nature in the same spirit as the nineteenth-century traveler, yet women's journals in general offer an important alternative to the traveler as simply the appropriating conqueror or the stalwart pioneer. This is an important distinction, for women expressed various responses to the land. Uncertain at times, curious and bold at others, they were clearly not passive but commendably engaged in the rigorous demands of travel.

Narrative styles reflecting these various responses to the land are often intertwined, especially if there was a significant gap between the time of the journey and the time of composition. As previously noted, Lydia B. Bacon's journal was initially composed in 1811–12 and then reconstructed in the 1830s and thus provides an interesting combination of travel narrative and travel writing. She in fact notes this gap between composition and reconstruction with caution, warning that her memory may have deceived her: "[W]hile reading you must keep in mind, Dear James, that these events, transpired, more than *twenty years since*" (371). The journal adheres to the travel narrative's descriptive style and adds a romanticized sense of nature. Bacon often blends these styles, for example, on June 26, 1811, from Pittsburgh: "We arrived here 10 days since after a tedious yet delightful journey, tedious in consequence of the extreme roughness of the road, but rendered delightful by the beauty of the surrounding landscap. On every side was exhibited, to our admiring eyes, a constant succession of scenery, at once *grand, sublime, awful & sweet*. A variety of emotions, fill my mind, at the survey of God works, everything is calculated, for our instruction, comfort, & pleasure" (371). Adapting the language of the picturesque, Bacon acknowledges spiritual elements of beauty that reinforced "our dependence on the Author . . . could we be sensible of our obligation to him" (371). In retrospect, Bacon could cast the scene in philosophical language—a discourse that she may or may not have initially used when dealing with the daily rigors of travel. Twenty years after the journey, Bacon remembered her experiences in religious terms and wrote in a style closer to travel memoir in both its reminiscence and its lengthy descriptions. Women's travel writings reflect the range of their connections to nature. Stephane Elise Booth, for one, sees the relationship between the land and the traveler as an interactive one, in which the frontier would "modify" women's eastern values: "But just as these women were altered by their frontier experience, the frontier was likewise transformed as the women built new lives for themselves and their families" (2). In hindsight, the pioneer's vision was based on notions of progress that embraced the frontier with a sense of entitlement. But to read the woman's travel narrative as a contemporary document, she did not necessarily consider her slow, arduous journey as an obvious sign of improvement. The more familiar and settled the lands became, the more confident and stylized the responses, as they reveal cultural and aesthetic preferences.

The distinctions between a scene rendered realistically and one rendered idealistically are especially apparent when a nineteenth-century author recounted an eighteenth-century pioneer's tale. Elizabeth Dewey Follett's experiences in the Wyoming Territory in 1775–83, for example, were initially passed down as oral history.[9] They were transcribed in 1880 by Jane Elizabeth Parker Ward and titled "A Few Pages from My Great Grandmother's Diary," and then edited and published in 1931 by Ward's daughter, Annette Persis Ward. Though the narrative is not a primary source, its very reconstruction provides some interesting differences between these sensibilities. For example, in the first entry, Ward's version of Follet's perspective of the Wyoming Valley includes this description: "[January 1st, 1775] Our farm is on the left side of the river, bounded by it on one side. The house faces the stream, and is about fifty rods from it. I never tire of watching its ceaseless flow; and looking beyond at the evergreen summit of the mountain ridge. I could not wish to be in a more lovely spot; and, had I my dear friends with me, should call it a Paradise on earth" (1).[10] As do other women, Follett notes a lack of friends and social connections that detracted from the setting. Still, the images are bucolic and peaceful, and they refute notions of nature as threatening and dangerous. Ward's romantic rendering of Follett's story is again suggested on June 27, 1778: "The sun has just set behind a mountain, and the heavens are still bright from his rays, altogether it is a perfect evening. As I sit here on the porch and feast my eyes upon the beauties of this lovely valley, and inhale the fragrance of the rose-scented air; a feeling of sadness creeps over me, a premonition of approaching evil" (6). Although Follett's fears were immediately realized—her house was attacked the next day by a combined Tory-Indian assault that left her without home and husband—the scene has a definite romantic cast, as per Ward's late nineteenth-century perspective. By 1880, the now settled frontier had taken on its own mythology, reinforced here by restful moments and flower-scented air.

Regarding style and travel writing, a final comparison accentuates differences that are particularly evident in comparing narratives that cover similar territory. Elizabeth House Trist's 1783–84 *Travel Diary* and Washing-

ton Irving's *A Tour on the Prairies* (1835), for example, each describe journeys in the Ohio frontier, one with the urgent intensity of a potential
settler, the other with the bemused attitude of an adventure seeker. Trist
records the names of the rivers, towns, forts, and landmarks and emphasizes the novelty of her surroundings with realistic details, as on May 22,
1784: "After a good nights rest we arose, had a comfortable breakfast.
By 9 Oclock got as far as the Muskingum, 171 miles from Pittsburg: a fine
River about 300 yds wide, about 200 miles in length, takes its rise from
a swamp about 40 miles this side lake Erie" (216). By contrast, when Irving ventured west four decades later, the routes were well established and
the narrative record could go beyond simple place identification. On October 13, 1832, he wrote: "The encampment now presented a picturesque
appearance. Camp fires were blazing and smoldering here and there
among the trees, with groups of rangers round them seated or lying on
the ground, others standing in the ruddy glare of the flames, or in shad-
owy relief" (59). The scene is further framed as a pleasant, enjoyable out-
ing. October 14, 1832: "It was a bright sunny morning, with a pure trans-
parent atmosphere that seemed to bathe the very heart with gladness"
(63). Irving also enhances *Tour* with the antics of the camp and the dangers of the buffalo hunt and conveys the excitement without the danger.
Hunting buffalo might even lead to a sublime moment, while watching
bees brought a vision of natural harmony: "[A]t present, the honey-bee
swarms in myriads, in the noble groves and forests which skirt and in-
tersect the prairies, and extend along the alluvial bottoms of the rivers.
It seems as if these beautiful regions answer literally to the description
of the land of promise, 'a land flowing with milk and honey'" (51). Although Irving intended his *Tour* as a travel narrative rather than a fictional
account, his narrative style embellishes and dramatizes his adventurous
plot, moving the travel narrative closer to the realm of entertainment.
Whereas Trist found the landscape formidable, for Irving, it was a source
of enjoyment. The pioneer travel narrative is also less self-consciously literary and thereby more informative about the realities of travel. Appropriately, in Cheryl J. Fish's study of women's nineteenth-century travel
writing, she notes: "Their emphasis on usefulness and reform distinguishes these works from popular travel writing by literary figures, such
as Washington Irving's *A Tour on the Prairies*" (3). Travel writing plays down

the everyday hardships of the journey in order to emphasize the pleasurable moments. The travel writer wants his or her adventure to be admired for the extravagance of the journey or the scope of the vista. As such, travel writing can tend toward embellishment, whereas the didactic travel narrative is often more laconic or sparely modified.

—❧

As women's travel writings link social, philosophical, and literary developments, they serve all the more clearly as a valuable index of cultural change. As this chapter suggests, the travel narrative focuses on the rudiments of travel and is written in a plain, descriptive style. Travel writing adapts a more embellished, romantic tone. To appreciate these different styles is to recognize their dual intentions: one to inform, the other to please. Audiences more accustomed to contemporary travel writing may recognize in it elements of both styles—the didactic and the descriptive. Nature writing, like travel writing, has often been considered to be the realm of the male author and explorer. As this chapter indicates, however, women were actively observing nature and studiously recording their findings. The onset of leisured travel and the American Grand Tour further encouraged women's participation in tracking the picturesque and marveling at the sublime. Women's records thus provide important evidence of how aesthetics came to bear on travel and travel writing.

To understand why women recorded their journeys is to uncover the importance of the record itself. In many cases, women took on the role of cultural purveyor, which explains the numerous passages that attempted to assert a social order. In the following chapter, I examine how women writers of travel narratives scrutinize public houses, accommodations, fashion, religion, and slavery with a shared concern for decorum and an interest in reinforcing a genteel social view. Although their reactions to rustic or unfamiliar conditions are appropriate to women of their genteel class, their avid interest in social interactions and their willingness to adapt speaks as well to a strength that oversteps class and gender.

2

Ordinary Travel

PUBLIC HOUSES AND TRAVEL CONDITIONS

*I*n addition to providing visual images of the landscape, the travel narrative offers key information about public houses and the conditions of travel. Not only did these institutions serve a civic function by sheltering travelers, but they also provided entertainment and thus a connection to local culture. When traveling along the eastern seaboard, a traveler might expect some conformity of lodging, with variations in food and entertainment. Accommodations along the western routes were by contrast sporadic and the quality inconsistent. Except for rare artifacts, such as the tavern signage from the Connecticut Historical Society and other institutions, we have little physical evidence of these once dynamic meeting places. Travelers fill this gap with descriptions that shed light on the material culture of travel and provide important historical documentation. Women's travel narratives are especially valuable in this regard, for they provide vivid descriptions of interior spaces and class interactions. Men also noted their surroundings, but with generally less attention paid to social factors. From the woman's travel narrative, we can reconstruct what taverns and inns looked like and their function as socially integrated meeting places for travelers and locals alike.[1]

From the start, accommodating travelers and traders was both a commercial venture and a civic obligation. In Boston on March 4, 1634, as Governor John Winthrop reported, Samuel Cole "set up the first house for common entertainment" to shelter travelers (1:110). By 1644, as Alice

Morse Earle explains, the Colonial Records of Connecticut "ordered 'one sufficient inhabitant' in each town to keep an ordinary since 'strangers were straightened' for want of entertainment" (2). Samuel Adams Drake notes that taverns were such "a recognized need" in early America that they were "licensed as fast as new villages grew up" (11). Public houses, also known as taverns, inns, and ordinaries, were established along popular trade routes and in towns, as Mary Caroline Crawford notes, they were frequently located "right next-door to the meeting house" (12). Earle adds a further note on nomenclature: "By the end of the seventeenth century the word ordinary was passing into disuse in America; public houses had multiplied vastly and had become taverns . . . the word inn, universal in English speech, was little heard here, and tavern was universally adopted" (30). When mail service was instituted in 1693, road conditions improved, and overland travel began to compete with water transportation, leading eventually to viable stage travel. In 1752, the first stagecoach service was thus set up to cover the fifty miles between Burlington and Amboy, New Jersey (Rice, 43). By the 1770s, a stagecoach ride between New York and Philadelphia took only two days. Until railroad travel supplanted the stage in the mid-nineteenth century, tavern culture thrived on the assumption that the coach required a stop every ten miles or so to replenish horse and traveler, and establishments were built accordingly at regular intervals. Thomas Prince's 1732 The Vade Mecum for America; or, a Companion for Traders and Travellers, in fact, marked distances between taverns and inns rather than between towns, as they are measured today. Tavern culture thus intersected early American commerce and paralleled the growing communication and social structures.

Public houses were clearly information centers where letters, newspapers, and gazettes were exchanged and traveler, merchant, and local clientele met. In early modern Germany, as B. Ann Tlusty explains, public houses had many functions, as "bookshops, post offices, lost and found depots, employment offices, advertising agencies, and even museums, where traveling showmen displayed collections of wonders. . . . Public taverns were also the natural choice for the open reading of ordinances, broadsheets, and other news items, as well as for reading and discussing the latest books" (162). Early American taverns continued in these traditions, as David Conroy reports: "Newspapers were delivered via taverns; thus

194   FAIRS &c.

BAPTISTS General Meetings.

AT Welch Tract in New-Caftle County, 2d Lord's Day in May.
At Cohanfie, Laft Lord's Day in May.
At Pifcataqua in New-Jerfey, 4th Lord's Day in June.
At Philadelphia, 4th Lord's Day September.
At Newport on Rhode-Ifland, 2d Lord's Day in June.

FAIRS are kept,

April	October
24 At Cohanfie,	16 At Cohanfie,
30 At New-York,	20 At Salem,
May	5 At Chefter,
1 At Salem,	16 At Jamaica,
3 At New-Caftle,	20 At German town
5 At Chefter,	29 At Briftcl,
8 At Briftol,	November
10 At Burlington,	1 At Burlington,
16 At Philadelphia	3 At New-Caftle,
12 At Providence,	5 At New-York,
18 At Amboy,	16 At Philadelphia
6 At Jamaica,	Amboy.

FAIRS in New-England.

At BRISTOL,
Third Wednefday, Thurfday & Friday, in May and October.

At LONDONDERRY,
Second Tuefday in May and October.

The

195   ROADS &c.

The Principal ROADS, with their feveral Stages and Diftances.
I. From BOSTON North-Eaftward, to PORTSMOUTH & KENNEBECK River.
N.B. R ftands for River.

1. From Bofton over Charlftown Ferry.

Public Places	Miles		Towns.
Town Ho			Boston.
Long's	1	1	Charlftown.
The Bridge	4¼	5¼	Medford.
Moor's	4¼	10	Lyn.

2. From Bofton over Winifimet Ferry.

Town-Ho	Miles		Boston.
Watt's	2¼	2¼	Winnifimet
Moor's	6½	9	Lyn
Pratt's	8	17	Salem
		20	Beverly over the Ferry
Fowler's	4	24	Wenham
Staniford's	7	31	Ipfwich
	4	35	Rowley
Woodbridge's	7	42	Newbury Ferry
			Salisbury over the Ferry
Collins's	9	51	Hampton
Fellows's	13	64	Portsmouth
			Kittery, over the Ferry
York Ferry	7	71	York
BricTavern	2	75	Ditto
Ferry	4	77	Cape Nedduck
Storer's	10	87	Wells
Little River	3	90	Ditto
Moufam R.	1	91	Ditto
Ferry	2	93	Kennebunk
M Houfe	4	97	Arundel
Batfon's R	1	98	Ditto
Randal's R.	3	101	Ditto
Ferry	6	107	Biddeford

Goofe Fare

THOMAS PRINCE, "FAIRS AND ROADS &C." This detail lists local fairs and indicates principal routes, with distances measured between taverns and inns. Thomas Prince, The Vade Mecum for America; or, A Companion for Traders and Travellers, 1732, 194–95. Courtesy American Antiquarian Society, Worcester, Massachusetts.

public houses were probably the most important gathering places to hear the news read and interpreted" (236). David Flaherty finds that public houses were "much more significant as regular centers of community life than the religious or political meeting houses" (105). Quite simply, as Edward Field claims, "all news emanated from the tavern" (4). In 1794, Madame de La Tour du Pin confirmed this observation: "[O]n the road to Canada, stood a large inn where all the news, gazettes and sales notices were to be found. Two or three stage coaches stopped there every day" (241). This reciprocity—shelter for information—contributed to making the public house an equitable space in which class differences were suspended out of courtesy and mutual enterprise.

The public house as communication hub facilitated social interaction, and the mixing of classes contributed to new social environments. Conroy notes that taverns were a "fertile breeding ground for new possibilities in social and political relationships" (2). Carl Bridenbaugh agrees that the tavern was a "great center for middle and lower class activities" (426). David S. Shields finds that the coffeehouse, in particular, became "the space where gentlemen communed with merchants because news became their common idiom" (xx). Conroy adds that as the "vast majority of colonial patrons were men," this pattern "reinforced patriarchal control of the diffusion of information" (43n59). Where drinking was particularly prominent, women were largely excluded as regular visitors to taverns and tended to gather around the marketplace or to meet in homes. By contrast, men "shared a sense of privacy in the public sphere," as Flaherty explains, by congregating in "one of the several small rooms into which the usual tavern was divided" (105–6). Though predominately frequented by men, public houses became increasingly egalitarian spaces, and, as Shields elaborates, these venues "enabled persons to bridge distinctions" based on rank or profession (xx). The rising hotel industry followed suit, as Eliza Williams Bridgham verified such interaction on July 29, 1818, from Saratoga Springs: "Here are rich & poor, old & young, sick & well, learned & illiterate, all in the same dwelling, some whose manners are superior, for refinement & elegance, others who are really clownish" (22). Whether frequented for business or pleasure, the public house was a scene of unprecedented intermixing of classes and gender. Women contributed to this interaction by partaking in meals and taking up lodging and, as did all travelers, became part of the larger transference of culture and news.

Travelers played another role in disseminating information through the distribution of letters, which were often passed on by travelers, some-

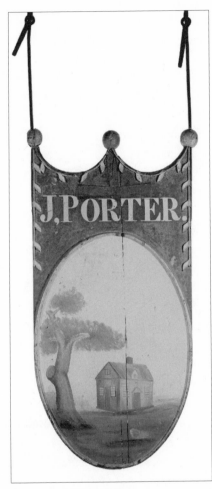

TAVERN SIGN FOR J. PORTER'S INN. This small establishment for the accommodation of travelers was located in Farmington, Connecticut. "Sign for Porter's Inn," Farmington, Connecticut, ca. 1820–25, Connecticut Historical Society Museum, Hartford, Connecticut.

times left on a front table for the willing traveler to pick up and take along. Following a practice carried over from London, the tavern and coffeehouse often served as postal depots for gentlemen, who could stop by, receive their mail, and catch up on local business matters. William Merrill Decker affirms that "generally [letters] proceeded by courtesy of overland travelers or ship captains who happened to be going in the direction of the addressee; such unofficial carriers might upon arrival at their destinations leave the letter at a designated drop point, turn it over to a local post, or deliver the letter personally" (58). This practice had become commonplace enough in 1722 for John Lloyd, postmaster general, to warn in the *American Weekly Mercury* on October 25: "Passengers travelling the Post-Roads" caught carrying letters or packets to be delivered "to the Person they are directed [to]" would be fined "Five Pounds Sterling for every Letter or Packet." Perhaps such warnings prompted a stagecoach advertisement from the *Salem Gazette*, April 16, 1784, to actually list the letters remaining at the local post office. In notes to the Abigail Franks letters, Leo Hershkowitz and Isidore S. Meyer elaborate on mail distribution: "Mail Delivery in the eighteenth century was a fairly haphazard affair but with all its faults worked quite well" (2:4n). They note that in addition to the official postal service, people often used "the services of ships captains or of friends traveling abroad" to send letters, or mail pouches were simply left in local taverns and coffeehouses. Moreover, "in London mail was delivered by the post. In the colonies, mail had to be picked up at the post office" (2:4n). For greater convenience and faster delivery, then, overseas letters were often conveyed by personal means, as the ships' schedules were more regular than the post.

Entrusting a letter to strangers or leaving it in a public house, moreover, kept it relatively safe from prying eyes, for, as Flaherty notes, even though "letters were objects of intense curiosity . . . [a] large majority of the male population and the overwhelming majority of women in colonial New England were not capable of reading or writing a letter" (117). Letters left at the tavern were also assumed to be semipublic, so any revealing information would most likely have been omitted. Elizabeth Hewitt points out that "while the 1792 Post Office Act explicitly made illegal the public scrutiny of letters, distinguishing itself from Britain where the public interrogation of letters by post office officials was sanctioned, the law depended on the notion that such arbitrary and intrusive measures were unnecessary simply because no real American would write a letter that would violate laws" (32). These protections were further aided by the assumption that "obedience is made identical to freedom." Self-restraint assured that the virtuous colonist would safely distribute letters along with the news. One would stop by the tavern, then, for mail and entertainment, with the traveler occasionally acting as postal agent.

Although men operated the majority of public houses, women often shared proprietorship duties with their husbands and if warranted assumed ownership as widows, for women could not legally own licenses otherwise. Elizabeth Dexter explains that a widow could "find no readier means of maintaining her home than that of entertaining travelers" (2). In New England from 1620 to 1699, 71 percent of female tavern owners were widows, and of the twenty-five female tavern owners in Boston, nineteen were widows (Rice, 51). In 1647, for example, the widowed Mrs. Clark of Salem was licensed "to keep an ordinary with 'liberty to draw wine,'" and in 1666, Elizabeth Sharret (Sherrod) was licensed "to keep the ordinary at Haverhill" (Dexter, 3). Stipulations were imposed, however, as Mrs. Clark's license was issued "under the condition that she provide a fitt man y^t [that] is goodlie to manage ye business," and Elizabeth Sharret eventually lost her license after being sued for "not paying for a pipe of wine and other goods" (Dexter, 3). Larger, more densely populated areas provided women better opportunity, as Sharon Salinger elaborates: "Women were more likely to be the proprietors of taverns in cities, especially port cities, than in smaller towns or the countryside" (162). Alice Morse Earle finds that in 1714, women ran twelve out of the thirty-four inns in Boston (25). Salinger's records indicate that in Boston of 1764–65, 119 women held 41.6 percent of the total tavern licenses; in Philadelphia of 1762–63, 69 women held licenses, or 24.4 percent of the total; in Charleston of 1762–63, 75 women were licensed, or 48.3 percent of the total (163). Other examples in Boston and the surrounding area include Alice Thomas in the 1670s, Hannah Bishop of the Green Dragon Inn in the 1670s, Frances Wardell in the 1710s and 1720s, Susanna Carter in Boston in 1704, Rebecca Holmes of the Bunch of Grapes Tavern in the 1720s, Deborah Chick of the Half Moon Inn in 1752, Judah Richardson on the Boston Road in the 1750s, Mrs. Joseph Mann in Wrentham in the 1750s, Mrs. Dorothy Whitney Coolidge in Watertown in the mid-1770s, and Mary Cranch in Boston in the mid-1770s.[2] Tavern licensure laws did stipulate that "only honest and upright, and preferably male, persons were qualified," but, as Salinger notes, "officials did take into account the petitioner's economic position" (164). Thus, depending on their financial and marital status and in certain regions, women managed taverns in respectable numbers.

When competition was especially fierce, ownership and licenses were more intensely scrutinized. This factor may have contributed to a steady decline in female tavern keepers. For example, as Conroy notes, in 1768 in Boston 11 of 25 new retailers were women, but by 1796, only 9 of the 128 retailers in Boston were women. By 1812, there were no female tavern owners registered of the 56 licensed (318). In southern Rowan County, North Carolina, Daniel B. Thorp adds, "female tavern keepers were almost unknown" (680). Demographics offer one reason, as there were simply fewer women, which "meant that remarriage was more likely for widows" (681–82). This decline in female tavern ownership may also be explained by a shift to other lodging alternatives that could

provide women with more
privacy.

This desire for privacy is
further indicated by changes
in tavern furnishings in the
1760s. Separate chairs supple-
mented benches in the common room, and single beds and
private rooms were added for
the wealthier patrons (Thorp,
684). Alice Morse Earle notes
that one indication of a good
inn was the additional comfort of a parlor, which was used
as "a sitting room for women
travelers" (41). In keeping
with this trend of offering more individual space, the popularity of the
boardinghouse had increased by midcentury. And whereas the tavern and
inn required a license for serving alcohol, the boardinghouse was a simpler operation. The proprietor let out separate rooms and offered a
weekly rather than a daily rate; this made the boardinghouse less expen-
sive and allowed the proprietor to be "selective about his/her lodgers"
(Rice, 42). Mary Beth Norton finds that "a woman could make a comfortable living from taking in lodgers" (145). Elizabeth Murray, who adver-
tised for needlework classes in the April 8, 1751, edition of the Boston
Evening Post, added that she "likewise accommodates—young Ladies with
Board and half Board, at a reasonable Price." Two weeks later, in the

April 22, 1751, Post, Elinor and Mary Purcell placed an almost identical ad for sewing lessons and boarding for "young Ladies." Four years later, we have Mary Jackson's ad in the Pennsylvania Gazette on June 5, 1755, for her public house, "where all travelers, and others, who may be kind enough to favor her with their custom, may depend on being well accommodated." Jackson's ad was one of many placed in the Pennsylvania Gazette, for as Elsie L. Lathrop explains, Pennsylvania was the gateway to the frontier for the "adventurous young men [who] were always going in search of new lands. . . . All of these travellers passed through Pennsylvania" (142). Additional advertisements and notices from the Boston Evening Post for boarding include Elizabeth Pike in Portsmouth, April 5, 1742; Mrs. Margaret Pratt in Salem, April 5, 1742; Yetmercy Howland in Bristol, April 2, 1744; Rebecca Wetherell in Plymouth, May 7, 1744; Mrs. Abigail Jarvice in Roxbury, April 15, 1751; Mary Perkins in Gloucester, January 6, 1755; Dorothy Coolidge in Watertown, February 20, 1775; Ann Slayton in Portsmouth, May 26, 1755; and Sarah Cutler in Weston, January 4, 1762 (Dexter, 12).[3] As proprietors, women participated in this social commerce by opening their homes to boarders and assuming ownership of taverns and inns, and as travelers, they contributed to this industry by patronizing these establishments and taking shelter.

Public Houses and Accommodations

Taverns and inns were compact, multipurpose buildings, often with a downstairs for dining, socializing, and entertainment and an upstairs with several small rooms for accommodations. According to Kym Rice's estimation, "most taverns were equipped with between 6 and 8 beds, enough to accommodate 12 to 16 men" (103). Larger quarters were described in the Philadelphia Chronicle, August 31–September 7, 1767, when Jonathan Haight placed an ad for the "Ferry-House" tavern in Bristol, "pleasantly situated on the River Delaware, and on the Post Road to New York," and noted that the house was "sufficient to accommodate 30 Travellers at one time," and the stable was "large enough to accommodate 30 horses as well." By 1818, these numbers had increased dramatically, as Eliza Williams Bridgham indicated in an entry previously cited from Saratoga Springs on July 29: "[T]his house, which is called 'Congress Hall,' accommodates

150, at this present time. It is 197 feet in length & three stories in height"
(22). Although most inns were rather simple, nondescript buildings,
Bridgham noted an exception while traveling to Cambridge on July 28,
1818: "The public house at this place goes by the name of the 'Chequered
Inn' for many miles, it being painted entirely in large squares of <u>deep red</u>
<u>& white</u>—you don't know, what a curious effect it has" (21). Bridgham's
astonishment suggests a sharp contrast to the public house's rudimentary
beginnings, as the public house began to serve a more leisured travel
market.

In both the modest and the more elaborate establishments, the rule of
the marketplace dictated that tavern keepers receive two sources of income per bed, and all travelers were expected to share beds. Public houses
logically adapted these customs, and with men as the majority of travelers, the practice was unremarkable. Alice Morse Earle reminds us that
communal accommodations were simply the norm: "Many of the rooms
were double-bedded, and four who were strangers to each other often
slept in each other's company. . . . Mr. Twining said that after you were
asleep the landlord entered, candle in hand and escorted a stranger to
your side, and he calmly shared the bed till morning. Thurlow Weed said
that any one who objected to a stranger as bedfellow was regarded as ob-
noxious and as unreasonably fastidious" (78–79). A woman who traveled with a female servant or friend would then share a bed with her, but
the other beds in the same room could easily be occupied by men, especially if the rooms were not divided or the whole house shared a common
sleeping area. Sleeping arrangements complied with general communal
norms, for, as Earle notes, "manners were rude enough at many country
taverns until well into the century. There could be no putting on of airs,
no exclusiveness. All travelers sat at one table" (78). Dr. Alexander Hamilton, on June 8, 1744, dined at a tavern in Philadelphia with "a very mixed
company of different nations and religions" and described this scene:
"There were Scots, English, Dutch, Germans, and Irish; there were Roman
Catholicks, Church men, Presbyterians, Quakers, Newlightmen, Methodists, Seventh day men, Moravians, Anabaptists, and one Jew. The whole
company consisted of 25 planted around an oblong table in a great hall
well stoked with flys. The company divided into comittees in conversation;
the prevailing topick was politicks and conjectures of a French war" (191).[4]

As Hamilton suggests, the communal arrangements not only collapsed social hierarchies but offered opportunity for lively conversation as well.

In keeping with these overall communal practices, travel narratives are filled with references to being awakened in the middle of the night by the innkeeper to make room for another occupant in one's bed. There was often an extra charge for a fire in the room, which may have reinforced the practicality of doubling up (Forbes, 2:3). Within the public house's homosocial world, which catered to the male traveler, this practice went unnoted unless accompanied by unusual commotion. Madame de La Tour du Pin confirmed this general custom in her account of her journey through Massachusetts and New York in 1794: "[W]hen the bed was fairly wide, you would even be asked, as if it were the most normal thing in the world, to allow someone to share it with you." Upon spending the night at an inn at Lebanon that was "very good, and above all, impeccably clean," La Tour du Pin shared this account:

> This is what happened to M. de Chambeau that very evening at Lebanon. In the middle of the night, we suddenly heard a stream of French oaths, which could come only from him. In the morning we learned that towards midnight he had been awakened by a gentleman who was sliding, without so much as a "by your leave" into the empty half of his double bed. Furious at this invasion, he promptly leaped out at the other side and spent the night in a chair listening to his companion's snores, for he had been in no way disturbed by M. de Chambeau's anger. This misadventure led to much teasing from everyone. When we arrived that evening at Albany, a small room was reserved for him alone, and that consoled him. (236)

Although Chambeau's response to this "invasion" appears somewhat comical and his anger out of place, his reaction does identify class issues and presumptions of privacy, concerns also expressed by many female travelers. While sharing beds was practical, resistance suggests that travel challenged personal codes of behavior, with the traveler—not the public house—expected to conform.

It was common to share beds in one's home for the sake of warmth, moreover, and double occupancy in the tavern bed was merely a continuation of that practice. David Flaherty adds that the "representative home in seventeenth-century New England had one-half to two stories with a central chimney" (35), and, that being the case, "communal living was still expected" (37). From this perspective, sharing beds for warmth was both sensible and practical. Richard Godbeer concurs: "New Englanders did not expect to sleep alone: they shared bedchambers and beds with family members, servants, and strangers in need of accommodation" (93). Sydney Geo. Fisher elaborates that not only were strangers welcomed into the same bed as a matter of courtesy and general hospitality, but the practice extended to courtship, in which "the young woman and her friend covered themselves [with blankets or skins] to carry on their conversation. The custom gradually spread until it was universally accepted and believed to be entirely innocent. . . . One reason always given in justification was that it saved fuel and lights and prevented suffering from cold" (284–85). Andrew Burnaby also noted this custom, known as bundling, during his colonial journey in 1759–60: "[T]he young ones . . . get into bed together also, but without pulling off their undergarments, in order to prevent scandal. If the parties agree, it is all very well; the banns are published, and they are married without delay. If not, they part, and possibly never see each other again." Burnaby adds that if by accident the "forsaken fair-one prove pregnant," the man was obliged to marry her "under pain of excommunication" (141–42). Privacy could not be fully expected when most eighteenth-century homes lacked space and beds. Richard Godbeer adds that given the "challenges of traveling home late at night . . . allowing suitors to stay overnight may have represented innocent hospitality in some instances" (246). Sharing beds was thus considered a polite act, for, as Godbeer elaborates, it was "not unusual for travelers to share beds even with single young women who lived in the household that was providing them with lodging" (246). The adoption of household customs by public houses was a logical extension. Not until reading these narratives, in fact, did I fully appreciate Ishmael's predicament, in Herman Melville's *Moby Dick*, when the whaler awakens to find Quequeq embracing him. Rather than throw a fit, Ishmael wryly comments, "Better to sleep with a sober cannibal than a drunken Christian." Alas, one could do worse.

Even though these dormitory-like conditions proved problematic for the female traveler, concern for virtue was often overshadowed by the need for a proper night's sleep. For Margaret Van Horn Dwight, who embarked on a six-hundred-mile, four-month wagon journey from New Haven, Connecticut, to Warren, Ohio, accompanied by the Reverend and Mrs. Wolcott and their daughter, Susan, conditions were especially challenging. On October 31, Dwight had this to report about Leonard Shaver's Tavern, Highdleburgh: "I was extremely tir'd when we stopt, & went immediately to bed after tea—& for the first time for a long while, undress'd me & had a comfortable nights rest—. We are oblig'd to sleep every & any way—at most of the inns now—. My companions were all disturb'd by the waggoners who put up here & were all night in the room below us, eating, drinking, talking, laughing & swearing" (23). This raucous atmosphere elicited critical commentary as both protest and testimony. In this way, the public house hastened, if not initiated, the socialization process whereby the eastern traveler was introduced to the frontier.

Concern for propriety may have been exasperated by fatigue, for a typical day's journey could take an exhausting twelve to fourteen hours. The stage often went from five in the morning until ten in the evening, and the Boston to New York stage left at 2 a.m. (Lathrop, vii). Even as late as 1832, the sixty-six-mile journey from Fredericksburg to Richmond took seventeen hours, as the stage stopped at ten taverns along the way (Earle, 363–64). The stage itself was not built for comfort. Marjorie McNinch describes the stage coach of the 1820s and 1830s as a "light wooden vehicle built to navigate dry as well as muddy roads. The stage was basically a wooden basket supported by iron bars with a slightly curved roof bordered by a rail. Leather pieces were draped around the basket where the passengers sat three across on three benches. The driver(s) sat in front on a high narrow boot. The wheels were high and generally painted red. Luggage was placed on the roof. Each coach was pulled by a team of horses" (230). Moreover, passing another stage once on the road was not acceptable, so travelers might rise even earlier to ride in the first coach to avoid the dust created by seven to fourteen stages traveling along. In addition to these inconveniences, travel could be quite slow, especially when hampered by wet conditions, as Abigail Adams indicated in a letter to her sister, Mary Cranch, on April 29, 1792: "My first stage was only twenty miles. I bore it better than I expected. The next day rode only 18. Rain came on & the Roads were miry indeed" (*New Letters*, 84). Not surprisingly, when Susan Johnson arrived in Fayetteville on December 24, 1801, after a four-day journey from New Bern, North Carolina—approximately 120 miles—she found herself "very much fateagued with so long a journey; and was obliged to got to bed after dinner from which [she] did not arise until the next morning" (15). Fatigue, it seems, could also lead to mishaps, as perhaps with Elizabeth Trist on May 20, 1784: "In preparing for bed, I unfortunately fell from my birth backwards; bruised my head and shoulder and otherwise hurt myself sufficient to make me a little more carefull in future. However, I got a pretty good nights rest" (214). From such reports, it can be surmised that the desire for proper rest outweighed concerns for propriety, as travel broke down barriers, if not patience. In such assessments, women complied with the travel narrative's perceived importance: to instruct fellow travelers on the rudiments of travel.

Conditions may not have been ideal, but for the weary traveler, basic comforts were quite welcoming. On Sarah Kemble Knight's five-month, two-hundred-mile expedition from Boston to New York, which included a stop in New Haven to settle her cousin Caleb Trowbridge's estate on behalf of his widow, she noted her surroundings with an eye for gentility and a desire for comfort. Throughout her account, Knight makes clear her genteel status and high standards, as she describes her accommodations and encounters. Knight traveled the Post Road that followed what were initially Indian trails and that was first traveled by a postal rider on January 13, 1673, who made the 250-mile round trip in a month. Knight, in fact, followed the lower (southern) route, approximately 270 miles. When Knight embarked on her journey, October 2, 1704, the route, while established, was still cumbersome, and the five-day journey required numerous river crossings, the changing of horses, and the hiring of guides. With Boston clearly established as the cultural center of early America, Knight looked askance at all other locales. On December 6, 1704, for example, Knight arrived in Rye after a long day's ride and de-

"AMERICAN STAGE WAGGON." In his journal, Isaac Weld notes, "The waggons are used universally for stage carriages" (27). Kym Rice identifies this tavern "as the Spread Eagle, which stood in Stafford, Pennsylvania on the 'great Road' between Philadelphia and Lancaster" (51). Engraved plate by James Storer after Weld's *Travels through the States of North America . . . during 1795, 1796, and 1797, 1798*. Photo courtesy of The Beinecke Rare Book and Manuscript Library, Yale University, New Haven, Connecticut.

scribed lodgings that included a "little Lento Chamber furnisht amongst other Rubbish with a High Bedd and a Low one, a Long Table, a Bench and a Bottomless chair" (67).[5] The bed had husks for ticking, but, as Knight explains, "being exceeding weary, down I laid my poor Carkes (never more tired) and found my Covering as scanty as my Bed was hard." Just as she surrendered to these conditions, Knight was awakened by a servant making up another bed "for the men," presumably those with whom she had been traveling. Knight comments rather matter-of-factly about this intrusion, as she commiserates with the men, who were too tall for their bed. She ends this section with "poor I made but one Grone, which was from the time I went to bed to the time I Riss, which was about three in the morning" (67). Knight carefully notes the rustic furnishings as if to dramatize her ordeal and to explain that only her great fatigue would justify such a compromise of standards. In Julia A. Stern's analysis of Knight's journey, she notes that Knight "participates in the genre of female complaint" ("To Relish," 1). To complain also marks one's identity, which for Knight separated her from the surroundings and underscored her genteel status. Travel may initiate social interaction, but participation and compliance may not necessarily be forthcoming.

Communal accommodations in public houses contributed to some awkward moments. For Elizabeth House Trist, the lack of privacy clearly required some adjustment. Accompanied by Alexander Fowler, a friend of her husband's, and a female companion, known only as Polly,[6] Trist had been used to sharing quarters with Polly, but not with the men, as she explained on December 25, 1783: "Were obliged to Sleep in the same room with Mr. Fowler and another man. Not being accustom'd to such inconveniences, I slept but little" (201). On October 23, 1810, at Cook's Inn, Margaret van Horn Dwight described these conditions: "Our room is just large enough to contain a bed a chair & a very small stand—our bed has one brown sheet & one pillow—the sheet however appear'd to be clean, which was more than we got at Nash's [previous inn]—there we were all oblig'd to sleep in the same room without curtains or any other screen—& our sheets were so dirty I felt afraid to sleep in them" (6). Although frontier conditions and public houses made sharing private spaces necessary, Knight, Trist, and Dwight mark such moments as stressful, if not offensive. Practicality did not diminish their genteel preferences. Why the resistance at all? In part, Trist and Dwight expressed the burden of woman as conveyer of certain moral and social codes. To uphold these standards was also to register their absence, and yet to insist on them was often impractical. Begrudgingly, Dwight admitted to some degree of adaptation on October 24 at Buskirck's Inn: "We were again oblig'd all to sleep in one room & in dirty sheets—but pass'd the night very comfortably" (9). She was rewarded on October 26, when her group stopped in Chester, New Jersey, to find "an excellent tavern here compar'd with any [they] have yet found & [they] had for the first time clean sheets to sleep in" (12). For the third time in four days, Dwight notes the state of the sheets, as if to document her hardships. Dwight's overall attention to impoverished tavern conditions also suggests that by 1810 there was an even greater distinction between good and poor lodgings than Trist, for example, may have observed three decades earlier.

Mary Coburn Dewees describes equally crowded sleeping quarters, but with a much more accommodating attitude. As she recounted in her "Journal from Philadelphia to Kentucky, 1788," Dewees followed Trist's route to Pittsburgh before heading south on land to Lexington. On October 10, 1788, while crossing the Allegheny Mountains, just past Bedford, she noted: "We put up at a small house, where we were not made very Welcome but like travellers we learn'd to put a few sour looks unnoticed" (11). She too commented on dirty conditions when her party was "obliged to put up at a Cabin" on October 9, after crossing Sidling Hill at the foot of the Allegheny Mountains: "The people very Kind but Amazing dirty. There was between twenty & thirty of us, all lay on the floor, except Mrs. Rees, the children and your Maria, who by our dress, or address, or perhaps boath, were favoured with a bed, and I assure you we that thought ourselves to escape being fleaed Alive" (11). Dewees' gentility, evident by appearance, apparently saved her from sleeping on the floor, and though the fleas and the close quarters were not pleasant, she did not exaggerate the situation, but had a healthy sense of reality. She wrote two days earlier, on October 7, "Believe me, my dear friends, the sight of a log house in these Mountains after a fatiguing day's Journey Affords more real pleasure that all the magnificent buildings your city contains" (8). Her insistence on keeping matters in a positive light may have been influenced by these "dear friends" for whom she wrote the journal. According to R. E. Banta, who edited its 1936 publication, the journal was "written from notes made on the journey, with the idea that it was to be sent back to Philadelphia for the entertainment of friends and relatives there" (i). The certainty of Dewees' destination and the relative brevity of her journey may have contributed to her account's positive tone; she knew that her inconveniences would soon end, and so she enjoyed the journey for the adventure. The repetition of such observations in women's narratives emphasizes their concerns for standards of cleanliness and privacy, which, in turn, signify a desire for maintaining social order. And while the journey testifies to the woman's fortitude, her cataloging of unpleasant conditions affirms her gentility.

Other travelers were more magnanimous yet, as on June 19, 1789, when Abigail Adams wrote to Mary Cranch with high praise for Mr. and Mrs. Joseph Mann of Mann's Inn in Wrentham, Massachusetts: "[W]e dinned upon roast veal, roast chicklings, sallad, &c. West India sweet meats. I ought not to forget the dessert. It is really a very good Inn" (9). Adams's recommendation was most likely appreciated and probably passed along. During Madame de La Tour du Pin's 1794 travels through New England, she too was quite pleased with her stay at an "impeccably clean" inn at Lebanon in Massachusetts, yet noted: "But the luxury of white sheets was still unknown in that part of the United States. To ask for sheets that had not been used by others would have been considered a quite unreasonable caprice" (236). This standard may not seem unreasonable today, but was nearly impossible to fulfill on the frontier, where water for cleaning was scarce and, as La Tour du Pin notes, the possibility of clean sheets a luxury.

In some cases, just finding a room proved difficult, and travelers were not always welcomed, a situation exasperated by increasingly crowded, sometimes scarce, accommodations. For example, Sarah Kemble Knight noted on December 21, 1704, that she departed New York with her "Kinsman Trowbridge, and the man that waited on [her]"; they lost their way and were "overtaken by a great storm of wind and snow" four miles short of Rochelle. They were forced to seek shelter as darkness fell: "[W]e were very uneasy. But meeting one Gardner who lived in a Cottage thereabout, offered us his fire to set by, having but one poor Bedd, and his wife not well, &c." Given these limitations, the man kindly escorted them to a house "where he thought, we might be better accommodated." Knight then describes a most unaccommodating, if not hostile, landlady: "a surly old shee Creature, not worthy the name of woman, who would hardly let us go into her Door, though the weather was so stormy none but shee would have turned out a Dogg" (70). Fortunately, her son was more obliging: "[B]ut her son whose name was gallop, who lived Just by Invited us to his house and shewed me two pair of stairs, viz. One up the loft and tother up the Bedd, wch was as hard as it was high, and warmed it with a hott stone at the feet" (70–71). The story does not have an entirely pleasant ending, though, for when Knight requested some food to warm her, "[t]hey had nothing but milk in the house wch they Boild and to make it better sweetened with molasses"; upon drinking it, Knight promptly vomited. Ever practical, she concludes, "But I believe it did me service in Cleering my stomach" (71).

Julia A. Stern observes this moment as particularly complex and notable: "That a woman obsessed with her own refinement should feel vindicated in the very throes of bodily disorder is itself a fascinating commentary on the way in which Knight contemplates differences of class. Vomit becomes a righteous conduit through which the elite woman traveler may register her disgust over distasteful service by an inferior" ("To Relish," 9–10). East Chester was all in all "a very miserable poor place," but it did serve as yet another benchmark for comparison. For the next day, from New Rochelle, she could more cheerfully report that she had "good Entertainment" and that there "are three fine Taverns within call of each other, very good provision for Travailers" (71). Knight took seriously her role as travel guide, however singular her own journey.

Landlords could also be quite choosey, regardless of gender, as men also suffered from poor conditions and rude comments as they traveled westward. Fortescue Cuming, for example, had this trouble to report while trying to find a bed for the night in Carlisle, Pennsylvania, in February 1807: "The twilight shutting out further view, I hastened through a tolerable compact street to Foster's, to which I had been recommended as the best inn. I asked if I could have a bed that night, and was answered rudely, by an elderly man, in a bar who I took for the landlord, after he had eyed me with a contemptuous scrutiny—that I could not . . . I turned on my heel, and entered the next tavern kept by Michael Herr, an honest and obliging German, where I found nothing to make me regret being rejected as a guest at Foster's, except want of bed linen, sheets not being generally used in this country in the inns, excepting at English ones, or those of fashionable resort. A very good bed otherwise" (47). Cuming's good-natured response suggests that this may not have been an unusual experience and that the business of lodging travelers was good enough that landlords could indeed turn away a potential customer. Foster's "contemptuous scrutiny" counters the image of a public house as a mixing ground, as it suggests instead the traveler as "outsider." Philip D. Zimmerman adds another dimension to the overall sense of traveler as outsider in his analysis of tavern signage: "A tavern sign must have conveyed to travelers a sense of genteel domesticity, an awaiting haven from the apprehensions and discomfort of the stranger's world. Because strangers had no recognized place or status in unfamiliar communities of colonial times, signs that directed them to sources of 'provisions and lodging in some comfortable manner' enforced social order and codes of conduct that surpassed mere physical comfort" (30). Thus, even though public houses were legislated in the seventeenth century, the traveler's presence remained somewhat suspect. The first emigrants quickly grew suspicious of the newly arrived, who must then be treated with caution. The fluidity of the frontier demonstrated that the "center" was constantly subject to revision, as populations of "outsiders" passed through or settled in.

Public Houses and Sociability

In addition to commenting on tavern keepers or the quality of accommodations, women keenly noted the sociability of the public house. Their persistent notice of matters genteel and civil reinforces their perceived role as arbiter of social codes. Female travelers seemed particularly compelled to express criticism, as if to justify their presence in an "inferior" setting. Their comments to some extent simply reflect the crude conditions of most frontier and outlying establishments. And yet, women's observations are fraught with a self-consciousness of traveler as outsider who must confront a certain uneasiness. Despite predisposed attitudes, public houses appear animated as key centers for the entertainment of travelers and locals.

Drinking was indeed part of the entertainment, as an ad in the February 9, 1767, *Philadelphia Chronicle* for the Hudibras tavern in Princeton confirms: its owner claims to have "laid in a stock of liquors, &c. for the Accommodation of Gentlemen Travellers and Others, who may depend upon his utmost Endeavors to oblige." The abundant supply of rum and the subsequent low prices led to taverns opening at increasing rates, as in Boston, where "licensed premises rose from seventy-two in 1702 to one hundred and fifty-five in 1732" (Rorabaugh, 33). During the 1760s attempts to maintain order in the public houses included the prohibition of Sunday sales and gambling. To curtail decadent behaviors, regulations discouraged inactivity and overconsumption of alcohol, and tavern keepers had to comply to keep their licenses. In some places, laws were passed to prevent service to "blacks, apprentices, Indians, servants, or seamen without the permission of their masters or ships' captains" (Rice, 70). Time limits of one hour with a restriction of one-half pint of wine at one sitting were imposed. In 1700, as Bridenbaugh reports, "strict tavern laws" regulated licensing and levied "heavy fines for illegal sale of liquor and disorderly establishments" (271). Bridenbaugh also notes that New York avoided "any serious tavern problem" because of its "careful and continuous reinforcement of the liquor laws" (273). Elsie L. Lathrop notes that Tennessee law prohibited gambling in the taverns, and in Roger's tavern, "if any disobeyed, a kettle of burning feathers placed in a closet beneath their room soon ended the game" (298–99). Edward Field marks particularly stringent laws in Massachusetts wherein "drunkenness or tippling was prohibited, and the tavern keeper who permitted such irregularities was liable to a fine of ten shillings" (20–21). To restore public houses to their original intention, some towns required "all taverns to provide lodging for travellers" (Rorabaugh, 34). Mary Caroline Crawford reiterates that the early ordinaries, especially those in the country, were not intended for overnight guests, but to "circulate the festive flip up to nine o'clock in the evening and to thaw out pious pilgrims before and after meetings on Sundays" (13). From their rather innocuous beginning, taverns became increasingly subject to legislation. Compliance maintained order, allowing the public house to retain its standing, even when it went beyond its sole duty of accommodating travelers. Not surprisingly, then, women remarked as frequently on social behaviors as they did on the cleanliness of their sheets.

As locals spent more leisure time entertaining themselves in the taverns, some early Americans found this trend alarming. In spring of 1761, for instance, John Adams expressed concern for the tendency of "poor Mankind" to "waste their Time, spend their Money, [and] run in Debt" (1:206). Such activities threatened economic stability by decreasing output. Adams addressed these issues in a letter drafted to the *Boston Gazette* in May 1761: "In most Country Towns, in this County, you will find almost every other House, with a sign of Entertainment before it. . . . Multiplicity of these Houses, by dividing the Profits, renders the Landlords careless of travellers, and allures the poor Country People who are tired with Labour and hanker after Company, to waste their Time and money" (1: 214). In their defense, Salinger explains: "Taverns offered colonists

"WIDOW MCMURRAN'S TAVERN, SCRUB RIDGE." Upon lodging at this public house in the Tuscarora Mountains, Pennsylvania, Adlard Welby noted, "[T]averns are every where building." Welby, *A Visit to North America and the English Settlements in Illinois*, 1821, 191. Photo courtesy of The Beinecke Rare Book and Manuscript Library, Yale University, New Haven, Connecticut.

one of the few sources of secular diversion and amusement in early America. Locals or travelers could attend scholarly lectures, listen to musical entertainers, or gaze upon unusual animals" (57). Still, Adams identifies a social habit that would lead to unprecedented consumption: between 1790 and 1830 Americans "drank more alcoholic beverages per capita than ever before or since" (Rorabaugh, xi). Drinking songs and contests contributed to this overconsumption and moved critics, such as Adams, to condemn the growing number of public houses.

While drinking was popular for both sexes, women were generally discouraged from frequenting taverns. W. J. Rorabaugh finds simply that the "public was not tolerant of women drinking at taverns . . . unless they were travelers recovering from a day's arduous journey," and even then, they were offered "watered and highly sugared spirituous cordials" (13). That women did imbibe in taverns is clear, yet the records are essentially "invisible," as Daniel B. Thorp explains in his study of Rowan County in North Carolina, 1753–76. Single women who had tavern accounts may have purchased liquor to bring home, but they "did not drink in taverns, while married women drank with their husbands but did not have their own accounts." Thorp adds that the more likely reason for this lack of

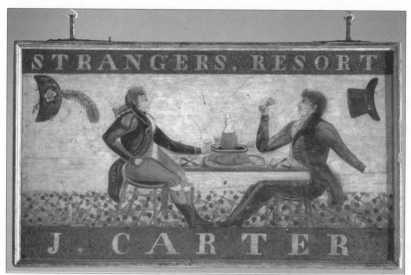

TAVERN SIGN FOR J. CARTER'S INN. This sign, depicting Jared Carter's Inn, ca. 1823, bears the slogan "Strangers' Resort" and shows two gentlemen enjoying a light repast. Sign for Carter's Inn, Clinton, Connecticut, ca. 1823, Connecticut Historical Society Museum, Hartford, Connecticut.

documentation is that "settlers in Rowan County simply considered taverns to be male space" and "did not look favorably on women who frequented taverns" (681–82). Sharon V. Salinger elaborates: "Women were clearly not part of the public culture of drink. If they bought liquor, they carted it off to the privacy of their homes" (223). In some instances, women were a welcomed addition, as this ad in the *Salem Gazette* on June 15, 1784, announcing that John Piemont, innkeeper of Ipwich, was back in business after having "the misfortune to lose his stables by Fire": "Any Gentlemen and Ladies that please to use his house, may expect genteel usage—and all favours will be gratefully acknowledged by their humble servant, J. P." This gender inclusion also suggests that women were traveling more frequently; not only did the female traveler spread the word about good or poor accommodations, but her remarks signaled a desire for a more individualized environment. Into these mixed, social spaces, women ventured in need of shelter and found maintaining their gentility a challenge.

Travelers responded variously to the lively, sometimes rowdy, atmosphere of the public house. In 1704, Sarah Kemble Knight could hardly sleep from the "Clamor of some of the Town tope-ers in next Room" (58). Such complaints persisted into the next century, as on April 24, 1802, when Susan Johnson observed similar excesses while passing through Georgetown, Maryland: "a great number of people about the tavern where we changed horses, & several quite intoxicated & noisy" (105–6). Matters did not improve that night; while in Dover, Delaware, she recorded, "we were much disturbed this night by some riotous people who were singing untill three in the morning" (106). Travelers themselves were usually "exempt from most tavern regulations" (Rice, 26), which might explain such noisy, late-night escapades. In February 1807, Fortescue Cuming recollected a particularly raucous scene in a public house on the road to Bedford: "It was not yet day, and the scene in the tavern was, to me, truly novel. It was a large half finished log house, with no apparent accommodation for any traveler who had not his own bed or blanket. . . . [T]he whole floor was so filled with people sleeping, wrapped in their blankets round a large fire, that there was no such thing as approaching it to get warm, until some of the travelers who had awoke at our entrance, went out to feed their horses, after doing which, they returned, drank whiskey under the name of bitters, and resumed their beds on the floor—singing, laughing, joking, romping, and apparently as happy as possible. So much for custom" (59). In 1829, Maria Sophia Quincy described just how difficult it was to sleep under some conditions: "August 8th. Last night, if possible exceeded the first night we were here in noise & confusion. The eight stages again flew up to the door, baggage was thrown about in all directions, people coursed about the house all night, talked & walked about the piazza, went off again at 2 & 3 o'clock" (10). In such moments, time collapses, as these travelers express complaints that a contemporary traveler might share: noisy patrons and early morning departures. Whereas Knight, Johnson, and Quincy were simply annoyed, Cuming was astounded by the lack of decorum, a reaction elicited by the carnival atmosphere before him. The female traveler may have complained about and even challenged this predominantly male scene, but tavern culture demanded that the woman adapt rather than the institution.

Compliance with rustic conditions, however, affronted some women's sensibility. Margaret Van Horne Dwight's criticisms were particularly sharp, ranging from accommodations and cleanliness to the impropriety of the wagoners with whom her group traveled. On October 28, 1810, Dwight recorded, "Our bed to sleep on was straw, & then a feather bed for covering—The pillows contain'd nearly a single handful of feathers, & were cover'd with the most curious & dirty patchwork, I ever saw—We had one bedquilt & one sheet—I did not undress at all, for I expected dutchmen in every moment & you may suppose slept very comfortably in that expectation" (17). The bedding drew criticism for its meager quality and unclean condition, while the threat of intrusion disrupted her sleep. Dwight strongly resented the lack of social boundaries and the inappropriate behaviors of her fellow travelers. On October 27, Dwight recorded this scene: "We are at a dutch tavern almost crazy—In one corner of the room are a set of dutchmen talking singin & laughing in dutch so loud, that my brain is almost turn'd—they one moment catch up a fiddle & I expect soon to be pulled up to dance—I am so afraid of them I dare hardly stay in the house one night; much less the sabbath—I cannot write so good night" (15). With privacy nonexistent, Dwight appears even more irate over the imposition of such loud "talking singin & laughing" in a language that she disapproved of by men whom she feared. She reported a particular lapse in decorum on October 28: "[A]fter we were all in bed in the middle of the night, I was awaken'd by the entrance of three dutchmen, who were in search of a bed—I was almost frightened to death—but Mr. W at length heard & stopt them before they had quite reach'd our bed" (17–18). Not only did this sudden intrusion startle Dwight, but she felt her reputation in danger. Following the conventions of the heroine in the sentimental novel, Dwight's protestations needed a proper audience. Writing with Elizabeth in mind, Dwight heightened the drama sufficiently while asserting control, even when conditions were deteriorating around her.

Despite her protests, this situation persisted. The subsequent retelling and recasting of events takes on the dramatic style of a novel. Dwight inserts her voice into the literary discourse and proves herself a fit narrator. Dwight recorded this incident on November 9, from Phelps' tavern: "I was very much frighten'd by a drunken waggoner, who came up to me as I stood by the door waiting for a candle, he put his arm around my neck, & said something which I was too frighten'd to hear—It is the first time the least insult has been offer'd to any of us" (36). Dwight was clearly vulnerable waiting in the dimly lit tavern for her candle, and, as if still living in a closely knit town, she fends off any possible rumors that she may have encouraged such advances. On November 11, upon reaching their lodgings in the foothills of the Allegheny Mountains, Dwight and Mrs. Jackson, another member of the traveling party, had yet another traumatic encounter. Dwight had just taken off her "frock & boots" and "scarcely lain down" when "one of the wretches [wagoners] came into the room & lay down" beside her: "I was frighten'd almost to death & clung to Mrs. Jackson who did not appear to mind it—& I lay for a quarter of an hour crying, & scolding & trembling, begging of him to leave me—At last, when persuaded I was in earnest, he begg'd of me not to take it amiss, as he intended no harm & only wish'd to become acquainted with me—A good for nothing brute, I wonder what he suppos'd I was—I don't know of any thought word or action of mine that could give him reason to suppose I would authorise such abominable insolence" (40). Not only was such behavior uninitiated, but, as Dwight clearly states, reciprocation was unthinkable. The scene was drawn out, as Dwight begged him to leave—a request that "at last" took effect. Before departing, the intruder showed that he has his own concerns, as he requested that she not "take it amiss." Dwight found the act egregious and wondered what possible communication or misperception had permitted him to consider that she had invited "such abominable insolence." While her account of the incident underscores the vulnerability of the genteel female traveler, Dwight did not allow herself to be victimized. Writing and audience reinforced her sense of authority.

The wagoner's attempted familiarities forced Dwight to defend her virtue, and the journal helped sort out matters. The breakdown of social codes was upsetting enough, and not having the appropriate context to underscore its horror appears equally disturbing. By writing in her journal, Dwight documented her disapproval and reassured her audience that she had not been corrupted by such crude conditions. When Dwight recorded such incidents, she departed from simply keeping a record of travel and maintained instead a journal of personal experience. As such, Dwight's framing and casting of these scenes parallels popular sentimental novels of her day that mirror social expectations for female behavior, complete with beleaguered heroines, sympathetic audience, and suspicious rakes. In some respects, Dwight's predicament resembles aspects of these fictional depictions, which, as Elizabeth Barnes explains, "typically chronicle a young woman's triumph over physical hardship and rebellious pride to gain the security of a newfound family" (12). The scene also complicates and, in some ways, reverses Barnes's description of an "eighteenth-century seduction fiction [that] traces the fall of the ingénue to the verbal manipulations of the persistent, charming, and better educated male." For in these scenes, Dwight, the wagoner's social superior, was clearly in charge. While Dwight boldly rejected the wagoner, however, the context for her responses was displaced. For though Dwight reacted as would a Lucy Sumner or an Eliza Wharton, upon being caught in a similarly compromised position, Dwight quickly learned that she was not living in Hannah Webster Foster's world. Unlike New Haven genteel society, the frontier did not conform to the codes of the sentimental novel.

Dwight may also have been frustrated by the absence of proper courtship ritual that would have allowed her to respond accordingly. Expectations of courtship ritual were carefully articulated in eighteenth-century novels, as Paula R. Backscheider points out: "The time of courtship could be made into subversive space. Women writers throughout the century remarked that it was the single moment in a woman's life when she had power, and it was also the time in which identities were clarified and hopes for the future formulated" (21). Although in Dwight's case the intruder did apologize, the context was all wrong: "He begg'd of me not to take it amiss, as he intended no harm & only wish'd to become acquainted with me." There was little triumph, for the wagoner had nothing socially valuable to offer. Dwight minimizes any potential damage to her reputation by recording this scene to her advantage; she is the overwrought genteel traveler subject to the crude manners of this unrefined wagoner. In this sense, the travel narrative serves as time-tested conduct book, whereby genteel codes are applied to actual situations. The single, female traveler feared for her reputation in the same way that married women worried about propriety. In each case, the genteel female confronted a frontier reality that insisted on her compromise.

Women's concerns reveal the responsibilities they faced to uphold moral codes and the subsequent anxiety lest these standards not be recognized or honored. Though some women adjusted quite easily, others

strained to comply and fit in. For Trist, on January 3, 1784, an overnight
stop in a one-room log house presented an ongoing problem, shared
sleeping quarters. Although, as she explains, it was "customary for the
Men and Women to sleep in the same room," Trist decided to rise "before day light" to dress. To the local countrywomen, however, Trist's modesty appeared out of place; "some of the Women look upon a Woman as
affected that makes any objection to it" (206). Trist was thus deemed by
another woman to be "very incecure in her self that was afraid to sleep
in the room with a strange man." This woman found "nothing indeli-
cate in the matter," and from her perspective "no man wou'd take a liberty with a woman unless he saw a disposition in her to encourage him"
(206–7). The desire for privacy drew accusations of prudishness. Caught
between conflicting standards, Trist and Dwight appeared unduly fastidious in their modesty. But to them, compliance with frontier standards
would have constituted too great a compromise. For the wagoner and the
countrywoman, though, such complaints did not register and seemed,
instead, out of place.

In some instances, the basic need for shelter outweighed genteel preferences. Elizabeth House Trist was relieved, for example, on January 7 when
her party took shelter from the intense cold at "a good farm house"
owned by the Waltowers and "found a comfortable room, warm with a
stove. I felt quite happy for we were allmost frozed. We had a good comfortable supper of fat bacon fried and some Coffee. I eat it with a mighty
good appetite. We met Mr. Irwin, a Gentleman from Pittsburg at this
House." When it was time to retire for the night, Trist's concerns over
privacy were well met with the simple addition of curtains around her
bed: "Old Mr. Waltowers and Mr. Irwin had one of the beds, Polly and
myself the other—but we found no difficulty in being private, having
good worsted curtains round the bed. We allways made it a practice to
dress and undress behind the curtain. Therefore, found no difficulty,
notwithstanding there were Six or 7 men in the room. Mr. Fowler and
the rest of the people had some clean straw spread on the floor. I must
confess I never slept better" (209). Such incidents underscore the interplay between travel and social construction, as Trist registers her approval
of a seemingly logical compromise.

Women's narratives thus show the link between travel and states of
mind. As women ventured from home, the public house served as a sur-

rogate domestic sphere and a scene of intense social interaction. Commentary was often harsh, reflecting the substandard, though not unusual, conditions and the mixing of social classes, which threatened to undermine genteel distinctions. Dwight's passages in particular express a theatrical quality, as characters react to unpleasant situations with a sympathetic audience looking on. Why would meager bedding or night intrusions matter, unless they represented contrast and threatened identity? Recording the event helped these women to process and to understand the experience. If one agency of the frontier was to collapse social distinctions, these women clearly illustrate the tensions between settlement and frontier. When these two entities collided, change, if not compromise, was inevitable.

Physical Hardships and the Rigors of Travel

In addition to making psychological adjustments, these women exerted tremendous physical effort. Travel was arduous, and journeys west proved especially demanding, requiring perseverance and adaptability. At times, practicality outweighed gentility, and as women persevered, they challenged gender barriers regarding stamina and resourcefulness. Ultimately, their journals reinforce William Bartram's observation, "We are, all of us, subject to crosses and disappointments, but more especially the traveller" (69). Travel on horseback proved particularly demanding, as Alice Morse Earle explains: "Women rode with as much ease and frequency as men. Older women rode behind men on pillows, which were padded cushions which had a sort of platform stirrup" (226). As previously noted, the stage, which was often slow and tedious, could also be quite uncomfortable; Lydia B. Bacon described her journey after arriving by stage in Pittsburgh on June 26, 1811: "[A]t one time the seats were taken out, plenty of straw put in the bottom of the Stage, & the Passingers stowed in, like baggage." It was not a good solution, though, as they could not view the landscape: "[I]t soon became wearisome, & concluded we should rather endure the pounding than be deprived of this pleasure" (371). So, Bacon held on "with both hands," and as she explains, "exerting *every nerve* to maintain my Equilibrium, on one side of me, my neighbours elbow pushing in to my side, on the other, the side of the stage which was not stuffed, rubbing against me, till I was black & blue, & then bounce would go my poor head, against the top of the Stage, till my brains were ready to fly." Still, she endured the discomfort "for the sake of beholding the scenery" (371). Twenty years later, in 1833, Mary Lyon described similar discomfort while on a journey that began in Boston, went on to New York and Philadelphia, and eventually headed west to Detroit before returning east. In a letter from Philadelphia to Zilpah Polly Grant on July 10, 1833, Lyon wrote, "I rose in the morning with the headache, which increased till I reached Amboy. When I took the railroad car, my seat was rather confined; the motion of the carriage increased the pain in my head, and produced an excessive nervous restlessness. It did seem as if I could not go forward; but still I must" (115). Confinement and incessant jarring motions were common complaints about both stage and rail travel. As women encountered difficult conditions and confronted danger, they stepped outside of prescribed gender roles and found ways to survive.

Women's narratives thus offer singular examples of women's strength and fortitude as they dealt with rigorous physical demands. Dangerous travel conditions are described repeatedly; we learn of stony, steep roads, inclement weather, rising and falling rivers, and relentless mosquitoes. In late December 1783, for example, Elizabeth House Trist described the stresses of winter travel: "[O]n the 31st we set off; the Snow up to the Horses bellies. After rideing 2 miles we began to ascend the Tuscarora Mountain. . . . Upon the Summit of the Mountain, my saddle turn'd. It was with great difficulty I cou'd stick upon the Horse. . . . On one side of me was a thicket and on the other a precipice. . . . We suffered another inconvenience for want of a breastplate to our saddles, for some places that we had to ascend where allmost perpendicular, and our saddles slip'd so that we cou'd scarcely keep our selves on by holding the main. We were Six hours going 10 miles to fort Lyttleton" (205). Barely one week into her journey, Trist recorded these conditions with little time to consider her own bravery. The details themselves testify to the challenges of travel. Six months later, on June 17, 1784, Trist reported on a different kind of obstruction as she traveled down the Mississippi toward Natchez: "The Musquitos bite and tease me so much that my life is allmost a burthen to me. I do sincerely think that all the wealth of the Indias wou'd not induce me to live in a Musquitoe country. I had no Idea they cou'd possibly be so intolerable" (227). Again, on June 18, 1784, she remarked:

"My patience is allmost exausted. What with the Musquitos and head winds, I am allmost sick" (227). Trist encountered these obstacles, and yet she never expressed a desire to head back or forgo her journey. Such passages provide a distinct contrast to suggestions that women, particularly genteel women, were passive, if not sedentary. Travel narratives testify to women's impressive courage, determination, and stamina.

Rough conditions are thus duly noted, and complaining is as much a part of the description as triumph. Far from whining, women offer the harsh realty of their experiences, neither shying from the disappointment, nor backing off from the celebration. Sarah Kemble Knight, for example, described difficult travel conditions on October 6, 1704: "Wee advanced on towards Seabrook. The Rodes all along this way are very bad, Incumbred wth Rocks and mountainos passages, wch were very disagreeable to my tired carcass; but we went on with a moderate pace wch made the Journy more pleasent. But after about eight miles Rideing, in going over a Bridge under wch the River Run very swift, my hors stumbled, and very narrowly 'scaped falling over into the water; wch extreemly frightened mee. But through God's Goodness I met with no harm." Not only does Knight identify a long-standing complaint of both early travelers and today's commuters—bad roads—but she retells the story nonchalantly. She continues, "[M]ounting agen, in about half a miles Rideing, come to an ordinary, were well entertained by a woman of about seventy and vantage, but of as Sound Intellectuals as one of seventeen." The woman shared a gossipy story about an elderly man "being about her Age or something above, Saying his Children was dredfully against their father's marrying, wch shee condemned them extremely for" (62). Thus, Knight concludes with a respectful comment on the woman's sound objection to age discrimination regarding marriage. In such passages, Knight collects stories that illustrate local color, playing the role of the critical, if not condescending, observer. The passage thus moves from complaints about road conditions to remarks on gender bias—all in a lively mix of venting and observing.

Eight decades later, Mary Coburn Dewees shared similar frustrations with roads when crossing the South Mount outside of Hunter's town, 113 miles from Philadelphia on the way to Chambersburgh: "[Oct. 5] the road in places for a mile in length so very stony that you can Scarce see the earth between" (6). She was tested again when climbing the North Mountain on October 7: wherein she finds "this the most fatiguing day's Journey we have had, the roads so very bad and so very steep that the horses seem ready to fall backwards, in many places" (8). In June 1812, Lydia B. Bacon summarized another common difficulty: "[I]t is very tedious traveling through roads that are cut as you procede, sometimes the Horse is in danger of Mireing, than of Breaking his legs going over log bridges" (65). Crossing mountains was indeed one of the more treacherous parts of these travels, but though these women expressed their fears and doubts, they endured and did not abandon the journey.

Comments and complaints about road conditions persist throughout the narratives of travelers, especially those heading west and over the Alleghenies, which presented a definite physical and psychological barrier. In W. M. Verhoeven's discussion of Gilbert Imlay's epistolary travel account *Topographical Description* (1792) and novel *The Emigrants* (1793), he cites Imlay's view of the Allegheny Mountains as a "moral watershed" that separated "the pastoral innocence of the western settlements from the social evil, political corruption, and religious blindness that dominated life in the eastern states" (192). For Imlay, westward migration represented an opportunity for financial gain and for greater individual freedom. By contrast, the genteel female traveler described the move as challenging and arduous. Elizabeth Van Horne was particularly realistic about the difficulties: "I already think it a great undertaking to remove a family from Jersey State to the State of Ohio. Was their no Invalids numbered among us it would be something easier. Yet for any family— *Strength, fortitude, resolution,* and a good share of *Patience* is absolutely nessary" (13–14). Still, on October 24, 1807, she had this to report: "Laurel Hill is justly & properly named indeed—it crowns all the Hills for length and roughness—We found men at the foot of the Hill at work upon the road as we came down—I told them they could not be employed in any business that would please me so well. Altho I never expected to rise the hill again I was glad to see them making it better. He told me their was a handsome sum collected to defray the expencs of making the road good to the top of the Hill" (15). Van Horne thus expressed oft-repeated complaints about rocky, poorly maintained roads and a lack of amenities, indicating fundamental comparisons to a more urban life.

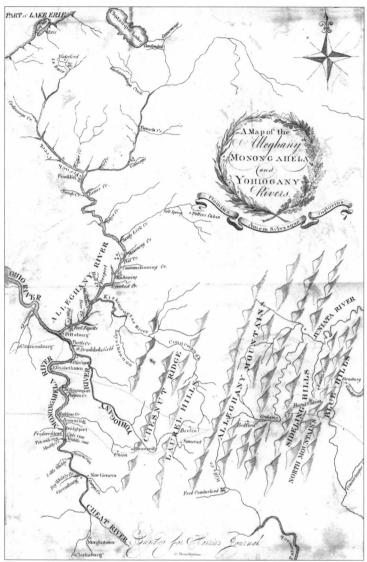

"A Map of the Allegheny, Monongahela, and Yohiogany Rivers." This map highlights the mountain ranges confronting westward travelers. Many of the women in this study comment on the difficult crossing of "Laurel Hill." This map was engraved by Thomas Wightman for Thaddeus Mason Harris's *Journal of a Tour into the Territory Northwest of the Alleghenny Mountains Made in the Spring of the Year 1803*, 1805. As reproduced in "The First American West," http://memory.loc .gov/cgi-bin/query, icufaw bbc0020. Courtesy of University of Chicago Library, Special Collections Research Center.

Water travel proved another formidable challenge, and its dramatic conditions contributed to compelling narratives. For example, on December 1, 1817, Lucy Newton departed Union, Ohio, for a ten-day, one-hundred-mile journey to Anderson Township. Her brief record, which she titled "A Journal or memorandum of my Journey from Union, Ohio to Mechanicksburgh, & from there to Anderson Township, Ohio," recounts a journey that she calls "remarkable." Newton offers a lengthy description of a near disaster on the third night, when she "awoke out of a deep sleep" after sensing "immediate danger but what [she] did not know." Newton elaborates: "I heard an uncommon nois but thinking it might be the ice I tryed to compose my mind, but all in vain, for I was still under the impression that there was danger near. I considered a moment, the continuation of the sound led me to think it was running water. I sprang out of bed and was mutch surprised when I found the boat had sprang leak & while I stood in the water I called Mr. Parker, for he was the only man on board" (2).[7] Though she shared her alarm with the other passengers, Newton notes, "[F]or my own part I was not in a flutter." She simply took her candle, went to the bow of the boat, and, as she explains, "while standing in the coald water I baled as fast as I could." Mr. Parker meanwhile managed to "asuage the flood" by using wedges and corks, while the others bailed "several times in the night." Notwithstanding her quick reaction, Newton ultimately acknowledges the "hand of God in the peculiar display of his providence and preservations. I owe my life to that God that never sleeps nor slumbers" (2–3). Newton seems to have taken her adventure in stride. The rest of her account includes the much less dramatic, though impressive, description of her family finding out about her arrival on December 10 through a series of unexpected connections. Strangers on the boat passed on information to her cousin and eventually to her brother: "[H]is arrival was not a little surprising to me for I did not suppose he knew whare I was" (3). This concluding detail illustrates the precarious nature of travel while demonstrating the effectiveness of oral culture.

For Lydia B. Bacon, rivers were also challenging, if not dangerous. In one incident, after crossing Blanchards Creek, Fort Finly, in Indian country, she recalls: "[I]n fording the rivers, the current is so strong, oft times, it is almost impossible to gain the opposite shore, & many a one has a fine bath ere they reach *terea firma*, but as yet I have been exempt from this

"A VIEW OF THE BOATS AND MANNER OF NAVIGATING ON THE MOHAWK
RIVER" Flat boats aided by poles were used to navigate shallower rivers. From
Christian Schultz, *Travels on an Inland Voyage through the States of New-York, Pennsylvania,
Virginia, Ohio, Kentucky and Tennessee, and through the Territories of Indiana, Louisiana, Mississippi,
and New-Orleans: Performed in the Years 1807 and 1808; Including a Tour of Nearly Six Thousand
Miles,* 1810. Photo courtesy of The Beinecke Rare Book and Manuscript Library,
Yale University, New Haven, Connecticut.

disaster which would take all my Philosophy to bear, I assure you it takes
all my strength, & prowes, to maintain my equilibrium, sometimes the
rivers are so deep, I am obliged to put my feet on the horses neck to keep
out of the water & she has pretty long legs too" (65). Bacon forthrightly
confesses her fears but did not retreat. This reporter's style is one of the
more endearing qualities of these narratives. The lack of self-conscious
reflection in these dramatic narratives makes their feats all the more impressive. In each account, these travelers do not question whether they as
women should be traveling, but matter-of-factly describe the conditions
and their reactions. Unlike in the apologetic introductions of the sentimental novel, for example, there are no qualifications. In this regard,
travel allows these women to transcend gender roles. When they are so
engaged, physical demands outweigh social expectation. Travel challenged
women, but they faced rugged roads and crowded taverns with determination and resourcefulness.

∼◦∽

In this chapter, I focus on the physical and material elements of travel in
order to situate women travelers more fully within the historical record.

The public house as focal point for their commentary initiated their transition from urban to frontier life. These intermediary spaces intensified class and gender issues by bringing women into close contact with others from less privileged levels of society. Confusion often followed, with an impulse to impose order evident in lengthy passages and, at times, dramatic representations. Considering that the travel narrative records only transitory states, the record is subject to some degree of distortion. But at the same time, this very uncertainty encourages a straightforward, honest accounting. Women thus provide a valuable record long after the taverns themselves have ceased to exist or been remodeled. Written to the moment, the travel narrative offers a rare glimpse into the daily experience of early American travel. I expand and explore this quality more thoroughly in the next chapter by taking a closer look at women's reactions to their newfound frontier and rustic environs through the lens of gentility.

3

Writing into the Ohio Frontier

GENTEEL EXPECTATIONS AND RUSTIC REALITIES

hile some female travelers evaluated the public houses and urban centers for evidence of gentility and signs of decorum, others assessed the open lands and frontier spaces for potential community and sociability. At times compliant, women were graceful ambassadors of republican generosity; at other times, they forthrightly asserted their desires and opinions. With these assertions, women alerted local populations to a new kind of traveler, and indeed, a new kind of woman. In doing so, they complicate perceptions of westward migration and settlement as a predominantly male enterprise. Aware of social forces urging them to maintain genteel values, women chronicle many areas of American life, including fashion, religion, and slavery, with a focus invigorated by personal perspective. Showing admirable fortitude while negotiating challenging terrain, women delineate the cultural and physical infrastructure of early America.

These encounters were, as the following discussion makes clear, not always congenial. For women who promoted a genteel social view were often at odds with this new, more pluralistic society. Faced with cultural expectations that they emulate virtuous behaviors, women were alternately stymied and invigorated. In interesting, somewhat unexpected ways, these tensions and burdens sharpen women's perspectives as they scrutinize their surroundings. In the process, gentility, particularly in regard to manners and address, becomes a type of imperialistic stance—conquest by social position rather than brute force or militarist prowess.

89

Not surprisingly, then, when women tried to impose their genteel standards, they were often rebuffed. One way they reacted to their discomfort was to criticize others. Some travelers aggressively imposed their own standards and sense of social order; others simply bemoaned the contact. Moreover, contrary to gender stereotypes, in their writing women often perpetuate hegemonic sensibilities rather than express a more inclusive attitude. In part, this reaction reveals anxiety about relocation and the prospect of adapting. Their irritation not only makes these travelers appear out of place to the locals, but also brings into question their own motives and expectations—just what were they hoping to find, and what were they planning to create? Considering that the travel journal addresses the time between one home and another, it speaks only to an interim state, and such questions go largely unanswered. Still, women were expected to maintain, if not promote, certain behaviors. So inspired and determined, women document the settling of America as a dynamic series of interactions followed by reflection. The act of writing helps women to sort out matters by rehashing difficulties and by projecting an orderly social vision. For the traveler who envisioned the frontier as an extension of the East, moreover, these challenges would be especially pronounced. The idea of vehemently reinforcing class distinctions in a new democracy may seem odd. Yet, in numerous entries, these female travelers do just that, as they demonstrate their desire to re-create and reinforce familiar, genteel society. Rather than voluntarily casting off social preferences in order to embrace an egalitarian society, many travelers were intent on reinforcing class hierarchy by asserting their standards and judging others accordingly.

Whether traveling onto the Ohio frontier or along the eastern seaboard, therefore, women made keen assessments, whereby they affirmed their own authority. Sarah Kemble Knight, for one, consistently remarks on the fare in the local ordinary and inn, noting her experiences with frank and at times brutally honest descriptions. On October 3, 1704, for example, on her way to the Providence Ferry, Knight stopped for a meal and "called for something to eat," whereupon the landlady brought in a "Twisted thing like a cable" and "tugg'd for life to bring it into a capacity to spread." Knight then described a dish of pork and cabbage: "The sause was of a deep Purple, wch I tho't was boil'd in her dye Kettle; the bread was Indian, and every thing on the Table service Agreeable to these.

I, being, hungry, gott a little down; but my stomach was soon cloy'd, and what cabbage I swallowed serv'd me for a Cudd the whole day after" (54–55). Though she did sample the meal, Knight emphasizes its inferior quality by noting the color of the sauce and the "Indian," or lowergrade, bread. By only offering her version of the encounter, rather than setting it in dialogue, Knight leaves us to wonder at the landlady's response to her implicitly imperial airs. By contrast, on December 7, heading to New York, she stopped at noon in Norwalk, Connecticut, and enjoyed a good dinner: "Fryed Venison, very savoury. Landlady wanting some pepper in her seasoning, bid the Girl hand her the spice in the little *Gay* cupp on the shelfe" (67). Here, the landlady was commanding as she directed her servant and corrected her seasoning, and Knight appears as impressed by the venison as by the "Gay," or colorfully decorated, cup. That evening at 9:00 p.m., however, she arrived in Rye, and she describes a different meal at an ordinary "wch a French family kept": "Here being very hungry, I desired a fricassee, wch the Frenchman undertakeing, managed so contrary to my notion of Cookery, that I hastned to Bed superless" (67). As do all travelers, Knight had her mix of good and bad meals, and her remarks speak not only to her culinary preferences, but also to her assumption that her opinion as a genteel woman mattered. Mary McAleer Balkun makes the point that "Knight imposes her own standards upon whatever and whomever she encounters in her travels and foregrounds her point of view" (9). Knight's demands also signify the female proprietor's responsibility to maintain certain business standards, which in this case includes producing an edible meal. More than simply keeping track of what she ate, Knight's account is thus located in her dissatisfaction as a consumer and the assumption that she could expect a decent meal. If she were a guest in someone's home, such remarks might be considered rude, but as a traveler and a paying customer, Knight places the landlady outside of the conventional, domestic role of provider. Instead, the landlady is judged as a vendor whose paid commodities are subject to Knight's scrutiny.

For Margaret Van Horn Dwight, dissatisfaction with frontier accommodations was compounded by Deacon Wolcott's attempts to "*save expence*," which often forced an uneasy compromise. On October 22, 1810, for example, she described their room at Cook's Inn in County West

Chester as "very small & very dirty" and complained about the stifling atmosphere: "The air is so impure I have scarcely been able to swallow since I enter'd the house—. . . . The men have been swearing & laughing in the store under me this hour—& the air of my room is so intolerable, that I must quit my writing to go in search of some that is *breathable*" (7). Rejecting the "intolerable" air and intrusive noise, Dwight makes clear her familiarity with better arrangements. Writing in her journal was almost impossible with the "swearing & laughing" coming from below. This complaining tells us of her sense of decorum, as does the fact that Dwight considered it "grating to [her] pride" that she must go into a tavern and "furnish & cook" provisions. To do so would further collapse boundaries. Just as Knight and Dwight modeled genteel standards, they were keen social critics who unapologetically identified poor conditions and ill-mannered behavior. Rather than compromise their standards, genteel female travelers deliberately reminded others of these distinctions. Travel allowed Knight and Dwight to be assertive about their preferences and standards. By voicing their concerns, women impacted the larger social scene and influenced the transportation of culture.

More than mere snobbery, however, such comments express a certain anxiety. For in their displeasure, these writers collectively ask, "What kind of woman found herself in such surroundings?" Richard Bushman explains their discontent in light of the "outward signs of gentility" that functioned as an "assurance of common assumptions and predictable behavior, of a commitment to reason, tolerance, and respect." In this regard, genteel women would have felt especially out of place without certain activities, for, as Bushman notes, "dancing, personal grace, and manners signified engagement to a code of conduct" ("American High-Style," 359). Without these familiar markers, genteel women were disoriented. Eliza Bridgham, for example, illustrates these sentiments when

WESTWARD ROUTE VIA THE FORBES ROAD TO PITTSBURGH AND DOWN THE OHIO AND MISSISSIPPI RIVERS (C. 1800). John Forbes's Road, built in 1758, starts in Dauphin County, Pennsylvania; continues west to Fort Ligonier in Westmoreland County, Pennsylvania; and ends at Fort Duquesne (later Fort Pitt), at the junction of the Ohio, Allegheny, and Monongahela rivers. The profile drawn by James Monteith appears on a map titled "Middle Atlantic States," printed in James Monteith, *Barnes' Elementary Geography* (New York: A. S. Barnes, 1895), 41. Jody Bendel, art director, Minnesota State University Moorhead.

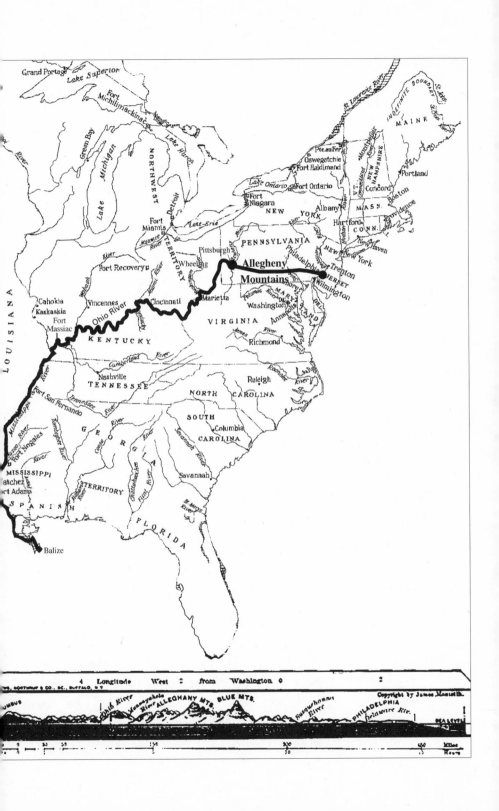

Grand Portage

Lake Superior

Fort Michilimackinac

Green Bay

Lake Michigan

Lake Huron

NORTHWEST

Detroit

Fort Miamis

Maumee River

TERRITORY

Lake Erie

St. Lawrence River

INDEFINITE BOUNDARY

MAINE

Pte au Fer
Oswegatchie
Fort Haldimand

Montpelier
V. T.
NEW HAMPSHIRE

St. John

Portland

Lake Ontario
Fort Ontario

Concord

MASS.

Boston

Providence

Fort Niagara

NEW YORK

Albany
Hartford
CONN.

New Haven

Fort Recovery

Wabash River

Pittsburgh

Wheeling

Susquehanna River

PENNSYLVANIA

Philadelphia

Trenton

NEW YORK

**Allegheny
Mountains**

NEW JERSEY

Wilmington
DEL.

Cahokia
Kaskaskia
Fort
Massac

Vincennes

Ohio River

Kentucky River

Cincinnati

Marietta

Potomac River

MARY LAND

Washington
Annapolis
D. C.

VIRGINIA

James River

Richmond

LOUISIANA

KENTUCKY

Cumberland River

Nashville

TENNESSEE

Tennessee River

Roanoke River

NORTH   CAROLINA

Raleigh

Fort San Fernando

Mississippi River

Yazoo River

Fort Nogales

GEORGIA

Coosa River

Tombigbee River

Savannah River

SOUTH
CAROLINA

Columbia

Savannah

MISSISSIPPI
Natchez
Fort Adams

SPANISH

TERRITORY

Mobile River

Alabama River

Chattahoochee River

Flint River

St. Marys River

FLORIDA

Balize

Longitude   West   from   Washington   0

2

UMBUS

Ohio River

Monongahela River   ALLEGHANY MTS.   BLUE MTS.

Susquehanna River

PHILADELPHIA

Delaware River

Copyright by James Macbeth.

4ALBYH

Miles
Hours

addressing her sister in her journal on July 26, 1818, from Guilford: "I wish you were here, if it is only to see the <u>difference</u> of manners & deportment in these people, from what <u>we</u> have been used to—not that we are <u>very</u> refined, in <u>my</u> estimation, but that they are most <u>unfortunately</u> <u>rough</u>" (19). Bridgham's attention to "manners & deportment" suggests that her behavior would also be held to certain standards. Bushman elaborates on this presumption: "Every detail of behavior had to be carefully practiced. Any false move could come under the scrutiny of a critical eye" (*Refinement*, 57). A woman's manner, dress, and posture were thus subject to evaluation, and this scrutiny was heightened for women travelers. Anticipating criticism, women turned their gaze outward and expressed their displeasure. Although travelers generally imagined western frontiers as an extension of the eastern metropolis, and therefore in need of some serious guidance, the West would eventually become associated with innovation rather than replication. With so many elements in motion, the traveler and the frontier would certainly undergo change rather than maintain stasis. The woman's travel narrative documents the tensions and conflicts born from culture change.

Women who traveled west were subject to scrutiny, for as outsiders, they were, quite simply, interesting. Travelers not only brought news; they were themselves newsworthy. David Conroy reminds us that "the exchange of news and information at taverns invested every new arrival, however humble, with the potential of being a news-carrier" (48). Lydia B. Bacon and her husband, heading home to Boston in 1812 after a seventeen-month journey, experienced this phenomenon firsthand while sitting in a hotel parlor in Albany "in one corner of which sat a Quaker Lady of very pleasing aspect, who informed us as a piece of news, that the Eve previous, An Officer, & his Wife, had arrived directly, from Detroit, who had been taken Prisoners by General Brock, & added, have you heard any thing about them? We observed we were the Persons, upon which she expressed her pleasure at seeing us, & made many enquiries, respecting the transactions, which had excited such commotions, throughout the United States" (78). Almost at once, her husband was surrounded by other military men and "diligently employed in answering innumerable questions." Bacon was thus surprised, if not delighted, to find that they had become part of the "news cycle."

For Sarah Kemble Knight, such attention could be distracting, as she quickly learned. Having departed Boston on October 2, 1704, with her kinsman Capt. Robert Luist, Knight visited Reverend Belcher in Dedham, where she hired a guide, John, at Fisher's Tavern. Upon arriving at Billingses "twelve miles further" for her first night, Knight described this encounter with Debb, the landlord's eldest daughter: "[I] had not gone many steps into the Room, ere I was Interogated by a young Lady . . . with these, or words to this purpose (viz.) Law for mee—what in the world brings You here at this time a night?—I never see a woman on the Rode so Dreadfull late, in all the days of my versall life. Who are You? Where are You going? I'me scar'd out of my witts . . . I told her shee treated me very Rudely, and I did not think it my duty to answer her un-mannerly Questions" (54). Although Knight had a guide, traveling with-out a male relative as chaperon appeared irregular. Knight simply did not conform to notions of how and when and with whom women should travel—certainly not alone and definitely not so late. In Julia A. Stern's discussion of Knight's journal, she notes the "paradoxical nature of Knight's identity" as "both a genteel women *and* a female traveler." As such, Knight transgresses gender roles. In noting this particular scene, Stern finds that "Knight is mistaken for a prostitute," for given the late hour and Knight's "fine clothes [this] could be understood in no other way in rural Connecticut in 1704" ("To Relish," 3). Once Knight explained that she was there only to await the next day's post, however, tensions subsided; Debb rushed upstairs to adorn herself with rings and returned for a long chat. While the landlord's daughter initially reacted fearfully and cast Knight as a dangerous figure, an outsider both geographically and socially, Knight's refusal to answer the "unmannerly Questions" placed the inquisitor in the same category as outsider, which for Knight was de-termined by social class. Still, Knight remained distant and condescend-ing. This interaction not only points to gender expectations about women travelers, but also shows that traveler-innkeeper relations were a source of information, news, and gossip. As Knight and Bacon verify, the trav-eler was indeed the focus of great interest and accommodated under watchful eyes.

Woman's presumed role as ambassador of culture not only inspired critical commentary but also influenced journal style. When surrounded by familiar trappings, the woman traveler wrote confidently and in great detail as she catalogued her findings. Faced with less familiar situations, women deflected insecurity by framing scenes as minidramas, a discursive choice that allowed them to distance themselves by class and ethnicity. Knight, for one, often punctuated such scenes with biting caricature, as on October 7, in New Haven, when describing "a tall country fellow" who entered a merchant's house to inquire after some ribbons: "—he advanc't to the middle of the Room, makes an Awkward Nodd, and spitting a Large deal of Aromatick Tincture, he gave a scrape with his shovel like shoo, leaving a small shovel full of dirt on the floor, made a full stop, Hugging his own pretty Body with his hands under his arms, Stood staring rown'd him, like a Catt let out of a Baskett. At last, like a creature Balaam Rode on, he opened his mouth and said: have You any Ribinen for Hatbands to sell I pray?" (65–66). This slow-motion portrayal of this country fellow implicitly contrasts him to a more sophisticated shopper who would have been less hesitant to inquire after the goods and approach the merchant. The awkward nod, tobacco spitting, and dirty shoes create a sad portrait that justifies the narrator's ridicule. To accentuate the class differences, Knight names this man "Bumpkin Simpers" and his female companion "Jone Tawdry." As Knight continues with her caricature, "Jone" enters, "dropping about 50 curtsees," and proceeds to examine the ribbons with exaggerated delight, claiming them to be "*dreadfull pretty*" (66). Mary McAleer Balkun calls attention to Knight's role as "deputy-husband," which allows her to become "more self-assured in her dealings with the variety of strange and fascinating settlers she encounters" (19). Knight moreover intended this sketch to be both humorous and instructive, for it concludes: "We may Observe here the great necessity and bennifitt both of Education and Conversation; for these people have as Large a portion of mother witt, and sometimes a Larger, than those who have bin brought up in Citties; But for want of emprovements, Render themselves almost Ridiculos, as above. I should be glad if they would leave such follies, and am sure all that Love Clean Houses (at least) would be glad on't too" (66). In this concluding gesture of sympathy, Knight suggests that education would complement natural wit, though crossing class barriers by "such follies" as buying hat ribbons should be discouraged. Such passages confirm Sargent Bush's observation that Knight "surely

wrote for an audience other than herself" (74). For as a "colloquial narrator," Knight used humor and earthy language to enliven her prose and,
at times, assert her own education and status (77). William L. Andrews
elaborates on this tendency: "From today's perspective, Knight's reliance
on manners, dress, dialect, and behavior as indices to character may seem
superficial, even unfair, though it makes for some excellent broad comedy. We should not forget, however, that behind the joking, some of
which is at Knight's expense, there is a more discerning narrator" (8). As
both director and narrator of her travel account, Knight attempted to
control and to reinforce class structures.

The dramatization of events and insertion of dialog not only exaggerate differences but coincide with moments of insecurity. Breaking from
the journal's typical prose style to insert dialog signals authorial control.
When Margaret Van Horn Dwight found herself and her traveling companions objects of great curiosity, she also framed such moments theatri-
cally, using lively dialog, as on October 19, 1810: "We stopt to *eat oats* at a

FISHER'S TAVERN, DEDHAM, MASSACHUSETTS. Caption that appears on the
image: "'The Old Tavern.' Joshua Fisher, father and son, 1658–1730; Nathaniel
Ames 1735–1766; Richard Woodward during the Revolution, and 'The Sign of
the Law Book' 1794. Taken down 1817. Drawn from the memory of the oldest
inhabitant of Dedham 1891. The large elm tree was planted by Fisher Ames about
1800." Photo courtesy of Dedham Historical Society, Dedham, Massachusetts.

Tavern in Fairfield, West Farms, an old Lady came to the room. . . . 'Well! Gals where you going?' 'To New Connecticut' 'You bant tho—To New Connecticut?' 'Why what a long journey! do you ever expect to get there? How far is it?' 'Near 600 miles' 'Well Gals, you Gals & your husbands with you?' 'No Ma'am'—'Not got your husbands! Well I don't know—they say there's wild Indians there!'" (2). Dwight emphasizes the colloquial here as if she had traveled farther than the twenty-five miles to Fairfield. Curiously, Ohio does not yet warrant its own identity, but is "New Connecticut," an extension—or colony, as Edward Watts might argue. The woman's concern that Dwight and her cousin were traveling without husbands, while intrusive, also marks a certain discomfort about their status. As Elizabeth Barnes explains, "republican marriage contributes to the domestication of authority by embodying a patriarchal structure and representing it as benign" (67). Elizabeth Maddock Dillon, in speaking to connections between gender and liberalism, offers this insight: "The elevation of personal happiness to a moral good is further extended, in many cases, to a national good as well: that is, the ideal marriage is linked to an idealized American nation founded in consent and affection" (126). As single women, Margaret Van Horn Dwight and Susan Wolcott challenged and upset these idealizations, and so evoked an uncomfortable response. Whereas Knight records Debb's series of questions to illustrate her impertinence, Dwight notes dialect—"eat oats" and "Gals"—to signal class distinctions. Knight and Dwight both use dialog to emphasize differences that are then reinforced by their amused, exasperated responses. Both travelers also bristle at the assumptions that they wanted protection, for, to their minds, their very gentility should have provided some safety from impertinent inquisitions—and yet, on the road, such distinctions apparently collapsed.

Not all travelers were as antagonistic, but they were all subject to commentary and advice. On October 9, 1807, Elizabeth Van Horne experienced similar inquisitiveness two days out from Scotch Plains, New Jersey, while in Somerset, where "an old Lady asked Clara how far we were traveling—Clara answered, to the State of Ohio—What no further? How far should we go? Says Harriet. Why, to Kentucky!!! Was the answer" (9). It seems that everyone had an opinion about travel. Curiously, Ohio has lost some ground to Kentucky as a preferred destination. Van Horne also

noted acts of kindness on October 10 in Potters Town, outside of Bethle-
hem Township, where her group "[a]scended a hill and came in sight of
an elegant garden and summer house." The Van Horne family, all nine of
them, were then invited into the house for cherry bounce—a distilled
drink made from cherries[1]—and as it was Saturday, the lady regretted
that previous engagements prevented her from escorting them "some
miles." Van Horne then reflected: "The politeness of Miss Bray (who is
the Lady mentioned) was signally pleasing—as travelers and strangers it
was so unexpected" (11). By noting the singularity of Miss Bray's kindness, Van Horne reinforces the status of traveler as outsider. Not surprisingly, then, Van Horne's large party, sixteen including family, friends, and
servants, again attracted attention while on their way to Easton, October
11, 1807: "It being Sunday and no meeting we were gazed at from morning to night—indeed it is much the case every day—I believe we are a
wonder to the country through which we pass—Our numbers or something take their attention they want to know who we are, where from,
and where we are bound" (11). Surveillance, it seems, worked both ways.
Moreover, the town appeared aimless without a Sunday meeting, leaving
the travelers as the main attraction. Van Horne's entry illustrates traveler
as an event, whereupon locals passed judgment and, to various degrees,
assimilated or rejected the outsider's influence.

Although Van Horne did remark on these queries, she lacked Dwight's
rancor or Knight's spunk. Perhaps Van Horne's gentler nature led Elizabeth Collette, the 1939 editor of the journal, to distinguish The Journal of
Elizabeth Van Horne, 1807 from "another Van Horn journal," the Dwight narrative of 1810. Collette notes, "Margaret, born in 1790, was a girl not quite
twenty when, in 1810, she set out. Eliza Van Horne, born in 1776, was
thirty-one." Collette makes further distinctions: "It is doubtful if the two
journal writers were related in any way or ever heard of each other. Their
accounts are interestingly different in outlook and in content" (8–9).
Dwight may have been a bit too forthcoming, if not caustic, for Collette's
tastes. Gentility prevails even in the editing of these journals.

Although women were often subject to scrutiny, they understood the
curiosity shown toward them, for travel certainly did offer occasions for
"people watching" and could prove quite entertaining. Eliza Williams
Bridgham, for example, noted on July 29, 1818, while passing through

the popular spa resort at Saratoga Springs: "This is one of the finest places, to see human nature, you can imagine—here you see all sorts, from all parts—there are several gentlemen here, from Europe, & the West Indies, & four ladies from Spain" (23). Bridgham was traveling with her father, Samuel Willard Bridgham, a Brown University graduate, state attorney general (1814–18), and mayor of Providence (1832–40). As a privileged traveler, she appreciated this international mixing of guests. Bridgham is also less caustic in her descriptions than Dwight, perhaps because she was just passing through rather than contemplating relocation. For example, in Brattleboro on July 22, 1818, she was delighted by local colloquialisms: "Oh! I was quite amused to find that some of our beaux, favorite expressions, had reached even to Vermont & New Hampshire. In Fitz-William I was startled to hear a man tell a young lad, 'to clear out!' & in Fitchburg a boy was fearful a horse was going 'to clear out'; it really sounded like home" (16). And on July 24, she noted: "I have been much amused by the different expressions I have heard since I came here; they have an addition to the famous 'clear out,' when they wish a person to leave the room, they say 'com, cut your cable, & clear out!' They abound in phrases of this sort, which makes it quite amusing" (17). While Bridgham noted how regional differences could be heard in language, she was also reassured to hear familiar, shared phrasing, as if it bonded the new nation.

Again and again, it is evident that travel naturally inspires comparisons as travelers seek perspective. Some find inspiration in the new and exotic, while others find comfort in the familiar. Elizabeth Gilpin, for example, marks the rhythms of travel with a distinctly worldly view, as on October 15, 1830: "[A]rrived at Utica nearly at dusk—only just in time to take our supper, and then go on board the Canal Packet 'Ohio' at 7 o'clock. We read tiresome books, looked at our fellow travellers, enjoyed the scene of making the beds for the night, and then retired to sleep if we could" (25). Thomas O. Beebee complicates such reactions when he notes a "fictional twist" in "letters of travel" of the late seventeenth and early eighteenth centuries, which were often embellished. According to Beebee, these letters "reverse the situation of the traveler and the object of his inquiries" and rather than depict "a European in Isphahan or Constantinople, epistolary traveler's fictions present a Tahitian in Paris or a Persian in

Berlin" (86). To draw on this example, women in this study, such as Dwight and Bridgham, portray the easterner on the frontier or in the out-skirts as having the cultural upper hand. As outsiders they seem almost obligated to critique local culture. For example, Bridgham wrote on July 31, while passing through Albany: "The inhabitants are mostly of Dutch extraction; to walk a few rods and view the curious names on the signs, is really amusing. To give you a specimen, I will write what is directly in front of the window where I am now sitting, 'Van Veghten & Talbert,' 'G. La Grange,' 'Gerrit Gates,' 'Conrada Teneyck,' 'T. Van Schaick,' 'Win-schoof Gaineswoort,'—these are all within my <u>present</u> sight; don't they about break your jaws in trying to pronounce them? It is really quite as disagreeable as the German" (27). Whereas common expressions had elicited humorous, kind responses, here Bridgham is less charitable, as she declares Dutch names disagreeable. She is, however, not without humor when she describes one particular sign: "As we were passing through, one of the lower streets of the City, I observed so <u>fine a specimen</u> of <u>wit</u>, I cannot forbear noticing it. A man, kept a common kind of huxter's-shop, over the door was written on a large white sign, 'I, John P. Jones, Put this sign here, To let you know, I keep good beer, I have made my board, A little wider, To let you know, I keep good cider'; don't <u>you think</u> some one exercised his poetical talents very finely? There were several other signs, of the same kind, but I don't recollect any more, the <u>Albani-ans must be courting</u> the Muses, with a great deal of success" (29). Even as she points out behaviors as distinctly rustic, Bridgham identifies clever advertising and an increased use of lettering, innovations in signage re-sponding to increased literacy.

Comparisons thus ranged from critical to amusing as women gauged their position and evaluated their surroundings. Above all, women were expected to be charitable rather than condescending. When women devi-ated from this cultural expectation, their harsh critiques seemed particu-larly out of place and communicated insensitive intolerance. In keeping with these perceptions, Cheryl J. Fish notes of three nineteenth-century women—Nancy Prince, Mary Seacole, and Margaret Fuller—that travel was "connected to benevolent work, uplift, and the desire to improve the quality of life for oppressed and wounded people as well as open up pos-sibilities for the traveler herself" (13). Rather than express sympathy for the less fortunate or suffering, however, some women seemed to forget their genteel manners altogether and expressed their unguarded displeasure. In late August 1812, Lydia B. Bacon, for example, was quite displeased when she and her husband, Josiah, "arrived at a wretched tavern" eighteen miles from Niagara Falls, around nine o'clock at night. After passing by an adjacent room with a "young Soldier sick with the camp fever," they entered a small room with two beds, one occupied by another traveler, and a broken window that "admitted the full moon which shone with uncommon brilliancy, & helped to make more visible the *extreme filth* of the place. . . . [T]he pillow cases was the color of coal & on turning down the cloaths they were worse *if possible, & emitted such an effluvia* that with difficulty I was kept from being sick." Sharon Salinger notes that such descriptions are all the more dramatic in that "the threshold for tolerance of dirt was quite high in early America—a time before regular laundering and bathing constituted normative behavior—[so] the taverns that elicited negative comment must have been quite awful" (215). The filth was notable, but Bacon's displeasure not completely justified. Her husband, who tried to "make the best of every thing," countered her reaction and "observed, dont say a word, they have given us the best they could." They then agreed to stay but to sleep in their clothes: "but sleep had fled, & the bugs which begun their repast soon as we got warm & from the voraciousness with which they regaled upon our poor wearied bodies, evinced they had not made a meal for a long time, combined with the piercing groans of the dying man & the stench which came from his bed, precluded even the possibility of such a thing" (76–77). As they were leaving in the morning, Bacon saw the dying man's brother attending him: "but I asked no questions & hasted away fearing we had imbibed the disease." Fear of disease thus drove Bacon to abandon common decency, let alone gentility. Bacon's entry shows how genteel manners may be forsaken when a traveler's sensibilities are tested. As Bacon "hasted away," in her own discomfort, she could not muster any sympathy for the sickly soldier. Though she knew better, the immediate concerns for her own welfare overshadowed her gentility.

When writing in the moment, Bacon was overcome by her unmediated reaction. In hindsight, upon completing the journal, Bacon regretted her behavior: "In reviewing this scene I have often thought how supremely selfish I was, instead of passing the night, in useless regrets, that we were so situated, it was my duty to have endeavored to alleviate the sufferings of the sick stranger, possibly I might have rendered him some service that would have been beneficial, at any rate my own reflections would not have been so painful at the retrospect" (77). Bacon's anxiety to reach home after her own ordeal as prisoner apparently clouded her otherwise charitable impulses. Given that in her later writing, she was "relating incidents intirely from memory, which took place twenty years since," such discrepancies are more striking. By contrast, a few nights later Bacon was delighted with her stay in Utica: "Mr. Baggs Hotel renowned for its elegant accommodations as its LandLord is, for his attention & sauvety of manners" (78). Regret seemed to have faded or at least been allayed by comfortable surroundings.

Gender expectations were apparent not only in women's comments on accommodations but also in attitudes toward unmarried travelers. For although traveling to establish a domestic life was not unusual, these narratives illustrate again and again the assumption that single women heading west were looking for husbands. On October 25, outside of Elizabeth Town, New Jersey, Dwight heard about a woman who, like her, was traveling "to a new, if not western country [but was] married on her way & prevented from proceeding to her journey's end" (10). Dwight was concerned that she too might be "prevented" from continuing her journey, which suggests a certain anxiety about remaining single. Seeking a marriage partner while en route seemed to be a popular motive, for in the same town, she and Susan Wolcott met a man who "enquired, or rather *expected* we were going to the Hio—we told him yes & he at once concluded it was to get husbands—He said winter was coming on & he wanted a wife & believ'd he must go there to get him one—I concluded of course the next thing would be, a proposal to Miss W or me to stay behind to save trouble for us both; but nothing would suit him but a rich widow, so our hopes were soon at an end" (11). For this man, finding a wife before winter was a practical matter. Apparently, then, an active marriage market was yet another reason to make haste toward Ohio. The man's determination to find a rich widow underscores marriage as a business venture in which one could shop around for a suitable match. While Dwight's conclusion that "our hopes were soon at an end," may at first glance seem like disappointment, it becomes clear that she was actually relieved, if not annoyed that the man "concluded" the purpose of their journey was "to get husbands."

Dwight found the presumption that single women were in search of a husband irritating, and from her frequent remarks on the topic it is clear that she remained troubled by it. Her ambivalence about marriage manifests in several passages in which she worries either about never marrying or about what she will do if she does marry. On Wednesday, October 31, in Highdleburg-Penn, she described this curious test: "If I were going to be married I would give my *intended*, a gentle emetic, or some such thing to see how he would bear being sick a little—for I could not coax a husband as I would a child, only because he was a little sick & a great deal cross—I trust I shall never have the trial—I am sure I should never bear it with temper & patience" (23). A week later, on November 8, she added: "After giving an emetic. I would take a long journey with my *intended*, to try his patience" (36). Dwight was anxious not only about finding a husband but also about her ability to put up with one. Whereas Dwight had been questioned about traveling without a husband and was left to feel defensive, she was later glad to discover that there were alternatives. On November 16, for instance, she was quite relieved, in fact, to discover "a curiosity in the house—a young lady who has come from N Connecticut *unmarried*—after staying in Warren a year—a thing I never before heard of, & had begun to think impossible. I feel quite encouraged by it—& do not believe the place as dangerous as is generally reported" (46). Dwight found relief in the possibility that a woman could remain single for an extended period in Ohio, though she probably understood that marriage could offer protection. The imperative disturbed her. Pressure to marry was indeed significant; as Elizabeth Barnes notes, "republican marriage exemplifies the perfect balance between personal fulfillment and collective commitment" (66). Marriage thus signified status, reinforced gender roles, and strengthened social harmony. By contrast, Dwight's protestations evoke dissonance, signaling inappropriate attitudes and embedded cultural assumptions. (As a side note, on December 17, 1811, a year after arriving in Warren, Margaret Dwight married William Bell Jr. Margaret Dwight Bell, according to Max Farrand's introduction, "became the mother of thirteen children" and was an active member of the community until her death in 1824 [vi].)

Dwight's concern for women's social position, however, did not always extend to the less fortunate. A week earlier, on November 7, from Phelps' Tavern in Peach Orchard, Pennsylvania, Dwight commented: "We found a house at the foot of the steepest part—A woman & her 2 sons live there & keep cakes and beer—The woman told us she had no husband at *present*—I suppose she has one in expectation." Dwight grows even more disparaging in her next passage: "We stopt at noon, at a dismal looking log hut tavern—The landlady (I hate the word but I must use it,) talk'd about bigotry, bigotted notions, liberty of conscience &c— She did not look as if she knew the meaning of conscience, much less of bigotry" (34). Rustics who engaged in popular debate affronted Dwight, and she found it necessary to chastise them, if only in her journal. Dwight was also confounded when appearance belied efficiency, as here, noting the keeper at Cook's Inn: "The landlady is a fat, dirty, ugly looking creature, yet I must confess very obliging. . . . She seems to be master, as well as mistress & storekeeper" (7). Although Dwight admits to the landlady's competence, the landlady's unkempt appearance runs contrary to her obliging manner. At Mansfield Inn, Dwight again critiqued women's behavior: "We found it kept by 2 young women, whom I thought *amazons*— for they swore & flew about 'like *witches*' they talk & laugh'd about their sparks &c&c till it made us laugh so as allmost to affront them. . . . [T]hey all took their pipes before tea" (14). By caricaturing these women as brazen and bold, Dwight makes them appear otherworldly, from mythical places. Dwight objected to their apparent gender violations, including swearing and smoking, and attempts in her writing to impose conformity. Ironically, Dwight's caustic depictions overlook the landladies' services, on which Dwight depended; her insistence on marking social class appears inappropriate. Such criticisms also suggest that female tavern owners may have lost some respectability by this late date. Indeed, their numbers were decreasing, as noted in chapter 2. As the tavern's function shifted from boarding travelers to entertaining locals, the role of the proprietor became less that of caretaker and more that of saloonkeeper. Dwight's remarks suggest these changing roles on the frontier as well. Dwight thus typifies the easterner who travels west and tries to enforce social codes, but who neglects to notice that the standards themselves do not necessarily apply. These moments of harsh interaction speak to the tensions previously noted: women were expected to behave with cordial gentility, and yet in reality they took up a more aggressive, assertive role as culture enforcers. To what extent this stance was inspired by frontier conditions is unclear, but it is notable that as social boundaries became blurred, women exerted greater authority to maintain them and, therefore, secure familiar identities.

The Sarah Beavis journal brings us to another part of the Ohio frontier and provides an opportunity to see how women from less prestigious families and with fewer resources endured hardships and expressed similar concerns about virtuous behaviors. Beavis's journal recounts a five-year struggle to find a new settlement in the Ohio Territory along the Mississippi and a subsequent series of misfortunes. The Beavis story begins in

SARAH BEAVIS JOURNAL EXCERPT (*on facing page*). Here Sarah Beavis describes the dramatic moment in summer 1781 when her brother-in-law, Joseph Young, proposed a lottery as a means of survival. Partial transcription: "This brings me to the most dismal and deplorible part of my narrative which as it [is] in the publick and therefore cannot be concieled is as follows. Shortly after I had buried my youngest daughter, already mentioned, Jas Young proposed to me that the children should be put in a lottery, but himself and me should be left out for the safety of the rest if any should survive the danger of death which we ware in at that time. For if we ware gone, thare would be none to take care of them. . . . Jas Young said hunger was too hard to bare and thought it no sin to kill one to save the rest. He then wrote down the names of the four youngest and the name of my sister-in-law's son, which lived with him, on tickets and put them in one hat, and as many blanks save one which he wrote 'death' in another. Then, by his orders, the tickets was drawn and given to me to read. At the last, out came his daughter Marey's name and next came out 'death.' As soon as she heard that the lot fel on her, she left the boat, though scarce able to walk, and as she made her way along the shore, she would cry out: 'O! daddy will you kill me? O! daddy will you kill me?' I sat confounded and silent till now but could no longer forbair, for I was persuaded that if he would stain our boat with the inosent blood of these dear creatures whose lives semed as dear to me as my own in a manner, although his children, that undoubtedly we would perrish and thare appeared nothing else to our short sight at that time. I then intreated that he would spare her life till tomorrow." "Sarah Beavis her pamphlet," 1783, MS pp. 7–8. Edward E. Ayer Manuscript Collection, Ayer MS 691, Newberry Library, Chicago.

ings me to the most dismal and deplorible part of my nara-
tive which as it in the publick and therefore cannot be concei-
d is as follows shortly after I had buried my youngest daugh
er already mentioned Jas Young proposed to me that the
ildran should be put in a lottery but him self and me-
ould be left out for the safety of the rest if any should
rvive the danger of death which we ware in at that time
r if we ware gone thare would be none to take care of
them. I told him that it was us that brought those inosent

Jas. Young
hunger was too hard to bare and thought it no sin to kill
one to save the rest he then wrote down the names of
the four youngest and the name of my sisterinlaws son which
lived with him on tickets and put them in one hat and
as many blanks save one on which he wrote death in another
then by his orders the tickets was drawn and given to me to read
at the last out came his daughter mareys name and n next
came out death as soon as she heard that the lot fel on
her she left the boat though scarce able to walk and as
she made her way along the shore she would cry out
o! daddy will you kill me o! daddy will you kill me I was
confounded and silent till now but could no longer forbair
for I was persuaded that if he would stain our boat with
the inosent blood of these dear creatures whose lives semed
as dear to me as my own in a manner al though his children
that undoubtedly we would perrish and thare appeared
nothing else to our short sight at that time & then intreated that he would spare her life till tomorrow.

1778 with her family's desire to migrate from upstate New York to Carolina, and, when that initial plan fell through, to Ohio via Kentucky. The account concludes in 1783 with Sarah Beavis's return to her mother's home in New York on the Yough River. Above all, Beavis testifies to travel as hardship. The journal unfolds conventionally, with Beavis following her husband's lead, first to Carolina and then to Ohio. Between lengthy waiting periods for her husband to return and for the river to rise, Beavis portrays westward migration as anything but painstaking and hardly glamorous. Upon her husband's untimely death and the death of her sister-in-law days afterward, Beavis's plight turned truly grim, for she was left to provide for twelve children, having only meager provisions and inadequate equipment.

To emphasize her plight, Beavis casts her narrative in biblical tones and appeals to the "Lord for guidance." Beavis's difficulties with uncertain river conditions and a lack of food were compounded by the erratic behavior of her brother-in-law, Joseph Young. When faced with starvation, Beavis prayed for divine intervention, while Young proposed another tack altogether—cannibalism. As Sarah Beavis explains: "This brings me to the most dismal and deplorible part of my narrative which as it [is] in the publick and therefore cannot be conceiled is as follows: shortly after I had buried my youngest daughter, already mentioned, Jas Young proposed to me that the children should be put in a lottery, but himself and me should be left out for the safety of the rest if any should survive the danger of death which we ware in at that time. For if we ware gone, thare would be none to take care of them" (7).[2] Knowing that the record would be made public, Beavis reluctantly reveals the unseemly details of Young's proposal. In doing so, she asserts control over the narrative and, more so than the other women in this study, dramatically underscores the tensions between virtue and survival.

As with other female travelers, Beavis was responsible for upholding the higher moral ground, despite her lesser economic stature. Unlike the self-interested Joseph Young, Beavis would defer her own survival to prevent any further loss of life, especially as concerned the children. To counter Young's bizarre plan, Beavis proposed that they hunt for bear, but when this proved unsuccessful, Young insisted on proceeding with the lottery:

> Jas Young said hunger was too hard to bare and thought it
> no sin to kill one to save the rest. He then wrote down the
> names of the four youngest and the name of my sister-in-
> law's son, which lived with him, on tickets and put them in
> one hat, and as many blanks save one on which he wrote
> 'death' in another. Then, by his orders, the tickets was
> drawn and given to me to read. At the last, out came his
> daughter Marey's name and next came out 'death.' As soon
> as she heard that the lot fel on her, she left the boat, though
> scarce able to walk, and as she made her way along the
> shore, she would cry out: 'O! daddy will you kill me? O!
> daddy will you kill me?' (8–9)

This horrific scene of the starving child pleading for her life tells of a
darker side of westward travel, one that makes complaints about sheets
and accommodations seem quite insignificant. The description of Mary
Young jumping on shore to avoid her fate speaks to strong survival urges.
Moreover, the weight of this moment prompts Sarah Beavis to break out
of her gendered submission: "I sat confounded and silent till now but
could no longer forbair, for I was persuaded that if he would stain our
boat with the inosent blood of these dear creatures whose lives semed as
dear to me as my own in a manner, although his children, that undoubtedly we would perrish and thare appeared nothing else to our short sight
at that time. I then intreated that he would spare her life till tomorrow
when who knows but the lord will provide something for our relief"
(8–9). By calling on the higher law of Providence, Beavis confronted
Young and convinced him to spare his daughter. She takes survival to a
higher level as well by framing the potential murderous act as a certain
cause for eternal damnation, and so evokes a more profound meaning of
"perrish." Fortuitously, the next day, an "Indian who was out hunting
with his wife and one child had killed a bare" and after skinning it followed this starving crew down the river and gave them part of the meat
(9). Although Beavis interpreted the Native Americans' act of kindness as
providential, it may have been motivated by pity or indifference. Still,
Beavis avoided an act of "intended cannibalism" and imposed law where
no definitive boundaries existed, thereby thwarting the cruel intentions

of Joseph Young. The Native Americans who appeared offering food and Joseph Young's death soon afterward reinforced her sense of justice and belief in providential design.

Though Sarah Beavis began her journey with hopes of a frontier settlement, the realities of uncertain transportation, lack of food, and dangerous animals checked this dream. When travelers were faced with survival, moral codes were tested—or, in Joseph Young's case, abandoned. Beavis's journal dramatically illustrates frontier travel as a trial. As Beavis bears witness to the dangers of migration, her account is similar to a captivity narrative, in which the survivor clarifies rumors, exonerates his or her reputation, and demonstrates providential design. More dramatically than other narratives in this study, Beavis's narrative serves as a cautionary tale underscoring the vulnerability of the frontier traveler. The female traveler thus faced cultural assumptions about her role as promoter of virtue whether heading west or venturing north or south, whether impoverished or privileged.

For Susan Edwards Johnson, who embarked on a far more leisurely journey from Connecticut to North Carolina, the genteel pose reinforced her presumed superiority. By contrast to Beavis, Johnson could afford comfortable surroundings and conveyances, even if they were not always available. Whereas Beavis relied on her religious convictions to see her through disasters, Johnson assumed the shield of gentility with equal vigor. On November 2, 1801, Johnson departed home and family in New Haven for New York, where she would join her husband, Samuel William Johnson, to embark on a six-month round-trip journey to Fayetteville, North Carolina.[3] Johnson is similar to the other women in this study in that she notes the landscape, houses, and accommodations, and from a decidedly privileged perspective. En route to Baltimore on November 14, she was "highly pleased to observe, the very improved state of the lands, thro' the State of Pennsylvania; the best Fences, & most substancial looking Barns, I ever saw, many of them Stone, & very large; the lands appear principally in Grass, which must afford pasture, for an immence number of Cattle; & from the very indifferent houses, I observed, conclude, the farms to be tennanted, saw very few gentlemans house on the road; but some very elegant standing on the banks of the Deleware" (4–5). In Elkton, she noted "the best publick house we were in on the road; had an elegant dinner; the house kept with peculiar neatness, the furnature very good, & every accommodation to render it agreeable—kept by one Richardson" (6). On November 15, "about one oclock," they stopped at the Columbian Inn: "took our lodgings at Pecks, a very spacious house, an excellant table; & well attended—but not <u>very</u> clean" (6–7). Wilmington appealed to her, with its hilltop view of the Delaware River. After crossing the Albemarle Sound and arriving at an inn on November 22, 1801, Johnson wrote: "found ourselves at an ill looking house kept by Macky; but they gave us a decent supper—our bed was bad & the landlady who was young & <u>she</u> tho't, handsom; was much offended when I requested to have clean sheets; which I presume, they had not, but having a pair with me I was independent of her frowns" (23). Dismissing the landlady's authority, Johnson asserted her own standards by bringing along her own pair of sheets. On January 21, 1802, in Point Peter near Wilmington, she recalled a pleasant evening at Mr. Lord's, where she and her husband enjoyed "an abundance of <u>good</u> victuals, but the family not much to [her] taste intended to be very genteel but did not know how" (57). This backhanded compliment suggests that though genteel ways might be imitated, gentility itself was somehow inherent. As with "new" and "old" money, these distinctions suggest a shifting class structure within which one might acquire the appearance of proper manners. This discrepancy between real and assumed gentility qualified what to an untrained eye might have seemed to be the Lords' gentility. (As in the dinner scene in William Dean Howells's *The Rise of Silas Lapham*, the class signifiers are all too apparent to a refined observer such as Susan Johnson.) By casting the young landlady as unduly vain and the aspiring Lord family as well intended, Johnson filters these scenes through a genteel lens, reinforcing her own identity. As with Knight, Trist, Dwight, Van Horne, and others, Johnson deviates from a straightforward travel log to editorialize and evaluate behaviors that register social class and mark distinctions.

Johnson's social critique also demonstrates how the traveler can both transport and impose culture. On November 16, 1801, for example, Johnson had high praise for Mrs. and Miss Smith while visiting Baltimore. She also noted General Smith's "elegant house . . . very spacious, & finished, with great taste" and the "Ladies, [who were] very richly, &

SUSAN EDWARDS JOHNSON JOURNAL EXCERPT. These passages reflect Johnson's critical perspective, as she both praises and criticizes her lodgings while noting the many variable aspects of travel in early America. Partial transcription: [November 17, 1801] "We sat alone all the evening, as it rained, feared we shou'd not be able to sail for Norfolk in the morning. We lodged at the Columbian Inn, kept by Peck. They keep an excellant table & very good attendance, which I before observed. 18th. The wind being fair, we went on board Capt. Deagle's packet, & set sail for Norfolk about one o'clock, P. M. . . . . [November 18–19, 1801] We arrived at Norfolk, at twelve the next day, which made us a passage to 23 hours, & the distance is 200 miles. The late unhealthyness of the town, together with its very unpleasant appearance (from the wharf) determined us, not to go into it; so that we step't immediately into a ferry boat, which took us to Portsmouth. Nov 19th: I never was so much alarmed on the water as passing this ferry, the wind was violet, the waves ran high, & we had several dashes of water upon us; but the Negroes mannaged the boat very well." "Journal of a Trip from Stratford, Connecticut to Fayetteville, North Carolina (1801–1802)," MS p. 13, Susan Edwards Johnson Papers, 1792–1851, 2 boxes, at the Connecticut Historical Society Museum, Hartford, Connecticut.

gaily, dress't." Johnson found comfort in these surroundings and was particularly impressed with their elegance. She then describes the tea setting: "Mrs. Smith did the honors of the tea table; the furnature of which, was very elegant; everything of silver except the tea & Coffee cups, which were white, with deep gold edges: after tea was removed, the card tables, were set among other company. . . . The Fruit was bro't in, in, cut glass dishes, on a large oval silver waiter, with China plates the same, & the Tea cups, & desert knives, with mother pearl handles, & silver blades. Before tea we had punch served in punch glasses with handles & with the fruit, wine & punch" (8–9). The elaborate setting signified wealth and elite status, with its gilded teacups, cut glass, and pearl-handled knives. Silver, pearls, and glass create a sparkling scene, one that Johnson delights in recording with detail. Here, the rituals of tea reassured her and provided her with an opportunity for social connection. Johnson also reinforces the values of female conversation and polite discourse while modeling proper female behavior. By signaling her approval, Johnson affirms her place in the social world and acknowledges her own capacity for appreciating such finery. David S. Shields observes, moreover, that taking tea was a "central rite in the new feminine mysteries" (Civil, 112) and notes that the discourse of the tea table "alerts us to the development of a woman's domain in the public sphere" (105). Richard Bushman adds to these observations: "Drawing-room society often brought together influential people to create relationships over dinner or at tea that played directly into alliances in business and politics" (Refinement, 441). The inclusion of this carefully drawn scene in her travel journal, moreover, emphasizes Johnson's appreciation for social graces and identifies her journey as a social expedition—no elaborate descriptions of the landscape for her. Instead, her journey was a comparative expedition, in which the South and the North and genteel and rustic represented distinct cultures.

Genteel Expectations and Fashion

In addition to critiquing the domestic sphere and to noting accommodations, women remarked on clothes and fashion with varying degrees of approval. For many women, fashionable clothes not only signified class but also gave them a reassuring sense of identity in a still unfamiliar place.

Again, the travel narrative serves as a valuable archive of material culture and contemporary values. In November 1795, Mary Bishop Cushman, who departed Coventry, Connecticut, for New York with her family, sailed up the Hudson River to Albany, and arrived by wagon in Palatine on November 29. After a rather uneventful week, she was delighted on December 12 upon seeing a group of "Dutch Lads and lasses" on their way to church who were "drest in a manner that excited [her] curiosity very much." Cushman begins by directly addressing her journal's main recipient, Laura: "[T]he Lads tho did well enough, but the *Lasses* O were drest dear me, how they look'd will you have a description of them, indeed if you can idea it it will be most diverting of anything in the world." As noted with other travelers, Cushman finds authority and interest in matters familiar. For though travelers, and particularly tourists, claim to seek adventure and new experiences, they often gravitate to what they know and can therefore understand. Today's American tourist who finds comfort in a fast-food restaurant chain while traveling abroad suggests a similar impulse. Perhaps travelers need a break from new stimuli, a psychological resting place as it were. It follows then that the otherwise succinct Cushman describes this group in one of the journal's most detailed and lengthy passages:

> . . . in the first place to begin at the head they wear a strip
> cap made of lawn rite old cut like as my GrandMomma's
> us'd to be then a large bonnet with a ribbon straight round
> or perhaps a little bow of narrow ribbon before, well then
> [they] had a striped blue and white, (what we call linsy
> wollsy) petticoat a light coulard long gown very long be-
> hind to trail half a quarter in the mud for they come afoot
> two miles as they always do at this season of the year, and
> they had coarse holland half handkerchiefs for their neck.
> Their gowns were short sleeves and they had white wollen
> mits, you know they will always look white after they have
> been rinsd a few times; Well then they had a cloak made of
> blue broadcloth that came down jist below their elbows and
> cut round so it hemd as low behind as before and trimd
> with thread gimp[4] about ten shades lighter than the cloak,

tho none but the cape and collar are trimd and lastly they
have blue stockings with white clocks leather shoes with a
larger pewter buckle, these added to gether to make a most
beautiful appearance you may depend well. (269–70)

These Dutch young people appeared both strange and familiar, with certain aspects of their costumes common, such as "white wollen mits," and
other parts unusual, such as "blue stockings" set off by "larger pewter
buckle." Cushman finds these outfits have altogether a "most beautiful
appearance." Whereas most of her journal is made up of simple, brief description, Cushman's precise detail in this passage suggests that she may
have simply lacked a common reference needed to describe her surroundings. Here, she casts aside prejudice and writes enthusiastically, confident
within the language of fashion. Cushman relates the Dutch dress from
head to toe, and at several points identifies with the various problems of
maintaining fashion: the muddy petticoat and the well-rinsed mittens.
Men's travel narratives may note dress in passing as an sign of social
standing, but they rarely provide such extensive passages regarding fashion, nor delight in a finely polished buckle as if describing a painting. In
this regard, David S. Shields rightly identifies fashion as "a means of asserting power in public" and thus a source of female authority (108).
Cushman, in fact, seems almost relieved to find this shared pleasure in
ritual and pageantry.

Finding similarities in custom and dress allowed many women to feel
connected in otherwise uncomfortable situations and unfamiliar surroundings. Remarking on fashion trends, in turn, allowed them to transcend geographical differences. For example, in an entry dated June 10,
1812, Lydia B. Bacon and company were encamped five miles outside of
Cincinnati, on a "dry Ridge, in Franklin County, near a Tavern, where a
puppet show had drawn together all the Lads and Lasses for twenty Miles
round." They then went to the tavern "not to see the *puppet Show*; but to
see the dancing, & were much amused, it was intensely warm & they
danced with all there strength, dressed in their best, of course, *petticoats of
the present fashionable length*, leather shoes with sharp toes, the Lads took of
their Coats & Jackets, & thus disencumbered of a part of their clothing
performed feats of activity, while the perspiration flowed copiously down

their blooming faces" (63). Bacon offers a vibrant portrait of life in the new republic in 1812. By emphasizing that dress at the tavern is current with "present" fashions, she shows her own knowledge of trends, enjoying a sense of authority over such matters. The dancers' vigorous display and "feats of activity" are depicted realistically down to the sharp-toed leather shoes and copious perspiration. Bacon's genteel mask drops momentarily in her immersion in the scene's unexpected pleasure. In such moments, the pose of traveler-as-outsider gives way to a lively multicultural interaction.

As with other genteel markers, fashion also presented barriers and reinforced social difference. For Mary Coburn Dewees, a lack of fashionable clothes prevented her from fully participating in the Pittsburgh social scene in 1788: "October 21st: We are now laying about a mile from Pittsburgh and have receiv'd several Invitations to come on shore. We have declined all, as the trunks with our cloaths are not come up, and we, in our traveling dress, not fit to make an appearance in that Gay place" (20–21). Clothes signify class and either provide entry or restrict participation. Dewees also marked decor as a signifier of social class by extending this compliment on October 22: "Called on Mrs. Butler and saw a very handsome parlour, Elegantly papered and well furnished. It appeared more like Philad[elphi]a than any I have seen since I left that place" (22). Though her lack of gay apparel kept her away from some social events, Dewees describes several invitations to tea that she apparently could accept while dressed in her traveling clothes. The biggest disappointment came on November 7, after Dewees had waited for the river to rise, staying on an island: "Had the Company of the 3 French Gentlemen before mentioned to dine with us, who came to invite us to a Ball held at Col. Butler's, where 30 Ladys and Gentlemen were to assemble for that purpose. It is hardly worth while to say we declined going as it was out of our power to dress fit, at this time, to attend such an Entertainment or else (you know) [we] should be happy to do ourselves the honour" (31). For Dewees, fashion identified genteel society, so that without proper clothes, she was without power to participate in the social events she admired.

There were also limits, for too much attention to fashion could signal frivolity. Eliza Bridgham, for example, notes a particularly wealthy group of travelers while staying as the Sans Souci Hotel in Ballston, near Saratoga

Springs, July 30, 1818. The house itself was "large & commodious, being nearly 200 feet in length, & three stories in height." It was a bustling scene, as she described it: "There are 120 now at this house, & about 700 strangers in the village. The gentlemen amuse themselves by walking, riding, playing at Billiards, nine-pins, &c while the Ladies I suspect, must devote nearly <u>all</u> their time to dress, as they change it <u>four</u> times in course of the day. They have a Ball, at Ballston, every other evening, which makes it pleasant for all!" (24). Whereas Dewees finds her lack of fashionable clothes limiting, Bridgham identifies clothes changing as an occupation unto itself.

Geographical differences are apparent for Susan Johnson, who found that the North set fashion trends, whereupon the South followed. On November 20, 1801, when approaching Suffolk, for example, she remarked on two women in a chariot drawn by two horses "so lean that they cou'd scarcely crawl" and driven by a poorly dressed driver; it "appeared as if Ladies Charriot & all were made in Queen Elizabeth's day" (6). A few days later, Johnson arrived in New Bern, where she stayed for a month with her cousin, Mrs. Devereux, during which time Mr. Johnson left for a three-week business trip to Fayetteville, most likely to attend to his logging business, though she does not explain his absence explicitly. After attending an "assembly" one evening she recorded: "I was surprised to see all the ladies so far behind our fashions, & the greatest part of them were very awkwardly dresst; there was Mrs Sitgreaves, a middle aged lady, with a snuff-color'd sattin on spangled all over, & a quantity of tinsal fringe, & a tassle. . . . [T]his lady is the descendent of the Indian Queen who married a british officer" (13–14). To Johnson's taste, this awkwardly dressed woman had transgressed fashion codes and lacked all decorum, with her spangles and fringe—especially inappropriate, it seems, for a "middle aged lady." The reference to this woman's Indian heritage and mixed marriage may explain the fashion faux pas as an exotic variation, but within Johnson's frame of reference such deviation was duly noted as outdated. Not surprisingly, then, when Johnson turned her attention to the other women, she also found them ill arrayed in their "coloured silks with a profusion of tinsal flowers & feathers [and] bright pink head dresses" (14). Still, Johnson was able to enjoy the dance as a curious, if not superior, observer of local custom and dress. Whereas fashion connected some women to their new surroundings, Johnson uses it to affirm class distinctions.

Genteel Expectations and Religion

Travelers in early America witnessed a particularly enlivened spiritual period that inevitably brought them into contact with members from congregations or denominations other than their own. Brian J. L. Berry identifies the First Great Awakening, dated 1730–60, as "a religious revival that relegitimated emotional religiosity . . . and gave millenarian thought a distinctive American tone," and marks the Second Great Awakening, dated 1800–30, with a belief that "conversion is possible by an act of will" (10–11). Commentary on accommodations, manners, and fashion established class preferences, while commentary on religion distinguished cultural and regional differences. Religion also identified a person's character, and, depending on the traveler, signaled acceptance or exclusion. In this very personal matter of religious affiliation, travelers often experienced a keen sense of themselves as "outsiders," as their tolerance was tested and their manners were strained. For the sake of civility, travelers often found themselves sitting in a new church or sharing a meal with those of different religious persuasions, which meant some degree of compromise. Although a traveler expected change, many found alterations to their weekly Sabbath schedule upsetting, a response that marked religion's importance as a measure of comfort and stability. For others, visiting a new church was to some extent entertaining. For many of these women, keeping the Sabbath signaled civility and provided order, while neglecting these rituals suggested civic and moral decay. During Elizabeth Gilpin's stay in Johnstown, New York, on September 26, 1830, she remarked on a visit to the local Presbyterian church to "hear Mr. Mair—a Scotch gentleman of great talent and eloquence. His sermon was a very good one, but his accent was so truly scotch I could not with all my attention understand him sufficiently to derive much satisfaction from it" (13). Gilpin also indicates that church going was yet another activity to be included as an attraction in the traveler's journal; sermons were critiqued along with other social conventions and institutions. As travelers documented the rich proliferation of religious diversity in early America, moreover, their reactions were variously surprising, indifferent, hostile, and curious.

Margaret Van Horn Dwight, for example, was not only a critical observer of the accommodations she stayed in and the locals she encountered; she was equally discerning regarding church services. The niece of Timothy Dwight and the great-great-niece of Jonathan Edwards, Dwight had been reared in the Calvinist traditions of investigation and argument. Her scriptural training, replete with close readings, sharpened her vision, as she carefully interpreted and scrutinized her new environment. In Middlesex, Pennsylvania, on October 20, for instance, Dwight attended church with the innkeeper's granddaughter, Susannah Nash, and found: "The sermon had nothing very striking in it but if I had time I would write you the text heads &c just to let you see I remember it, though I fear it has done me no good for I heard it like a stranger and did not realize that I was interested in it at all." A self-identified "stranger," Dwight distances herself as she assesses, rather critically, the minister's performance for his rhythms and elocution: "I thought his 'gait to deliver' was better than his voice, for he has a most terrible *nasal twang*" (4). The minister's pacing was offset by his delivery—a negative, snobbish commentary on regional differences. Moreover, Dwight found violations of the Sabbath particularly distressing: "Sunday eve—East pensboro' township-P-[November 4] . . . I believe no regard is paid to the sabbath any where in this State—It is only made a holiday of—So much swearing as I have heard amongst the Pennsylvanians both men & women I have never heard before during my whole life—I feel afraid I shall become so accustom'd to hearing it, as to feel no uneasiness at it" (28). New Haven apparently had higher standards; Dwight disdained such crude behavior and unnecessary frivolity, for, to her mind, a proper Sabbath required community compliance with certain behaviors. With these codes violated, Dwight was left the uneasy observer. Adding to the woman's role as culture bearer and reinforcer, religious observation required special vigilance.

Eliza Williams Bridgham shared Dwight's concerns with an apparent deterioration of religious tradition. Traveling with her distinguished father, Samuel Willard Bridgham, she often framed her remarks as those of a social superior. On July 26, 1818, while visiting Guilford, she wrote: "The minister, who is a <u>wandering</u> Methodist, preached last Sunday, for a <u>bushel of oats</u>, & the Sabbath previous, for two dinners, he had eaten a long time before!! What a shocking state of society is this! I never was more struck with the necessity & utility of public worship. People here make their calculations, to avail themselves of the Sabbath for all '<u>kinds of jobs</u>'" (18). On August 2, Bridgham and her father passed through Lebanon Springs, which was established in 1787, according to Suzanne Thurman, as a key Shaker village (24). They attended a Shaker meeting, an event that Bridgham found most intriguing. She provides an elaborate description of Shaker dress and the ceremonial manner of the Shakers' entrance, with men and women entering two by two through separate doors, men with blue hats and women blue bonnets, women in shoes "with heels, about two inches high!!" After the Shakers seated themselves, silence ensued until they "all sang a long hymn, there seemed no tune, but, a kind of Methodistical cant. They really sang as it were from the bottom of their souls, & made such a screaming, that a few of us were fortunate enough to escape, without the head-ache" (35). Bridgham explains that between the singing and the dancing, "a kind of shuffle balance," the "<u>spirit moved</u> an Elder to speak, which he did very handsomely; they are very liberal in their sentiments, treat <u>all</u> denominations as friends, & admire & applaud <u>Virtue, wherever,</u> it is, to be found." Brian J. L. Berry confirms that the genders were separated in adherence to Shaker doctrine on celibacy and that dance was central to Shaker worship: "The dances ranged from mildly exuberant to highly explosive. On the mild side were rhythmic exercises in which the participants would march with their hands held out in front of the body, elbows bent, moving the hands up and down with a sort of swinging motion as though gathering up something in their arms. This motion signified 'gathering in the good.' They also believed in 'shaking out the evil'" (37). Bridgham concludes that it was "really worth the <u>trouble</u> of visiting" the Shakers, even though she finds their dancing a bit theatrical for her tastes: "though solemn, I could not realise [the Shakers] were <u>devoted</u> to God & when the dances began, it <u>actually</u> appeared more like a Theatre, than the house of the Lord!" (36). Bridgham preferred a more traditional, less dramatic expression of faith and so equated the Shaker service with a most secular institution. Such comments demonstrate that religion was evaluated and compared like any other social event or commodity in the traveler's world.

Religion was also a source of curiosity for some travelers. Popular guidebooks made visiting the Shakers a regular stop. *The Northern Traveller*, for example, describes New Lebanon Springs as "one of the most delightful resorts for strangers . . . calculated to please a taste for the softer beauties of nature" (38). Under the subsection "Shaker Village," which is described as "an object of attention to most visiters," the book provides a brief history of the sect, its founder, Ann Lee, and its various beliefs. The travel guide then adds that "their worship consists principally of a strange and disagreeable kind of dancing, whence they have their name, accompanied with a monotonous song" (41). In late December 1807, Elizabeth Van Horne included a lengthy report on the Shakers with general observations on the religious diversity of Lebanon, Ohio: "How many in the State are under strange delusions with respect to religion and forms of Worship—the Shaking Quakers for one sect—it is awful to behold them—I have [been to see them] once but can give you [no idea of] my feelings at beholding [them in] their wild Indian powwow, and [dancing]—some spectators faint—[some] shed tears—and others tremble while some laugh and ridicule them."[5] Whereas Bridgham was bemused, Van Horne appears to have been made uncomfortable by the Shakers. By drawing comparisons to native ceremonies, she presents the Shakers' rites as exotic and excessively emotional. This deviance was "awful to behold" and set a benchmark for comparison. In fact, Van Horne seems to have disliked the evangelical movement in general: "The new lights (as they are call'd) are nearly as wild or disorderly as the Shakers—their Society is composed of Baptists & Presbyterians &c. their is also a Methodist society—and a regular (*what we call a regular*) [Baptist Society in this place & vicinity. There are a good number of respectable & able families that belong to the Baptist society. Their Preacher is plain, good, serious, tender, feeling, firm, uniform, Revd Danl Clark. There are also some Presbyterians.]" (22). Van Horne clearly identifies the diversity inspired by the Great Awakening, while indicating her own preference for "regular" over "wild" society. In June 1827, Captain Basil Hall also noted a stop in Lebanon: "[T]hough I have witnessed some strange forms of worship in former travels, I cannot say that I ever beheld any thing, even in Hindoostan, to match these Shakers" (1:111–12). Hall was ultimately polite about, if startled by, his witnessing the "innocent caperings of these honest Shakers." As travelers read the spiritual landscape, they applied a comparative mode to religion, just as they did to secular events. Bridgham, Van Horne, and Hall collectively indicate religion as a signifi-cant element in travel accounts. Increasingly, as travel accommodated tourism, deliberate trips to view similar "caperings" became standard fare.

For some travelers, Presbyterian sects set the standard against which other denominations and religions were measured. For Lydia B. Bacon, Catholicism warranted comment on October 10, 1811, while she was staying in Vincennes in Indiana Territory along the Wabash River: "This place was first settled by the French, one hundred years ago, but from the appearance of it, & its *original* inhabitants, they never had much inter-prise or industry, they are Roman Catholic in their religion, but in their habits & appearance not much superior to the Indians" (381). Her under-handed compliment indicates that she could have tolerated their religion if only their manners and appearance had been improved. On January 29, 1812, still in Vincennes, she complained about the general lack of at-tention to regular spiritual duty: "I long to be in a place where some re-spect is paid to the Sabbath. There is an excellent Preacher here, of the Presbyterian Order, we attend his preaching, & are much pleased with him[.] he is an excellent Man & has an interesting family, but few keep holy time here, the generality are intirely engrossed with the world" (384). Even regarding her own religion, she criticizes the community for its disrespect and nonattendance. For Bacon and others, religion provided stability and comfort, so that its absence, or in some cases new denomi-nations, threatened social norms, and they generally feared what they perceived as a growing secularity.

For Susan Edwards Johnson, religion also served as an important so-cial and moral indicator. In Wilmington, on January 27, 1802, she attended a Methodist meeting and heard "a ranting sermon." She notes that "this congregation is principally of negroes; the Methodist have done much good, to the miserable people have made them more faithful to their Masters, & more moral, & decent, in every respect—the Society is mostly supported by the Black" (60). Johnson thus appreciates religion for how it imposed authority over the slaves, and equates religious author-ity and church stewardship with civic health. When services were poorly attended or churches were in disrepair, Johnson and others criticized

a town's failure as a whole. On November 22 from Edenton, for example, Johnson described the dilapidated condition of the town church,
which was

> large, & handsom, but the premature decay into which it
> has fallen cannot but make a melancholy impression on
> every reflecting beholder; there is scarcely a whole pain of
> glass remaining in large arched windows, the doors swingin
> on the hinges, & from the coupela which has never been
> finished were growing various wild shrubs which seem'd to
> wave their heads in (silent reproach) to every beholder, & as
> a token how little the sacred duties of public worship, are
> attended & that the Owl & the bat there chaunt their orisons
> to the supreme giver of all things & unmolested usurp the
> hallowed desk, which ought weekly to be occupied by some
> good man, whose precepts, & example, wou'd reform a cor-
> rupt age. (21)

The church as social bulwark had returned to nature, with plants substi-
tuting for parishioners and the owl and the bat serving as prelates. This
primitivism disturbed Johnson, and the unfinished, damaged building
reflected a deeper problem of spiritual neglect. As if this decay were not
cause enough for alarm, there were other ramifications: "The day we
were there was Sunday, so that I had an opportunity of observing the
pernicious effects which follow, from the want of public divine service;
the streets were fill'd with idle people of all descriptions, who for want
of employment at home, had flock'd there to gaize upon their fellows &
naturally amused themselves with such observations upon the passengers as were not calculated [to] improve head or heart" (22). Curiously,
she criticizes the locals for the very same people watching in which she
engaged. The overt neglect of the town church did not bode well for
Edenton's moral stature and further inclined Johnson to take a superior
view toward her southern neighbors. With the congregational church at
the center of social life for many in the New Republic, Dwight, Bacon,
and Johnson were particularly sensitive to lapses in practice and thus responded to a perceived failing of the outlying, frontier towns. Not only

was religion of key importance to these women, but its variety elicited great comment.

Though travelers commented with passion and detail on their accommodations, road conditions, and other travelers, religion was an even more personal subject, and from such observations a heightened sense of the traveler's exclusion is communicated. Without the church as social center, the traveler so accustomed felt uneasy, which only contributed to the sense of being an outsider. In their uncensored honesty, these women present an alternative to the idealized view presented in J. Hector St. John de Crèvecoeur's *Letters from an American Farmer* (1782). The fictitious narrator of *Letters*, James the Farmer, proudly explains that a Presbyterian and a Catholic could live side by side in America, tolerant of their differences because they were united by commercial enterprise. Though religious diversity was a notable characteristic of this new republic, it was variously tolerated and critiqued. These women may not have appreciated this diversity, but they did document what historians would later recognize as a proliferation of religious sects that would prevent any one religion from dominating American culture. Travel narratives thus cited religion as a key indicator of regional differences, marking character, social rank, and ideological perspective.

Genteel Expectations and Slavery

In addition to religion marking social and moral differences, slavery was alternately accepted or condemned. For some women, slavery was a morally corrupt institution, while for others slavery affirmed the social order. In Madame de La Tour du Pin's account of her 1794 travels through Albany, New York, for example, she includes a report of a "Negro plot" two years earlier wherein "the town of Albany had been almost entirely burned down." She then explains that in the state of New York "slavery had been abolished for children born in the year 1794 and later. They were to be given their freedom when they reached their twentieth year, a very wise measure both for the negroes and the owners of slaves. It obliged the latter to support their slaves during childhood and it compelled the slaves, in their turn, to work sufficiently long for the masters to repay the cost of their upbringing" (236). La Tour du Pin seems to approve of these "wise" measurers and implies that the slaves somehow owed something to their owners. As an exiled French loyalist, she does not extend much sympathy toward the workers, so it is no surprise that she frames the "Negro plot" as a matter of ingratitude: "One negro, a very bad lot, who had hoped that the Government's measure would give him unconditional liberty, resolved to avenge his disappointment. He collected a few other malcontents and they arranged to set fire to the city on a certain day, where most of the buildings were still of wood. This horrible plot succeeded beyond their wildest imaginings. The fire caught hold in twenty places at once." La Tour du Pin describes the devastation and subsequent inquiry, the result of which was that the town "condemned the negro leader and six of his accomplices to be hanged. The sentence was carried out there and then" (237). She does not question these acts, but instead praises the swift and effective clean-up efforts, adding this reassurance: "By the time we arrived in Albany, no trace of the fire remained" (237). La Tour du Pin concludes by reasserting order, as the rebellion was repressed, or, as it were, snuffed out.

The disregard for slavery's oppressiveness was notable in many of these narratives, despite concerns the women may have expressed for other disadvantaged groups. This attitude is particularly apparent in Caroline Olivia Laurens's entry for July 1, 1825, as she traveled through Pickensville, South Carolina: "Early this morning we were awoke by the bustling noises of the neighbouring people who were getting ready to go to Greenville where a Negro was to be burned alive for stabbing a white man. This fellow had made an attempt to kill his master, but not succeeded, he ran away and lodged in the barn of an old farmer, who having occasion for some grain, went thither at night; not knowing anyone was there, upon his entrance (the Negro who had just awoke out of a sound sleep and thinking he was pursued by his master) instantly jumped up killed the old man and made his escape, but after a few weeks was caught and sentenced to be burned" (172). With no pause between the punishment and the justification, Laurens does not register any horror, and the story is related without any concern for justice for the slave, but merely followed with "This morning Mrs. Robinson hearing me say how fond I was of green-cheese immediately set about making one" (172). Laurens thus includes this event as a notable, dramatic moment, but without condemnation for such behaviors or concern for the slave's rights. Though charged as guardians of gentility, women also engaged in the perpetuation of hierarchy rather than the promotion of democratic, egalitarian practices. In so doing, it would seem that they compromised the woman's role as moral center.

For other travelers, slavery was far less acceptable. When Lydia B. Bacon arrived in Louisville, Kentucky, on May 27, 1811, for example, she called it a "very handsome flourishing Town situated on the Ohio. . . . The State of Kentucky is like a perfect garden, but slavery is tolerated here, which is a great evil" (62). Cataloging her surroundings, Bacon finds the physical landscape appealing but the social foundation weakened by slavery; she does not, however, elaborate on slavery's ramifications. In her southern travels, Susan Johnson wrote favorably on the well-designed gardens and elaborately built houses, but could not ignore the striking differences between visiting a large farm in Connecticut and an extensive plantation, as here in Suffolk, on November 20, 1801: "The first time, my feelings have been shock't with respect to the treatment of Negroes, is since I came into Virginia this morning, which was very cold. I saw many with scarce rags to cover their nakedness, without shoes, or stockings, shivering with the cold—it is common to hear their owners, tell, how much, they earn, every year; & they can Literally be said to muzzle the mouth of the ox—their countenances are in general less impress't with their abject situation than I expected" (16–17). The impoverished conditions moved and surprised her, for she could not read suffering from the slaves' expressions, as they were "less impress't with their abject situation" than she had imagined they would be. As Johnson suggests, the discourse of slavery, particularly antislavery literature, evokes the sentimental and the sympathetic as a means of instruction. Philip Gould notes: "The emphasis on virtue and feeling that developed in antislavery literature marks the convergence of didactic projects of the magazine genre and antislavery politics. Each was premised largely on the virtues of sympathy and benevolence" ("African Slave Trade," 204). While Johnson may not accurately assess the slaves' feelings, she criticizes the slave owners for their objectification of the slave as property, whose value was accounted for publicly in everyday conversation. In registering her shock, she also distinguishes between poverty and slavery. Whereas the Suffolk

women in the carriage—who "appeared as if . . . made in Queen Elizabeth's day"—elicits a snobbish pity, the ill treatment of slaves is a morally
offensive scene. Johnson, however, fails to go beyond her moral objec-
tions to advocate an abolitionist position. Instead, she contains her criticism
within the larger acceptance of class and regional differences. Curiously,
Bacon and Johnson record their observations of slavery in a journalistic
rather than reflective mode and more as a condemnation of southern life
than as a criticism of slavery itself. Joyce E. Chaplin sheds light on such
comments as particularly stereotypical responses to the South: "Travelers
singled out black slavery, in addition to the heat and disease, as an important influence on whites' character" (79). Still, a modern audience might
expect more moral outrage.[6]

At one point, the Johnsons sought a black servant, as on December 7,
1801, Susan Johnson explains, they "wised to get one bound," but the
black family "had no boys of the age [they] wanted" (30). Although they
were seeking a servant rather than a slave, the implication of human as
commodity remains troublesome. Johnson may be sympathetic, but she
does not advocate radical social change. Writing to her husband from
New Haven on January 1, 1804, Susan Johnson expressed concern about
his labor shortage and was alarmed, though sympathetic, when he decided to purchase slave labor: "I have always feared you wou'd be reduced
to the unpleasant necessity of purchasing negroes for your business, but
am sorry to find it so soon happen but I am of your opinion that it is
now unavoidable, & I hope the success attending it will compensate for
the sacrifice of your feelings." Johnson's concerns for the family's income
prevailed over any indignation that she may have felt during her first visit
through Virginia two years earlier. The capitulation, though reluctant, is
unfortunate.

Although Johnson refrains from condemning slavery as an abhorrent
institution altogether, she praises religion for its redemptive capacity to
counter the evils of slavery. For example, when she attended the Methodist meeting in Wilmington in late January 1802 she noted, as previously
mentioned, that "the Methodist have done much good, to the miserable
people have made them more faithful to their Masters, & more moral, &
decent, in every respect" (60). Johnson seems reassured that Methodists
were promoting social good and appreciates the solidarity of the black

congregation. Johnson again assumes a decidedly moral and instructive tone, which concurs with Philip Gould's observation that "antislavery writings presumably helped to teach readers how to feel—how to feel in the right way" ("African Slave Trade," 208). While Johnson's remarks support the status quo, she also identifies key economic and moral issues that would challenge slavery. On March 22, 1802, for example, she and Mrs. Frances Pollock Devereux[7] visited a plantation on the Trent owned by Mr. George Pollock, who had 180 slaves, and Johnson gave this report: "[The negroes] have every comfort to render life <u>comfortable</u> that is consistant with their abject situation—their labour is easy, & they have rewards, for their industry, paid by their master they have as much cotton as they will raise & all their cloth wove, & for every yard of cloth they make for themselves, they are paid three pence—none of the children are required to work before they are twelve years old; nor after they are fifty" (87–88). The plantation appears as a thriving country village with reasonably applied age limits on labor and appealing profit incentives. Johnson's willingness to approve these circumstances suggests a pervasive acceptance of slavery itself. Moreover, Johnson reports that when Mrs. Devereux asked the slaves "'if they had any wants? if the overseer was too severe?'" they "happily had no complaints to make & the poor creatures were very grateful for the interest, she took in their welfare" (88–89). The slave's silence was easily taken as affirmation and acceptance, a naive misapprehension. Indeed, forty years later, Frederick Douglass would explain a slave's constant guard against the overseer's inquiries to detect potentially rebellious slaves. After one slave answered such questions, Douglass explains, he was "immediately chained and handcuffed; and thus without a moment's warning, he was snatched away, and forever sundered, from his family and friends, by a hand more unrelenting than death" (21). To secure their safety, therefore, slaves were careful to answer in the affirmative. In passages such as the one cited above, Johnson steps outside of the travel narrative's typical descriptive mode to comment on slavery as an aberration in a democratic system.

Johnson's remarks thus offer an eyewitness report of plantation life and slavery conditions in the beginnings of a century that would move from the optimism of a New Republic to the catastrophic turmoil of the Civil War. The travel diary concludes rather conventionally, as the Johnsons retrace their outward journey to return home on May 3, 1802, weary but comforted by familiar sights: "[T]ook the Stage in the afternoon which brot us home between five & six & found my dear children & other friends all in good health after an absence of six months" (109). Her northern home appeared safely distanced from the slave-run plantations and the ill-fashioned women of the South, and her narrative stands as a record of the curious and the interesting. Johnson may not have been transformed by her southern travels, but her journal does document cultural differences that find slavery at the center, thus foreshadowing a conflict that would require others to take action and end the "abject situation" altogether.

—☙

The narrative that tracks a journey is fundamentally invested in observation. It seeks different sights to report and often embellishes to make the trip seem grander. For its tendency to exaggerate, the travel narrative is enlivening, and when the traveler suffers from inconvenience or displacement, the narrative can be sharply critical and attentive. Women's travel narratives express a range of these reactions. Not wedded to a particular agenda and largely unconcerned with publication or public consumption of their writing, these women wrote eyewitness accounts of American history that describe arduous travel to uncertain territories. For though women may have viewed their surroundings with an eye for gentility, the demanding acts of traveling required hard physical work and assertive action. These narratives are not twice told through the lens of a novelist with a larger, grander story to tell. They do not look backward nostalgically to a lost innocence, nor fully assume the writers' frontier citizenship. Nor do these women promote their journeys as heralding a new world, secular or spiritual. They are both too late and too early for these expansionist themes. That is, they wrote before ideas about the frontier were romanticized and after the zealous utopian communities of colonial America had subsided. Instead, these women were preoccupied with finding decent accommodations, dodging the wayward wagoner, and cataloging plants and wildlife. In this regard, their observations contributed to a clearer image and understanding of the western lands. In their underwritten, nonedited state, these narratives are most appealing, for they are honest and unpretentious as they document westward migration and, by turns, a developing class and social structure in early America.

These narratives may never take the place of the more romantic narratives of later pioneers braving the Oregon Trail, yet they are notable for their straightforward accounting. They tell us about privileged women and women of lesser means who headed west for the chance of a better life. Most did not pick up and leave for the sheer adventure of it, for migration and its subsequent separation weighed heavily. The women's diaries reflect a mixture of mourning and anticipation. These are obvious points to make in retrospect, for these narratives could simply not express anything less. It is only in our rereading of the pioneers' journeys that we may find their hesitation and criticism disappointing. To read these narratives forward from the seventeenth century is to see that they are remarkable in the very singularity of women traveling into new territory at a time when most women were homebound. For these women, travel was not taken lightly, nor did it carry any guarantee of success. Still, they set off. These women read the landscape before other narratives imposed a legend. This eyewitness quality is to be valued, respected, and preserved.

In the next chapter, I change course a bit to examine women's travel narratives from a more literary perspective, further acknowledging their rich archival value as a record of women's cultural and intellectual interests. In these narratives of travel, women enter the literary realm on their own terms, addressing topics both local and national. Their sophisticated style regarding audience and narrative and their extensive use of allusion evidence their cultural engagement. Women were not only resourceful enough to navigate rough terrain but intelligent enough to frame their narratives as compelling tales, and they did so with great enthusiasm, heart, and wit.

4

Literary Crossroads

TRAVEL NARRATIVE, POETRY, AND NOVEL

In addition to being a chronicle of social interactions and a critique of gentility, the woman's travel narrative is an important record of intellectual life in early America and the New Republic. Complementing the descriptive aspects of these journals, the many literary references signal women's tastes and convey their sense of decorum. As the woman's role was closely aligned with modeling virtue, her literary discussions and educational concerns are especially valuable. Notwithstanding prevailing attitudes that reading works of fiction may be harmful for women, their travel accounts clearly document their knowledge of literature, both classical and popular, and their keen interest in matters intellectual and literary.

In referencing literary works, women reinforce a closely knit relationship between travel and literature. For travel narratives share a creative, long-standing link to storytelling in both oral and written literary traditions. The traveler on a quest always has a colorful tale to tell of overcoming obstacles and a triumphant return. Virgil's Aeneas and Homer's Odysseus prove themselves heroic after long, arduous journeys. Chaucer's *Canterbury Tales* and Bunyan's *Pilgrim's Progress* mark victories for the pious pilgrim. Be it for earthly or spiritual reward, the journey has an organic frame with starting and stopping points. What transpires in between makes for the seemingly inexhaustible variety of the traveler's tale. The narratives in this study follow this journey motif, as women cast themselves as curious, adventurous, compliant, complaining, or romantic travelers. Whereas the novel uses elements of travel to tell adventurous tales of character development, as in Henry Fielding's *Tom Jones* (1749), Laurence Sterne's *A Sentimental Journey* (1766), and Tobias Smollett's *Humphry Clinker* (1771), the travel narrative incorporates literary elements such as allusion, verse, and characterization, as in Sarah Kemble Knight's *Journal* (1704), Dr. Alexander Hamilton's *Itinerarium* (1744), and Margaret Van Horn Dwight's *Journey to Ohio* (1810). Sir Walter Scott significantly influenced travel narratives as well with his novels of high adventure and characters who find romance and glory on their highland journeys, such as *Rob Roy* (1715) and *Waverley* (1815). In keeping with this spirited tone, travel narratives also incorporate characteristics of the picaresque, in which the central figure, the picaro, embarks on episodic adventures and is often humorous and amoral and somewhat roguish in his or her actions. The following discussion shows how women integrate literature and literary elements into their travel accounts and explores how these sources serve as potential models for framing these accounts. The woman's travel narrative is thus distinguished from texts that represent experience solely within a data driven, empirical framework. For the integration of literary allusions into a travel account suggests that the traveler sought context not readily apparent and therefore attempted to contextualize self and travel in a more imaginative manner. As women cite novels, poetry, scientific accounts, and philosophical treatises, therefore, they demonstrate a cultural fluency that reinforces class status and illustrates the female traveler's perceived role in disseminating culture.

Although the travel narrative does not emphasize personal transformation, and the novel is not intended as a Michelin guide, each genre uses travel as a plot device with central narrators who comment on their surroundings. Joyce E. Chaplin elaborates on these parallels: "Travel accounts multiplied just when the novel was increasing in popularity; and, as the two genres grew up together, authors had a cheerful disregard of the distinction between fiction and nonfiction that emerged later" (74). Kevin J. Hayes draws similar connections: "Novels and travel books could be grouped together because, quite simply, they tell stories, or, if you will, both were forms of narrative discourse. . . . Most of the period's novels remained heavily didactic and travel books were full of information about diverse peoples and cultures throughout the world" (101–2). Cathy N. Davidson also finds a relationship between the novel and travel: "The novel as tract necessarily verges into the novel as travelogue and vice versa" (Revolution, 164). The picaresque tale in particular provided travelers an adventurous, somewhat mischievous model, for as Davidson explains, "the picaresque form in America borrowed from its Spanish antecedents a preoccupation with marginality, with extremes, with the most contradictory aspects of the society. . . . The picaresque novel is engaged in exploring the margins of society and not in trodding some middle way" (Revolution, 164–65). This outsider's perspective corresponds well with the genteel woman who, upon patronizing the rustic inn and the frontier tavern, espouses her social views and condemns the locals. The woman's travel narrative follows suit by offering advice from differing points of view: social critic, frontier adventurer, leisured traveler, or adventurous heroine. Davidson elaborates on such observations: "The traveler/hero must be both part of and apart from what he surveys. He is both witness and judge, and each role compromises the other" (Revolution, 171). This apt parallel characterizes the genteel traveler as the socially superior outsider who bestows criticism and offers suggestions for improvement. Citing texts and including literary allusions also signals the traveler's own sense of participating in a larger history of travel and explorations. Regarding nineteenth-century travelers, Mary Suzanne Schriber finds that "travel accounts are full of historical and cultural information taken in part from observation and in part from historians, novelists, poets, and other travelers" (61). Early American women travelers display a similar integration, or what Schriber calls an "invocation of intertexts," as they draw on outside sources and make comparisons to works of literature and art.

The travel narrative, in turn, serves as a rich source for discovering what women were reading and how they interacted with these readings. References to literature were especially significant considering that most reading materials for the general colonial population were devotional and concerned with edification. David D. Hall describes the library of "the common reader," who owned "at best but a handful of titles—perhaps a Bible, a steady seller, a psalm book—and with the probable exception of the yearly almanac, rarely added new books to this stock" (164). Hayes identifies devotional, conduct, and domestic manuals as the main "types of literature read by early American women" (102). This curriculum contributed to a shared assumption that, as Richard Beale Davis explains, books were "assigned a value in terms of usefulness" (*Colonial Southern*, 18). Reading materials were thus fundamentally instructive, if not highly contested, for as Carla Mulford confirms, the "era's cultural preoccupation with women's education and their social behavior and morality was evident . . . not just in the novels of the day but in the masses of books designed for their instruction in conduct" (Introduction, xxix). For those who had access to books and newspapers in early America, therefore, reading materials were primarily didactic and secondarily entertaining. In this light, Lydia B. Bacon noted an interesting selection of books along with other standard items on May 17, 1811: "My saddle containing some necessary articles, a Bible, Homers Illiad, & A Huge Spunge cake presented by one of our kind Friends the morning of our departure" (61). Appropriately, she selected titles relevant to journeying in all its symbolic and profound meanings.

Bacon included these texts along with her "necessary articles," which is significant when one considers that books were costly. Edwin Wolf explains, regarding colonial America: "A book was approximately the monetary equal of half an acre of land—(£150 for 873 acres)" (8). Davidson estimates that "a typical late eighteenth-century novel would have cost approximately three to four times more than an equivalent hardcover volume today (when measured against current wages and consumer indices)" (*Revolution*, 25). Given that a novel "cost between $.75 and $1.50," its purchase would require two days' work, as Davidson notes, for "a common day laborer in Massachusetts" (25). Only the privileged, then, could add the classics, Milton, Shakespeare, poetry, and the novel to the standard colonial library, let alone to their saddlebags. For women heading west, books would prove especially vital. Even though the Northwest Ordinance of 1787 had given the charge to encourage schools and education, it did not initially allow young women the type of education in the belles lettres found in the eastern academy. For the women who packed novels and other reading materials, therefore, travel would afford an opportunity for intellectual and cultural inquiry.

Women were not only carrying classical texts on their journeys, but were making a point to visit libraries as well, which further indicates their literary interests. On July 17, 1818, in Worcester, Massachusetts, Eliza Williams Bridgham and her father, Samuel Willard Bridgham, toured the American Antiquarian Society's "collection of Antiquities." Her father had been elected to the society in October 1813, and thus they were escorted by Mr. Isaiah Thomas, the "President of the Society and father's particular friend." Bridgham was "delighted" and found the "greatest curiosities in the Literary department," which included "a Bible printed 14 years after the art of printing was invented, at Venice; the Bible Archbishop Cranmer formerly owned, and the first newspaper and first book ever printed in America. The newspaper was done at Cambridge in 1704, and the book in 1740 [sic]. It was a book of psalms and was really diverting to see how curiously it was spelt and punctuated" (7). The remaining collection included "some ruins of the ancient Herculaneum and Pompeia, and a piece of a Wine Jug formerly belonging to Cicero," and Indian artifacts. Bridgham's familiarity with history and literary texts, not to mention her attention to spelling, reveals a curious mind and a privileged reader. Susan Johnson also found time to visit a library while in Baltimore on November 17, 1801: "I went into the library, which I suppose contains about eight or ten thousand vollumes—but I had not time [to] form any opinion of the collection of books, as I only staied long enough, to see they were well arranged, handsomly bound, & kept with great regularity" (10). Johnson's matter-of-fact report suggests that she had some basis for comparison, and that the size of the library's holdings merited no particular comment. Even the handsome bindings and neat appearance of the books do not move Johnson toward judgment; instead, she withholds approval until the contents be known. As travelers today gravitate toward sites of personal interest, Bridgham and Johnson found libraries and collections a worthy addition to their itineraries.

Women's references to literature, in turn, track popular, contemporary tastes in ways that may not be apparent by examining library subscription lists. Although women were generally discouraged from reading works of fiction, their travel accounts document a uniform rejection of such dictates. As such, they indicate a woman's intellectual curiosity. For example, on July 18, 1825, Olivia Caroline Laurens, who was in Pendleton, South Carolina, noted: "Miss Hugers called to see us in the morning and promised to lend me 'Patronage,' a tale by Maria Edgeworth"

(222).[1] On July 29, she noted, "This evening commenced reading astronomy" (224). On July 30, Laurens enjoyed a visit with the Whitner
sisters, who "displayed their musical talents, they sang some of Moore's
sonnets" (224).[2] On August 25, she recorded: "This morning I commenced reading Griscom's 'Year in Europe' find it extremely entertaining, it is in two thick octavo volumes 500 pages each" (226).[3] Laurens
thus enjoyed literary, scientific, and popular texts recommended by her
social world for education, conversation, and entertainment. As Laurens
suggests, books expanded women's interests beyond the domestic and
provided key points of reference for their journeys. As part of Elizabeth
Maddock Dillon's larger argument about gender and liberal theory, she
asserts that "understanding the presence of women as writers and readers in the literary public sphere dramatically changes our understanding
of the shape of literary culture in the United States, and of the relations
between gender and liberalism" (37). In Cathy N. Davidson's introduction to The Revolution and the Word, she finds the "novel's popularity lay in its
ability to address the widest possible demographic of readers—Federalists and anti-Federalists, liberals and republicans" (7). Building on these
points, understanding women as active participants in culture making and
as engaged readers expands our understanding of their dynamic lives.

The commonplace book provided another model for travel literature.
In this text, one collects notable works of prose or verse for memoriza-
tion, inspiration, or education. The travel narrative that includes literary
references serves a similar purpose. Adapted from classical models, commonplace books were grouped by common topics for easy reference.
Catherine La Courreye Blecki elaborates, "Whether a person followed the
methodology of Erasmus, Locke, or modified them, organizing transcriptions in a commonplace book reveals a transcriber's habits of mind and
emotion" (62). In Susan M. Stabile's excellent study of women's writing
and memory, she notes: "Contrary to the exclusionary gender codes in
colleges, commonplace books initiated a feminine genealogy of learning
in which mothers and daughters taught successive generations of women
by bequeathing their manuscripts" (12). Travel narratives, in turn, incorporate current events, such as election results, building projects, and trade
transactions. Amanda Gilroy makes similar observations about travel
writing from the Romantic period, which she describes as "a hybrid

discourse that traversed the disciplinary boundaries of politics, letter-writing, education, medicine, aesthetics, and economics" (*Romantic*, 1). When serving such wide-ranging interests, the travel narrative does more than just retell a journey; it becomes a compendium of reflective observation.

In these broad connections between women's literary tastes and their use of literature in their travel narratives, class issues parallel education. For as Cathy N. Davidson reminds us: "Anyone interested in the ways in which the printed word may have influenced thought and behavior in any particular place and time must address basic questions of literacy. Who could read? Who could write?" ("Introduction: Toward," 9). From most accounts, literacy rates were impressive. By 1750 in New England, literacy "approached 70 percent among men and 45 percent among women," and in the southern colonies, "50 to 60 percent among European men and 40 percent among European women" (Butler, 111). David D. Hall places female literacy in New England at "80 percent or higher by 1790" (172). Rosemarie Zagarri finds that literacy "transformed women's relationship to print culture. More widespread literacy meant that more women had access to a vast world of ideas. In addition to the Bible and other religious spiritual readings, women began to devour histories, biographies, travel literature, conduct books, periodicals, newspapers, and novels" ("Postcolonial Culture," 23). Although Hall cautions against making assumptions about the connections among book availability, literacy rates, book production, and cultural impact, books were, to various degrees, a modeling influence. As Richard Bushman notes, "novels had joined forces with courtesy books to spread information about genteel behavior" (*Refinement*, 281). Travel narratives thus offered their own "codes of behavior," punctuated by their disdain for crude, rustic manners. To embellish a travel narrative reflected genteel tastes, and in this context, for a woman to have knowledge of novels was far more acceptable than for her to enter the fictional arena as reader or even author. In this sense, a well-sketched description, carefully placed allusion, insightful cultural reference, and occasional citation of poetry signaled taste and reflected a woman's character. The connections between literature and travel narrative not only evidence women's access to novels, poetry, drama, and scientific literature but suggest that such texts provided important reference points for the journey at hand, however humble or grand.

Drawing on literary sources also allowed women to experiment with content and style and develop their own authorial voices in an otherwise male-identified genre. More often than not, they let fall any mask of timidity to record a true account of their journey. Although women suffered no pressure to please a wide, commercial audience, they were writing within a social context characterized by distinct ideas about female authorship and thus faced a complicated situation: they were responsible for promoting "morally sound" values while encountering frontier spaces and outlying areas, each with its own, very different social composition. Given these expectations, how does a genteel woman interpret a beautiful view or a disturbing scene? Does citing poetry or quoting from a novel enhance and empower her observations? Or, do such allusions distance a woman from the reality of travel by gentrifying the experience? As the following discussion shows, women's literary references are more than flourishes and afterthoughts. Women's remarks are important indicators of intellectual engagement with their culture and their surroundings.

Contrary to the prevailing recommendation that reading materials were to be solely instructive and edifying, women's travel narratives clearly reveal that women also read and enjoyed popular literature. Even so, they were cautioned against it, as William B. Warner explains: "The power and danger of novels, especially to young women not exposed to classical education, arise from the pleasures novels induce" (5). Mary Kelley concurs that novels were considered problematic in that women would be exposed to the "darker sides" of human nature (116). Such concerns explain why many women begin their travel diaries and journals with an obligatory apology lest their work be deemed fictional and therefore unsuitable. In 1808, for example, Anne MacVicar Grant opened her *Memoirs of an American Lady: With Sketches of Manners and Scenes in America, as They Existed Previous to the Revolution* with this explanation: "[A] fictitious superstructure built on a foundation of reality, would be detestable on the score of bad taste, though no moral sense were concerned or consulted. 'Tis walking on a river half frozen, that betrays your footing every moment. . . . You do not know exactly which part of the narrative is false; but you are sure that it is not all true, and therefore distrust what is genuine where it occurs. For this reason a fiction happily told, takes a greater hold of the mind than a narrative of facts, evidently embellished and interwoven with inventions" (5). Grant's memoir spans forty years, and while her primary concern in this quote is discrepancies, she also identifies the rich complexity of a mixed-genre text. Hannah Adams's 1832 *Memoirs* also attests to the dangers of fiction: "I was passionately fond of novels, and, as I lived in a state of seclusion, I acquired false ideas of life. The ideal world which my imagination formed was very different from the real" (4). She then acknowledges more beneficial reading by naming poetry, history, and biography as sources of "an inexhaustible fund to feed [her] mind, and gratify [her] curiosity" (4). In this con-flicted state, Adams hesitates to assert her own story lest it be considered a fabrication. When Theodore Dwight introduced Sarah Kemble Knight's 1704 *Journal* to the American public in 1825, he too was quick to distance it from flights of fancy: "This is not a work of fiction," the introduction begins, "as the scarcity of old American manuscripts may induce some to imagine; but it is a faithful copy from a diary in the author's own hand-writing, compiled soon after her return home, as it appears, from notes recorded daily, while on the road" (85). These concerns figure prominently in debates over female education, and it is no wonder that women's literary works and reading materials were carefully scrutinized. Notwithstanding this caution, women's interest in the novel was certain, and they vigorously engaged in critical debate and assessment.

Critical Discourse and the Novel

The insistence that reading materials be instructive encouraged women to seek moral lessons from literature, while critically discussing literature allowed them to enter public discourse with confidence. Understandably, then, women reference popular novels in their narratives and discuss novels in their letters, for the sentimental novel and the travel narrative share a mutual intention to be instructive, if not cautionary. The traveler, like the sentimental heroine, often faced crises that forced her to adapt. Whereas the travel narrative tracks a woman's changing perceptions and experiences on the road, the novel marks a female character's moral and social development. In Samuel Richardson's *Pamela* (1740–41) and *Clarissa*

(1747–48), for example, young heroines confront duplicitous male authority. Similarly, William Hill Brown's *The Power of Sympathy* (1789), Susanna Rowson's *Charlotte Temple* (1791), and Hannah Webster Foster's *The Coquette* (1797) ask their audiences to ponder the alternatives to seduction and abandonment for young women who transgress the prescribed social roles of female sexuality. Dramatic scenarios often involve choices between virtue and dissipation, with the fallen woman and profligate man featured in cautionary tales for contemporary readers. Characters who uphold republican values, such as Mrs. Holmes in *The Power of Sympathy* and Lucy Freeman in *The Coquette*, provide dignified alternatives. Appropriately, Nancy Armstrong links domestic fiction with politics, as "these stories of courtship and marriage offered their readers a way of indulging, with a kind of impunity, in fantasies of political power that were the more acceptable because they were played out within a domestic framework where legitimate monogamy—and thus the subordination of female to male—would ultimately be affirmed. In this way, domestic fiction could represent an alternative form of political power without appearing to contest the distribution of power that it represented as historically given" (29). In Lisa M. Logan's discussion of the "Original Letters" between Frederick and Felicia, she offers these insights: "If the project of early national periodicals is to instruct women in reading, writing, behavior, and taste—that is, to standardize and regulate ideas about femininity, the elegant, accomplished, and virtuous Felicia is a perfect model" (287). Accordingly, the novel provided context for female experience, with characters whose choices sparked passionate debate. Elizabeth Maddock Dillon rightly observes that "the literary genre of the novel, which gained ground in the eighteenth century, is heavily identified with women (as both readers and writers) and with an intimate sphere in which women are principal figures" (36). Women were drawn into this literary world with its controversial characters and provocative plots.

Whereas novels model behaviors, women's letters and travel narratives demonstrate how these behaviors were applied and reinforced. Richard Bushman finds that "sentimental fiction played the most critical part in the extension of refinement to the middle class," while the stories themselves "engaged the central problem of the period: how to adapt genteel values to middle-class life." In short, Bushman finds, "authors of sentimental fiction made aristocratic gentility accessible by domesticating it" (*Refinement*, 281). Richard Godbeer offers a key explanation for the keen interest in these novels: "Their championing of virtuous young women who resisted sexual temptation even under extreme pressure was hugely popular with early American readers" (289). Godbeer notes Brown's *The Power of Sympathy* and Foster's *The Coquette* as sentimental novels that condemn "predatory men who seduced and ruined young women" but also insist didactically "that women be held accountable as accomplices in their own downfall" (291). Virtuous behavior was therefore a key concern, and through their critical responses, women considered various scenarios and consequences.

In this regard, women's interaction with novels in their letters and journals indicates the significant influence of popular literature on their perceptions and on their style of writing. Cathy N. Davidson, in fact, credits fiction and novels with providing women a valuable mirror: "Only in fiction would the average early woman reader encounter a version of her world existing for her sake, and, more important, only in the sentimental novel would her reading about this world be itself validated. As an added bonus, in not a few of these novels, women readers encountered women characters whose opinions mattered" (*Revolution*, 123). William B. Warner finds reading itself central to the novel: "In order to prevent the insidious circulation of novels, Richardson must teach readers how to read. It is therefore appropriate that *Pamela* begins with parental alarm and an injunction to read vigilantly" (187). In Barbara Sicherman's case study of women's reading habits in the late nineteenth century, she cites the Hamilton family of Fort Wayne, Indiana, and notes: "Books gave the Hamiltons a way of ordering, and understanding, their lives. They provided a common language and a medium of intellectual and social exchange that helped the women define themselves and formulate responses to the larger world. [Books gave them] a symbolic code and shorthand for experience that continued throughout their lives" (209).[4] By extension, when women cited such texts in letters and travel journals, it bolstered their authority as writers. Reading as a shared activity, in turn, reinforced the novel's socializing influence. Marjorie McNinch describes a "literary" as an "activity where one person read a selection to the group of people in the room, who would continue to sew or write during the reading" (231). Elizabeth Gilpin, for example, recorded this description of a literary while visiting the Rural Resort in Trenton Falls, New York, on October 13, 1830: "We had tea, found an old backgammon board, at which Harriet and I played, whilst Henry read aloud to us a novel lent to us by the Miss Shermans" (19). Reading was indeed a leisured, fashionable activity, as indicated in the "Saratoga" section of *The Northern Traveller*: "Here, as well as at Ballston, a Reading Room is kept, where strangers will find newspapers from different parts of the country, and where they will be able to supply themselves with books of different descriptions, to beguile their leisure hours. The Reading Room is at the Book Store, a little beyond the United States Hotel" (147). Literature, even as background to other activities, connected women to their cultural world, and literary discussions afforded important opportunities for sharing ideas and reinforcing values.

Susan Johnson found books entertaining as she traveled from New Haven to North Carolina. In New Bern on November 27, 1801, for example, she "began to read the maid of the Hamlet an indifferent novel, by the author of the Children of the Abbey" (27). Johnson refers to works by Regina Maria Dalton, *The Maid of the Hamlet* (1793?) and *Children of the Abbey* (1796), the latter a four-volume gothic romance centering on two young lovers deprived of their inheritance. On December 2, 1801, Susan Johnson and her female companions read *The Beggar Girl* until 1:00 a.m. (29). Written by Mrs. Bennett in 1797, this seven-volume, seventy-two-chapter, 1,967-page sentimental novel is set in a small village in Surrey in "one thousand seven hundred and whatever the reader pleases" (1). The switched-at-birth plot traces the trials of Rosa Wilkins, whose alleged mother abandoned her for America. Rosa wanders the streets begging for food until the compassionate Colonel takes her in. Once Rosa is washed, fed, and clothed, the transformation prompts the Colonel to adopt her. Volume 1 ends with the Colonel's death and Rosa's inheritance of his estate. The subsequent volumes trace the Pygmalion-like transformation of a "beggar girl" into a genteel lady. At the end of volume 7, we discover that Rosa is the daughter of Lady Denningcourt and thus a bona fide woman of privilege. Curiously, the novel's class issues seem to undercut Johnson's own insistence on reinforcing social distinctions. What if, as in the case of the beggar girl, social position could somehow be a "mistake"? On the other hand, the novel may have held Johnson's interest because it asserts that class cannot be hidden. Johnson's choice of novels might also suggest that travel was not all that extraordinary for her, and that she read novels to supplement her travel experience and pass the time more enjoyably. Travel may have allowed her to "catch up," as one does on a trip today. In any event, literature was an integral part of Johnson's journey.

Reading materials thus provided a centerpiece for commentary, while correspondence served as an important outlet for female discourse. Whereas novels evoked responses, letters cultivated genteel discourse. Robert Adams Day marks similar connections and cites Samuel Richardson's *Familiar Letters* (or *Letters Written to and for Particular Friends on the Most Important Occasions*) (published anonymously in 1741) as particularly influential: "The stress on conduct, combined with the need of vivid examples for moral instruction and Richardson's own story-telling bent, led inevitably to fiction" (54). The correspondences of Esther Edwards Burr (to Sarah Prince in 1750s), Eliza Lucas Pinckney[5] (to Mary Bartlett in 1742), and Abigail Adams (to Lucy Cranch in 1780s), for example, all include lively, critical assessments of Samuel Richardson's *Pamela* (1740) and *Clarissa* (1747–48). Kevin J. Hayes prefaces his insightful discussion of these responses by noting their larger intellectual value: "Pamela Andrews's reading and, more importantly, her critical remarks about her reading set a standard of behavior which allowed eighteenth-century women to discuss their own reading more freely, without censure" (107). Richardson's heroines thus encouraged women to debate morals and virtues on a larger, semipublic stage. In Esther Edwards Burr's journal, with its daily entries addressed to Sarah Prince Gill and then sent in weekly letters, she records her various reactions to Richardson. For example, on March 10, 1755, Burr entered this note: "I have borrowed Pamelia and am reading it now. I fancy I sha'nt like it so well as I did Clarissa, but prejudice must have its weight. I remember you said that in your opinnion it did not equel her. Your judgment my dear has a very great influence on mine. Nay I would venture to report that such a Book surpast such an one, if you said so, if I had never laid my Eyes on 'em— but forall I intend not to be so complaisant but I will have a judgment of my own" (98). Burr reluctantly begins reading the novel, if only to participate in the critical exchange. A month later, on April 8, 1755, Burr had apparently lost all patience with the main male character, Mr. B, criticizing his profligate ways, and appealed to Prince for more insight:

> I have a poor judgme[n]t of my own. I wish you would be
> so good as to let me ha[ve] your thoughts on this affair, and
> I should be glad if it is not two much trouble on the whole
> History. I know you have made every usefull remark that
> could be made—there is sertainly many excellent observa-
> tions and rules laid down [so] that I shall never regret my
> pains. . . . In my humble opinion Riches, and honour, are set up
> two much—can Money reward virtue? And besides Mr Bs
> being a libertine he was a dreadfull highspirited Man, impatient of
> contradiction as he says of himself—Pamela had a task of it,
> with all Mr Bs good qual[i]ties. She was as much affraid of
> him as of a Lyon—If the author had [le]ft it to me to have
> intitled the Books, I think I should hav[e] chose Virtue tryed,
> instead of rewarded. (107)

Burr's spirited remarks endorse the novel's provocative themes and the valuing of female correspondence in matters of literary criticism. Eventually, Burr found merit in the novel, as she noted on April 12, 1755: "Well I have finnished Pamela. Tis realy a ve[ry] good thing for all my ill nature about it" (108). The dramatic scenarios in these novels inspired Burr and others to formulate stands on moral issues and to advocate female virtues. From these accounts, it is clear that Richardson's novels invited women to express their own values, whether in consort or in opposition.

Letters thus functioned as a type of literary salon for some women, as they discussed novels and exchanged critical views. Faith E. Beasley concurs: "The female-centered and female-dominated salons were a foyer for discussions of the standards and methods used to evaluate literary enterprises in general" (148). Eliza Lucas Pinckney's extensive correspondence, for example, shows just how women integrated literature into their discourse. Letters between Eliza Lucas and Mary Bartlett, the first Mrs. Pinckney's niece, who was visiting from London, also address

Richardson's novels.[6] In a 1742 letter to Bartlett, for example, Lucas finds Pamela to be "a good girl and as such I love her dearly," and yet goes on to criticize at length Pamela's seeming lack of modesty:

> but I must think her very defective and even blush for her while she allows her self that disgusting liberty of praising her self, or what is very like it, repeating all the fine speeches made to her by others when a person distinguished for modesty in every other respect should have chose rather to conceal them or at least to let them come from some other hand; especially as she might have considered those high compliments might have proceeded from the partiallity of her friends or with a view to encourage her and make her aspire after those qualifications which were ascribed to her, which I know experimently to be often the case. (47)[7]

Pamela's choices become symbolic for Lucas as she critiques the character's behavior and relates it to her own responses. Lucas then dismisses Bartlett's qualification that poor Pamela is but "a young Country Girl" and moves on to criticize Richardson himself: "Here you smile at my presumption for instructing one so farr above my own level as the Authour of Pamella (whom I esteem much for the regard he pays to virtue and religion throughout the whole piece) but, my Dear Miss Bartlett, contract your smile into a mortified look for I acquit the Authour. He designed to paint no more than a woman, and he certainly designed it as a reflection upon the vanity of our sex that a character so compleat in every other instance should be so greatly defective in this" (47–48). Lucas identifies the problem as one with generalization and characterization. The verisimilitude that endeared Pamela to her audience, moreover, offends Lucas, who views Pamela's character as drawn too simplistically by an author who plays on gender stereotypes. In the same letter, Lucas brings in two other authors to make her final point: "[I]t puts me in mind of the observation in Done Quixott How grateful is praise though it be from a madman. I have run thus farr before I was aware for I have nither capacity or inclination for Chritisism tho' Pamela sets me the example by criticizeing Mr. Lock and has taken the liberty to dissent from that admirable Author" (48). Ultimately, Lucas praises Richardson's realistic portrait, for "the Authour has kept up to nature (one of the greatest beauties in the whole piece) for had his Heroin no defect the character must be unnatural." Notably, Lucas identifies as much with Richardson as with Pamela, suggesting perhaps that she too considers herself an author.

As evidenced here, *Pamela* and Richardson's other novels elicited thoughtful, often impassioned reactions from women throughout the colonies and abroad. For example, Abigail Adams calls Richardson a "master of the human heart" and praises his studious portrayals of the "odiousness of vice, and the fatal consequences which result from the practice of it." Adams appreciates the characterizations in *Pamela* for their virtuous examples, and in this letter to her niece Lucy Cranch Greenleaf, dated August 27, 1785, Adams notes that Richardson "never loses sight of religion, but points his characters to a future state of restitution as the sure ground of safety to the virtuous, and excludes not hope from the wretched penitent." Adams also identifies the epistolary novel as a cultural, moral guide and thus an apt model for letter writing: "I believe Richardson has done more towards embellishing the present age, and teaching them the talent of letter-writing, than any other modern I can name. You know I am passionately fond of all his works, even to his 'Pamela.'" Whereas Lucas faults Richardson's Pamela for being "defective" in her vanity, Adams finds Richardson's characters valuable, even in their depravity: "The oftener I have read his books, and the more I reflect upon his great variety of characters, perfectly well supported, the more I am led to love and admire the author. He must have an abandoned, wicked, and depraved heart, who can be tempted to vice by the perusal of Richardson's works. Indeed, I know not how a person can read them without being made better by them, as they dispose the mind to receive and relish every good and benevolent principle. . . . He may have faults, but they are so few, that they ought not to be named in the brilliant clusters of beauties which ornament his works" (111–12). Adams is thus far more forgiving, if not politically sophisticated, about human frailty and contradiction than Lucas, and she particularly appreciates the potential for restoration of virtue. Richardson also inspires Adams to expand on her own philosophical and literary tastes: "The human mind is an active principle, always in search of some gratification; and those writings which tend to elevate it to the contemplation of truth and virtue, and to teach it that it is capable of rising to higher degrees of excellence than the mere gratification of sensual appetites and passions, contribute to promote its mental pleasures, and to advance the dignity of our natures" (111–12). Ultimately, Adams finds great value in Richardson's work for provoking and stimulating discussion. As Adams and Lucas contend, literature played an important role in the discourse of these women, who looked to the novel for potential models for moral and social behavior. Given these strong reactions, it is no wonder then that, in Joan DeJean's words, it was "generally accepted that women writers were responsible for the creation of the form we now know as the novel. It was also generally accepted that women played a decisive role as arbiters of literary taste. They had come to serve this function as a result of the influence exercised by the salons" ("Literary," 118). As the next chapter will explore in more detail, the epistolary novel capitalized on this intricate relationship and proved a rich source for literary criticism and a model for women's correspondence.

The travel narrative also shares similarities with the sentimental novel, with both centered on the general trope of the journey, one toward virtue, the other toward a physical location. In each case, the text follows the life of a narrator, often an adventurous female, struggling with gendered expectations about propriety. In each, the sentimental voice reinforces emotion as a source of truth. With heartfelt passions, the sentimental heroine confidently defies authority and strikes out on an independent path. Early American women's correspondence takes seriously such dictates. In matters of romance, for example, women often model their discussion after the sentimental heroine's dramatic, declarative voice. In spring 1740, for example, Eliza Lucas responded to her father's request that she consider two potential suitors, a Mr. L. and a Mr. Walsh, finding the first choice disagreeable: "[T]he riches of Peru and Chili if he had them put together could not purchase a sufficient Esteem for him to make him my husband." Lucas holds back from criticizing the second man: "I have so slight a knowledge of him I can form no judgment of him, and a Case of such consiquence requires the Nicest distinctions of humours and Sentiments. But give me leave to assure you, my dear Sir, that a single life is my only Choice and if it were not as I am yet but Eighteen, hope you will [put] aside the thoughts of my marrying yet those 2 or 3 years at least" (6). Lucas thus champions a life of reasoned study over any frivolous alternative and adapts the novel's dramatic voice to express her preference for the unmarried, uncompromised life.

Another example of this interaction between fiction and nonfiction is the woman's conversion narrative that adapts a sentimental voice to portray emotional and dramatic states. For example, Elizabeth Ashbridge's *Some Account of the Fore Part of the Life of Elizabeth Ashbridge* (1755) reads as much like a sentimental novel as like a conversion narrative.[8] Similar to the novel, it begins with a confession to draw in readers and to create empathy: "From my Infancy till fourteen years of age I was as innocent as most Children, about which time my Sorrows began, and have continued for the most part of my life ever since; by giving way to foolish passion, in Setting my affections on a young man who Courted me without my Parents' consent; till I consented, and with sorrow of Heart may say, I suffered myself to be carried off in the night" (148).[9] Elizabeth Ashbridge was, in fact, married three times: at fourteen to a stocking-weaver, at twenty-two to a teacher turned soldier named Sullivan, and at thirty-three to Aaron Ashbridge, a fellow Quaker. Taken alone, Ashbridge's opening would be hard to distinguish from a "seduced and abandoned" contemporary novel by William Hill Brown, Susanna Rowson, or Hannah Webster Foster wherein passions overrule innocence. For Ashbridge is not unlike her fictional counterparts, who also follow romantic urgings and are subsequently cast into exile. Consider Lucy Sumner's comment to Eliza Wharton in *The Coquette* after a moment of revelation: "You have now emerged from that mist of fanciful folly, which, in a measure obscured the brilliance of your youthful days. True, you figured among the first rate coquettes; while your friends, who knew your accomplishments, lamented the misapplication of them; but now they rejoice at the returning empire of reason" (191). The sentimental novel's realism gave hope to those like-minded, strong-willed readers who "earnestly" sought guidance. In a similar literary and moral vein, Ashbridge offers her own colorful story as a cautionary tale.

The *Account* is also framed by travel, as Ashbridge departed England for Ireland, sailed to America, and journeyed across Pennsylvania, New York, and New Jersey. Throughout her travels, Ashbridge navigated a complicated spiritual landscape, a process that often lead to despair, "wherefore I often went alone and wept; with desires that I might be directed to the right" (148). Immersed in her spiritual plight, she even contemplated changing genders: "[I] sometimes wept with Sorrow, that I was not a boy that I might have been one; believing them all Good Men & so beloved of God" (148). Upon arriving in New York on July 15, 1732, she characterized herself "a Stranger in a Strange Land" (151). Undaunted, even by an unfortunate intrigue on board that left her unwittingly indentured, she continued her search: "I used to Converse with People of all societies as Opportunity offer'd & like many others had got a Pretty Deal of Head Knowledge, & Several Societies thought me of their Opinions severally; But I joyned Strictly with none, resolving never to leave Searching till I had found the truth" (155). By distinguishing between "Head Knowledge" and "truth," Ashbridge reflects the "head and heart" dialog of her day and indicates that she will not be persuaded by dogma alone.

Like Richardson's *Pamela*, Ashbridge confronted her master and asserted her own authority. In the *Account*, she sets up the scene by cataloging his abuses: "He would not suffer me to have Clothes to be Decent in, having to go barefoot in his Service in the Snowey Weather & the Meanest drudgery, wherein I Suffered the Utmost Hardship that my Body was able to Bear, which, with the afforesaid Troubles, had like to have been my Ruin to all Eternity had not Almighty God in Mercy Interposed" (152). By embracing virtue and a higher law, the seemingly passive female was empowered and subsequently defended herself regarding allegations that she had complained about her master's sexual advances: "I was Called In; he never asked me Whether I had told any such thing but ordered me to strip; at which my heart was ready to burst; for I could as freely have given up my Life as Suffer such Ignominy. I then said if there be a God, be graciously Pleased to Look down on one of the most unhappy Creatures & plead my Cause for thou knows what I have said is the truth" (152). As pleading aspirant and humble servant, Ashbridge depicts servitude on both spiritual and secular levels. As a woman, she gathered her power obliquely by evoking both her heavenly and earthly fathers: "I then fixed my Eyes on the Barbarous man, & in a flood of Tears said: 'Sir, if you have no Pity on me, yet for my Father's Sake spare me from this Shame (for before this time he had heard of my Father &C. several ways)

& if you think I deserve such punishment, do it your Self.' He then took a turn over the Room & bid the Whipper go about his business, and I came off without a blow" (153). Using her head and heart, Ashbridge defies her master and triumphs. By blending spiritual autobiography, travel narrative, and sentimental novel, her *Account* illustrates a creative construction of narrative voice.

Additionally, women read classics and philosophy and referenced these works in their writings. Eliza Lucas, for example, often integrates classical and popular texts into her letters and expresses varied, wide-ranging tastes that include the eclogues of Virgil, the epics of Milton, the novels of Richardson, the essays of Addison and Locke, the histories of Plutarch, and the poetry of Young, Parnell, and Thompson.[10] From classical poets to contemporary novels, Lucas's curriculum rivals that of any genteel student of her day. Lucas also read law, as she describes in a letter of June 1742 to her friend Mary Bartlett: "I am engaged with the rudiments of the law to which I am yet but a stranger" (41). She was studying Thomas Woods's Institute of the Laws of England (1720), which led her to complain of "cramp phrases" and note the need to consult both French and English dictionaries. Then, in a conspiratorial tone, she tells Bartlett, "If You will not laugh too immoderately at me I'll Trust you with a secrett. I have made two wills already. I know I have done no harm for I coned my lesson very perfect and know how to convey by will Estates real and personal" (41). That she would confess such an act as a secret speaks to presumptions that she has transgressed the limits of female realms. Her apology notwithstanding, Lucas was clearly engaged and stimulated by her rich literary and scholarly investigations.

Notably, Lucas often cites a title within a year of its publication, indicating that she was either wealthy enough to procure a copy or that she subscribed to a lending library. Richard Beale Davis comments on such access, "In books and printing there was really no cultural lag, for the colonial received the latest volumes only a few months after his relatives back home did" (*Intellectual*, 1:498). Lucas confirmed this exchange, closing the cultural and intellectual gaps with her avid interest in engaging literary and classical models. In an April 1742 letter, Lucas describes her reading list, which included Virgil and Plutarch, to Bartlett: "I have got no further than the first volume of Virgil but was most agreeably disappointed to find my self instructed in agriculture as well as entertained by his charming penn; for I am pursuaded tho' he wrote in and for Italy, it will in many instances suit Carolina" (35). She had been reading the Eclogues, Virgil's pastoral poems in which he idealizes rural life in the manner of his Greek predecessor Theocritus. In fact, Walter Muir White-hall cites these works as Lucas's inspiration to plant a cedar grove at the Wappoo plantation (xi). Lucas was delighted that instead of finding "battles, storms and tempests" first off, she was presented with "the calm and pleasing diction of pastoral and gardening." She concludes this section of the letter with a regret: "[H]ad I but the fine soft language of our poet to paint it properly, I should give you but little respite till you came into the country and attended to the beauties of pure nature unassisted by art. The majestic pine imperceptibly puts on a fresher green; . . . the daiseys, the honeysuckles and a thousand nameless beauties of the woods invite you to partake the pleasures the country affords" (36). Such references show that Lucas was indeed quite earnest in her application of reading materials to her life and wrote with a keen sense of audience. When a neighbor warned Lucas about the potential debilitating effects of reading and plantation work on her appearance, Cynthia A. Kierner notes, Lucas staunchly defended herself, responding, "[W]hat ever contributes to health and pleasure of mind must also contribute to good looks" (281). Richard Beale Davis, in fact, finds Pinckney "displays a rare and independent spirit" and credits her with "an inquisitive mind and a knack for saying what she thinks may interest her reader" (*Intellectual*, 3:1430). Under Virgil's pastoral influence, country life stood in contrast to the town's artifice, as Lucas idealizes the country as a sanctuary for inspiration. Virgil inspired her to rhapsodize on natural beauty, and Locke will caution her to be wary of the luxury. Lucas's letters model a genteel woman's literary interactions, as she displays her skills of interpretation and thoughtfully applies literature to experience.

Lucas also turned to philosophy for understanding and interpreting her intellectual and emotional responses. In July 1742, after an extended visit to Charlestown, six miles by water and seventeen miles by road, Lucas wrote to Bartlett, upset to find "everything appeared gloomy and lonesome. . . . [T]he change [was] not in the place but in my self, and it doubtless proceeded from that giddy gayety and want of reflection which

I contracted when in town; and I was forced to consult Mr. Lock over and over to see wherein personal Identity consisted and if I was the very same self." She concludes with this apology: "I don't affect to appear learned by quoting Mr. Lock, but would let you see what regard I pay to Mr. Pinckney's recommendation of Authors—and, in truth, I understand enough of him to be quite charmed." Lucas adds that she imagines it will take another five months to read through Locke's essay, presumably his *Essay Concerning Human Understanding* (19). Though qualifying her commentary, Lucas recognizes the value of referencing Locke at her time of distress. For if identity is formed by experience, then why the apparent shift in perception upon returning from a pleasurable trip to Charlestown? How could the same place look so different contingent on mood? Lucas was clearly bothered by this difference and the possible implication that reality was less than constant. Travelers faced with changing landscape might do well to follow Lucas and consult Locke.

Romancing the Narrative: Literary Allusions

Whereas earlier, promotional tracts were eager to impose a theme and thereby present America as a "land of plenty" and a "new Eden," women's eighteenth- and early nineteenth-century travel narratives are more organic texts that derive their sense of narrative from contemporary travel culture and literary representations. As women contextualized their experiences within fictional, philosophical, or aesthetic frameworks, the travel narrative provided a creative venue for describing America along their own literary lines. To embellish a travel narrative also indicates a certain romance in one's approach to travel. For though women remained focused on the immediate demands of travel, their use of figurative language or inclusion of literary works interjects a more symbolic, metaphoric dimension into their accounts. By noting the literary elements in women's travel accounts, we learn about women's reading habits and levels of education, which are not easily apparent in male-authored contemporary and historical accounts.

Perhaps one of the most enduring examples of a woman's travel narrative containing literary elements is Sarah Kemble Knight's mock-heroic, picaresque dramatization of her journey. Often embellishing a mood or allaying fears, Knight transformed the events of her journey into other-worldly, imaginative scenes. On October 2, 1704, for example, she wrote, "Thus Jogging on with an easy pace, my Guide telling mee it was dangero's to Ride hard in the Night, (whch his horse had the sence to avoid,) Hee entertained me with the Adventurs he had passed by late Rideing, and eminent Dangers he had escaped, so that, Remembring the Hero's in Parismus and the Knight of the Oracle, I didn't know but I had mett with a Prince disguis'd" (53). Knight's allusions to two romances by Emmanuel Forde, The History of Parismus (1598) and The Famous History of Montelion, Knight of the Oracle (earliest surviving edition, 1633), inject a playful irreverence into her own sense of mission, if not her guide's stature. On October 3, she imagined the forest as a fantastic city: "the way being smooth and even, the night warm and serene, and the Tall and thick Trees at a distance, especially wn the moon glar'd light through the branches, fill'd my Imagination with the pleasant delusion of a Sumpteous citty, fill'd with famous Buildings and churches, with their spiring steeples, Balconies, Galleries and I know not what: Grandeurs wch I had heard of, and wch the stories of foreign countries had given me the Idea of" (57). Such projections transform a seemingly forbidding expanse into a charming, inviting cityscape, complete with inspired architecture.

As Knight does with particularly lively or dramatic scenes throughout her journal, she punctuates the previous quote with verse:

> Here stood a Lofty church—there is a steeple,
> And there the Grand Parade—O see the people!
> That Famouse Castle there, were I but nigh
> To see the mote and Bridg and walls so high—
> They'r very fine! sais my deluded eye.

Knight thus adapts the traditional child's verse to her own imaginative needs and departs from its original, more pious meaning:

> Here's the church, and here's the steeple
> Open the door and see all the people.
> Here's the parson going upstairs,
> And here he is saying his prayers.

Knight embellishes the verse to diffuse her anxiety about riding through unfamiliar terrain at night. Rather than fear the dark forest, Knight conjures a fortress and church, and rather than suppliant worshippers, she imagines parading people. Enjoying her "deluded eye," Knight concludes with a nod to her own mixing of entertainment and fantasy: "Being thus agreeably entertain'd without a thou't of any thing but thoughts themselves, I on a suden was Rous'd from these pleasing Imaginations, by the Post's sounding his horn" (57). Knight does seem to be enjoying herself. Verse is particularly appropriate here, for, as Sargent Bush notes, while "it is better than the 'doggerel' label sometimes laid on it," Knight's verse is "intentionally comic" (78). Case in point, Knight resisted attributing any profound significance to her illusions and gladly returned to reality and greeted the arriving stage.

In keeping with her play on spiritual imagery, Knight imagines herself after crossing a river as potentially drowning, looking then "like a holy Sister Just come out of a Spiritual Bath in dripping Garments" (55). William L. Andrews comments on this scene and finds that "Knight foresees her fate hovering between the sublime and the ridiculous. Her imagination delivers her from tragedy—a bloated corpse floating in the river—only to plunge her into comedy—a dignified and genteel woman slogging her way to shore in the middle of the night, cold and soaking wet" (7). By conjuring deliverance, Knight enlivens her narrative. Her journal in fact incorporates many imaginative elements, such as characterizations, including the aforementioned acerbic portraits of the traveling salesman and his female companion, a comedic retelling of a country trial with judges caricatured as pompous even as they sit on pumpkins, and a delightful sketch of New York as "a pleasant, well compacted place situated on a Commodius River" (69). For Knight, the travel narrative provided a chance to express many literary styles. In this respect the travel narrative not only reflects the picaresque, but also is most unlike an account interested solely in travel as accomplishment with measurable outcomes, be they products, discoveries, or acquisitions.

Early American women writers also use literary allusions and make comparisons to enhance setting and to emphasize character. In some cases, these references intensify effect and punctuate sublimity. Consider, for example, Lydia B. Bacon's description of Bedford, written on June 26,

1811: "[I]t was situated in a beautiful Valley watered by a very lovely stream called the Junitta [Juniata]. It reminded me of Johnsons Rassellas [Rasselas], who was born & educated, in a similar valley, surrounded so entirely by mountains, that he lived, to the age, of man, ere he learnt, there was any other world, beside the spot he inhabited, & then prompted by curiosity he climbed, one of the mountains, when lo, another world, burst upon his view, which he explored, but return'd (if I recollt right) not much delighted with his discovery" (372). By referencing *Rasselas* and its utopian imagery Bacon expands and deepens her portrait, associating isolation with the potential for imaginary and philosophical exploration. The parallels between Rasselas's reaction and her own response are curiously ambivalent. Perhaps such realms as Bedford were too far removed from reality to provide lasting satisfaction. Although Bacon was drawn to such places, she acknowledges that society may not understand such creative yearnings.

In another instance, while passing by Blennerhassett Island along the Ohio River, named for Harman Blennerhassett (1765–1831), Bacon compares the landscape with a contemporary travel guide, the Western Tour. Initially, she was disappointed that rainy, inclement weather prevented her from exploring it, "for it must be worth examining, if the description, which I will give in an extract, taken from the Western Tour if it be correct" (375). She then quotes a lengthy passage, which in part reads: "a most charming retreat, for any man of fortune fond of retirement, & it is a situation perhaps not exceeded for beauty in the world" (375). Having cited this passage, Bacon concludes: "This description was given several years ago. Since then Blannerhassett was concerned with Burr, in his attempt to sever the union, and was obliged to abscond from this charming retreat. At present its inhabitants are a few Slaves who raise hemp, the entrance is choked with bushes the whole has a romantic appearance" (375). Here, allusion provides a promising background while also lending Bacon's comments some irony. To anticipate a scene based on another's perception or experience, she implies, may be quite different from actually seeing it for oneself. Bacon was cautious and tried to protect herself against such potential discrepancy. After visiting a Swiss family and their vineyards in Vevay on September 3, 1811, she notes: "It was twilight, & one of the most brilliant, I ever beheld, we tarried till the full Orbed Moon, arising in Mild Majesty, reminded us it was time to depart, which we did with much reluctance, & like Our Mother Eve, on leaving Eden, we cast a long a lingering look behind. I had often read of such places, & thought they existed only in the Authors brain, but my eyes have been gratified with a sight, equal to anything I ever read" (378). With beautiful imagery, Bacon emphasizes feminine associations between the moon, "Mother Eve," and Eden, and thus includes yet another utopian image. Travel and paradise find close proximity in Bacon's account, as she balances fanciful interpretation with her own emotional response. In referencing an "Authors brain," Bacon empowers her own creativity, and she embellishes the scene quite fancifully.

Literary references and general allusions, then, complement the female traveler's own perceptions. As previously noted, Maria Sophia Quincy emphasizes a scene's picturesque qualities on August 12, 1829 by citing a painter known for landscapes: "If the Scenery in the Green Mountains would have afforded subjects for Salvator Rosa, the pencil of a Claude could alone do justice to the exquisite landscapes we have seen since we left them" (27). In a similar application, on August 5, 1811, Lydia B. Bacon described the Ohio River town of Marietta, whose ship building had been halted due to the recent embargo: "[I]t is now so thinly inhabited that the clover is quit high in some of the principal Streets, indeed in some of them, there is hardly a foot path. It reminded us of Goldsmiths deserted Village. It is well laid out & beautifully situated" (374). The reference to Goldsmith infuses the scene with sentimentality that emphasizes moral loss and distances it from the reality of economic decline. In keeping with their gentility and thereby reflecting their education and aesthetics, Quincy and Bacon place their journeys within a more literary, romantic context that coincides with the development of travel culture.

By contrast to official reports, travel narratives thus present the individual's personal, at times creative, view as influenced by literary and cultural models. Eliza Bridgham reflects these literary influences in the final entry of her three-week journal, written on August 7, 1818: "This is concluded the 'famous journal,' which I feel thankful is at an end, & that I have again returned to my darling home. With the hope that this series of Letters may not gain quite as much celebrity as Lady Montagu's, or Mrs. Chapone's, E. W. B. offers them to her sister as Light Reading for

"Maysville on the Ohio, Kentucky." Adlard Welby notes, "The town, which seems to be fast increasing in size and importance, stands high from the level of the river, and is screened by towering hills, affording in the immediate neighbourhood and also up the river situations for building that few places can surpass: the view from above the town looking down the river is beautiful and extensive" (214–17). *A Visit to North America and the English Settlements in Illinois, 1821.* Photo courtesy of The Beinecke Rare Book and Manuscript Library, Yale University, New Haven, Connecticut.

Leisure Hours" (94). In paying homage to Lady Montagu's extensive travels and to Hester Chapone—the spirited bluestocking who challenged Samuel Richardson and wrote on the need for greater freedom for women within marriage and education—Bridgham signals that women's writings were taken seriously and that they served as models for other women travelers. Citing outside sources and drawing comparisons to noted authorities enhanced a woman's observations.

In some cases, women defer to a male author even though their own comments are notable and interesting. When Eliza Bridgham visited Saratoga Springs on July 29, 1818, she modestly denied her own descriptive talents in hopes that a more renowned author might sketch the scene: "Oh! I have wished a dozen times that some man of talents & observation, would spend the summer, & study characters—& then let me see the result; I am sure he could not have a better opportunity to view human nature. Here are, rich & poor, old & young, sick & well, learned & illiterate,

all in the same dwelling—some whose manners are superior, for refinement & elegance, others who are really <u>clownish</u>. If the Author of 'Letters
from the South' were here, he would have ample foundation for something
amusing—the springs are finely described by *Salmagundi*—there are about
one thousand persons in the place, almost every house is a boarding-house"
(22). Bridgham alludes to James Kirke Paulding's *Letters from the South, Written during an Excursion in the Summer of 1816* (1817), a series of short, lightly humorous articles about the transition of the springs from a source of medicinal waters to a resort destination, and *The Salmagundi Papers* (1807–8),
coauthored with Washington and William Irving, a series of satirical essays and poems in the style of the *Spectator* and using pseudonyms. In *Salmagundi*, "No. XVI, October 15, 1807, Style, at Ballston," William Wizard, Esq.,
relays the findings of "Evergreen," who reports: "The worthy, fashionable,
dashing, good-for-nothing people of every state, who had rather suffer
the martyrdom of a crowd than endure the monotony of their own homes,
and the stupid company of their own thoughts, flock to the Springs; not
to enjoy the pleasures of society, or benefit by the qualities of the waters,
but to exhibit their equipages and wardrobes, and to excite the admiration, or, what is much more satisfactory, the envy of their fashionable
competitors" (388). While *Salgamundi* mimics the travel guides for the leisured traveler, Bridgham's delighted, ingenuous responses convey a refreshing immediacy. In a similar manner, Caroline Olivia Laurens referenced a
Sir Walter Scott poem while traveling through the Carolinas, on September 14, 1825, from Pendleton: "We went down to the water's edge, and as
we were gazing on the landscape presented to our view, a little boat suddenly issued from one bank of the river guided by a female who pushed
it to the opposite side—jumped out—chained it to a tree—and disap-
peared. It reminded me of the 'Lady of the Lake'—'A little skiff shot to
the bay'" (228). In describing what would otherwise be an unremarkable
moment, Laurens invests the woman's mysterious disappearance with en-
chantment, as per the allusion to Scott. Such allusions thus complement
rather than supplant the narrative. Unlike the novel, which signaled questionable material, poetry was associated with genteel culture as part of the
belles lettres that a woman would be expected to know for participation
in polite society. As with Lauren's Scott allusion, citations from poetry
could be incorporated into the travel account with fewer, if any, consid-
erations regarding a woman's morals or values.

Embellishing the Narrative: Poetry, Versification, and Romance

In other instances, travelers composed verse, cited poetry, and drama-
tized events to romanticize and to embellish their accounts. As previously
noted, Sarah Kemble Knight's *Journal* often includes poetry; in fact, there
are five poems of original verse composed in various styles and stanzaic
structures that favored the rhythm of iambic pentameter. For example,
she writes an eighteen-line ode to the moon in a succession of heroic
couplets, inspired while Knight traveled through a "dolesome woods . . .
encompased with Terrifying darkness." When Knight at last reaches the
top of a hill, she celebrates "the friendly Appearance of the Kind Con-
ductress of the night, Just then Advancing above the Horisontall Line.
The Raptures wch the Sight of that fair Planett produced in mee, caus'd
mee, for the Moment, to forgett my present wearyness and past toils; and
Inspir'd me. . . . My tho'ts on the sight of the moon were to this purpose:
Fair Cynthia, all the Homage that I may / Unto a Creature, unto thee I
pay; / In Lonesome woods to meet so kind a guide / To Mee's more
worth than all the world beside" (56). Only into the second day of travel,
Knight had not yet adjusted to the rigors of the road nor the fears of
night travel. Her relief at the rising moon signals her appreciation for
light and for nature as a guide: "E're thy Bright Aspect rescues from dis-
pair: / Makes the old Hagg her sable mantle loose, / And a Bright Joy
do's through my Soul diffuse. . . . From hence wee kept on, with more
ease thn before: the way being smooth and even, the night warm and
serene" (56–57). Evoking light and dark imagery, Knight contrasts the
bright moon and dark horse, allowing for the spiritual guidance of nature's luminary to protectively lead her on. The road levels out and joy
infuses her soul, as Knight enlivens and animates her adventure by rendering scenes in verse.

Knight's versification also reflects her familiarity with various poetic
styles. Her use of successive lines of iambic pentameter, for example, is
known as "stichic" verse. Poet-critic Timothy Steele explains: "Stichos:
in ancient prosody, a single verse that repeats through a long passage
or an entire poem. For the ancients, 'stichic' verse is one of the two
major divisions of poetry, the other being composed in lines of different
lengths and arranged according to strophic (i.e., 'stanzaic') reponsion"
(333).[11] Other forms of Knight's poetry include a light-hearted fantasy

of a European scene in a five-lined stanza in iambic pentameter (composed of a couplet and a triplet, *aabbb*); a plaintive ode to rum in a seven-lined stanza in iambic tetrameter (two couplets with a triplet in between, *aabbbaa*); a pun-driven nine-lined stanza to warn other travelers about a disheveled inn, in iambic pentameter ending in a triplet (*aabbccddd*); a twelve-lined stanza in compassionate admiration of an impoverished family, written in a series of heroic couplets, another example of stichic verse. Knight thus adapted the poetic form to suit her subject and used verse to embellish her response.

As with any travel guide, Knight offered helpful recommendations. Yet, in her case, she often employed verse to dramatize her points, particularly when venting frustrations. On October 3, 1704, Knight lodged at Mr. Havens' Tavern at Kingstown, for example, and was "very civilly Received, and courteously entertained, in a clean comfortable House." Exhausted from the day's journey and having nearly fallen out of a canoe, Knight's desire for rest went unanswered as revelers in the next room loudly debated the origin of the Narragansett country. At first, she simply complained, "I heartily fretted, and wish't 'um tongue tyed,"; but then she got down to business:

> I set my Candle on a Chest by the bed side, and setting
> up, fell to my old way of composing my Resentments, in
> the following manner:

> > *I ask thy aid, O Potent Rum!*
> > *To Charm these wrangling Topers Dum.*
> > *Thou hast their Giddy Brains possest—*
> > *The man confounded wth the Beast—*
> > *And I, poor I, can get no rest.*
> > *Intoxicate them with thy fumes:*
> > *O still their Tongues till morning comes!*

> And I know not but my wishes took effect; for the dispute
> soon ended wth 'tother dram; and so Good night! (58)

Knight thus apostrophizes rum to good results, apparently. This intermixing of verse and prose allows her to dramatize certain moments, as again on October 4:

I thought it proper to warn poor Travailers to endeavor to
Avoid falling into circumstances like ours, wch at our next
Stage I sat down and did as followeth:

> May all that dread the cruel feind of night
> Keep on, and not at this curs't Mansion light
> 'Tis Hell; 'tis Hell! and Devills here do dwell:
> Here dwells the Devill—surely this's Hell
>
> . . . .
>
> The Right hand keep, if Hell on Earth you fear! (59).

Knight puns on the name of the inn, perhaps "Davol," as she sounds this
warning. While verse in letters was fairly common, it was more unusual
to find, and in such quantity, in a travel journal—let alone to punctuate
such exciting scenes, mixed in with helpful advice.

Along with allusions, versification itself was a topic of interest. In a
March 1742 letter, Eliza Lucas exercises her critical talents while advising
Mary Bartlett upon seeing some first efforts, "The lines are very pretty,
tho' you take the poets licence to raise your heroine much above her
deserts. If this is your first attempt you will certainly be an excellent po-
ettress in time, but let a friend advise you to chuse a subject for the future more worthy of your muse than a penejerick on Yr. humble Servt.,"
followed by her signature (28). In May 1743, Eliza responds to Mary's request for a poem: "How came it into your head to ask me to write a
poem on Virtue for you; into mind to give you any hopes that I would
attempt it. I am sure I could as well read Homer in the Original as write
a piece of good poetry on any subject whatever; that on Virtue I own always gives an Alacrity to my mind, and was I equal to it, would Celebrate
each branch of it in Numbers suitable to the high sence I have of the Sacred theme. But tis too exalted for my diminutive pen and I must admire
in silence" (62). Here, Lucas weighs her options and thoughtfully de-
clines to aim too high. Obviously familiar with these texts, she writes
confidently, as one actively engaged in literary culture.[12]

For the leisured traveler, in particular, poetry and novels seemed to en-
rich otherwise noneventful journeys. Eliza Williams Bridgham, for one,
spent a rainy morning on July 19, 1818, "pleasantly" reading the ballads
of James Hogg's Queen's Wake, wherein seventeen bards compete in Queen

Mary of Scotland's supposed wake.[13] In Maria Sophia Quincy's 1829 journal of a three-week journey from Cambridge, Massachusetts, to Malta, New York, she mentions reading *Gil Blas*[14] several times: on August 3, "I established myself in a rocking chair at a cool window, & commenced reading 'Gil Blas' which amused me very well till the hour of setting off on our journey arrived" (3); on August 8, "Mama and Anna are at present stretched on the bed & I hope will procure some sleep. I feel quite bright & refreshed & am seated in a fine chair with 'Gil Blas' to amuse me this m[orning]" (11). Quincy's leisurely journey allowed for such moments, and her choice of subject matter reflects her interest in the literary world. The picaresque tale set in Spain may have also enlivened a rather predictable journey through New England and thus offered Quincy an alternative lens through which to view her own adventures. In this sense, reading materials provided a creative counternarrative, and allusions enhanced early American women's journals.

Not only did travelers fancy themselves as adventurers, but some showed signs of disappointment if they did not experience events worthy of their journals and presumably their audiences back home. Bridgham thus complains: "We have been <u>four days</u> from home & not yet met with either, a <u>curious</u> or a <u>romantic</u> <u>adventure</u>!!" (9). The journey appears to have fallen short. Fortuitously, two weeks later, on August 2, Bridgham could amend that lament, "Oh! Abby, now I <u>have</u> got an adventure to relate!!" (33). The thin plot finds father and daughter on their way to visit the Shakers village, a two-mile ride from Lebanon Springs, when "father thought the horse looked wishfully at every brook, we passed, & supposing the hostler had neglected his duty, he drove in & after the horse had drank, sufficiently, he sprang out to fasten the check-rein, when the horse gave a <u>sudden</u> step, rather <u>furiously</u>, & covered father's clothes with a kind of black, clayey mud!" (33). This seemingly disastrous turn is portrayed with great animation and drama—a "wishful" horse, a "sudden" step, her father's clothes covered in mud—all seemed ruined. Bridgham knows her audience, and her sentimental novel, and thus continues: "Now, gentle reader, pause! & imagine our situation!! It was nearly the appointed time! To proceed was <u>utterly</u> impossible, to turn back & change his suit, seemed <u>almost</u> as much so—however, the latter was the only alternative—& then we had the mortification of being <u>looked</u> <u>at</u>, in this plight, as we were obliged to pass through the village—& the people, like all others, <u>in a village</u>, ran at the window, at the sound of every <u>vehicle</u>! Now, was'nt our case lamentable?" (33–34). Just at the moment of greatest humiliation, Bridgham pauses, and thus draws attention to the traveler as outsider. Still she and her father persevere: "We drove back, at a rate, perhaps, seldom seen, in this sober town, father was exactly ten minutes, changing his dress, from '<u>top to toe</u>'; & then we commenced our ride again. We drove so fast, that we arrived exactly at the beginning of the meeting, & then, as the latest had the best seats, we <u>fared</u> better, <u>after all</u>, than the others. . . . —So much for the adventure, which in its early stage was pretty distressing!!" (34). At last, there is a happy ending. Bridgham's lively sense of narrative is further enhanced by her direct address to her "gentle reader," certainly her sister, Abby, but also a common address in the sentimental novel to emphasize a particularly dramatic, complicated moment for the protagonist. Her father's quick actions saved the day, and despite being gawked at, they managed to arrive in time and secure the best seats—quite an adventure, indeed. The sense of traveler as outsider is clearly evident in this self-conscious rendering of an exciting scene in an otherwise "sober town." Adapting this dramatic narrative voice allows Bridgham to frame a scene with thematic sensibilities and reinforce her sense of control over such calamities.

While making comparisons to literature and adventurous tales could prove one's own journey disappointing, travel accounts were interesting in their own right, as they taught important lessons of female courage that challenged fictional portraits of passive female characters. For seven-year-old Anne Grant in 1762, travel was indeed exciting, if not liberating: "I luxuriated in idleness and novelty; knowledge was my delight, and it was now pouring in on my mind from all sides. What a change from sitting down pinned to my sampler by my mother till the hour of play" (1:110). Travel provided new educational horizons as well. For after Grant became "captivated with the copper-plates in an edition of *Paradise Lost*," Captain Campbell offered her the book as a parting gift: "Never did a present produce such joy and gratitude. I thought I was dreaming. . . . I tried to read it; and almost cried with vexation when I found I could not understand it" (1:141). She memorized it "almost by heart . . . yet took care to go no farther than I understood" and pursued her study by asking adults for interpretations and turning to the dictionary, "a perpetual fountain of knowledge." A year later, now eight years old, Grant was reportedly "extremely sorry for the fallen angels, deeply interested in their speeches, and so well acquainted with their names, that [she] could have called the roll of them with all ease imaginable" (1:142–43). This one mention of travel in Grant's memoir is significantly linked with *Paradise Lost*. Milton's grand epic inspired Grant and was a fitting complement to her journey.

When Susan Johnson dramatizes scenes, they take on a more animated tone, and like Knight's writing, provide some comic moments. On November 23, 1801, she recounted this episode: "At ten we were ready to leave [Mr. Goelet's] house & I was much diverted at our mode of conveyance—there was a sulkey as old, & miserable as cou'd be, with a horse so lean as to appear unable to bear his load—all our baggage which consisted of two trunk a portmanteau & umbrella all of which were put upon the poor forlorn sulkey with myself to ride 90 miles & I am sure it was the merriest ride, I ever had in my life: Mr. Johnson, was mounted on a Rosinante, like the one I rode; the ridiculous figure made, was an incessant source of laughter for us—as the weather was fine we jog'd on quietly 45 miles this day" (24–25). Cast as sophisticated outsiders who have taken to local transportation, the Johnsons ride "on a Rosinante"— a reference to the unattractive horse in *Don Quixote*—as if characters on an adventure. Johnson crafts this episode with a comic tone certain to appeal to her family and friends. Such self-conscious portraits again point to the influence of literary models on the travel narrative.

In addition to fiction, women read works on science, history, and natural phenomena. Susan Johnson, for example, read travel and scientific literature, as on April 8, 1802 when she cites *Volneys Travels in Egypt and Spain* and "a little treatise of astronomy by Fontinelli [sic]" called *Plurality of Worlds* that she found "instructive," amusing, and worth a recommendation to her friends (95). Kevin J. Hayes explains that Bernard Le Bovier de Fontenelle's "introduction to Cartesian thought" was a science book commonly read by colonial women and describes it as "dialogues on the Copernican system . . . between a philosopher and a charming, inquisitive Marquise, [that] took place in her ornately landscaped garden. The male figure played the part of teacher and the female the part of eager though naïve pupil" (127–28). Reinforcing gender roles of the paternal teacher and his receptive female student, the dialogue format was intended to make scientific discourse more accessible. In translating it from the French, however, Aphra Behn notes that Fontenelle is inconsistent with the marquise's words, which range from silliness to profundity (cited in Hayes, 128). Behn resents such condescension. While Johnson makes no mention of these inconsistencies, she does indicate that she experienced a range of reading materials, including them quite naturally into her travel record.

Astronomy was another topic of interest to women, as noted in their journals and letters. Comets were apparently a cause for staying up late and rising early. On September 24, 1825, Caroline Olivia Laurens was keen to view a comet: "Saturday night—it is now about 12 o'clock, or Sunday morning. Eleanor & I made an agreement to sit up until the comet rises, which will be about one or two o'clock" (229). On September 29, she recorded, "Eleanor and I made a determination to sit up the whole of this night to see the comet. . . . About three in the morning we took another look at the heavens, but no comet appeared. The morning star Venus had just risen. . . . Half past 5—the sun had almost risen above the horizon so we thought it time to go to bed" (229). The event, though less satisfying than expected, was worth missing sleep for, as it promised discovery and contemplation. In a March 1742 letter to Bartlett, Eliza Lucas shares her own excitement upon seeing "the Comett Sir I. Newton foretold should appear in 1741 and which in his oppinion is that that will destroy the world" (29). A few weeks later, Lucas followed up with a gentle complaint to Bartlett: "By your enquiry after the Comett I find your curiosity has not been strong enough to raise you out of your bed so much before your usual time as mine has been" (31). She describes the comet as a "very large starr with a tail and to my sight about 5 or 6 foot long—its real magnitude must then be prodigious. The tale was much paler than the Commet it self and not unlike the milkey way. . . . The brightness of the Committ was too dazleing for me to give you the information you require." Lucas speculates about whether the comet "had petticoats on or not" and conjectures "by its modest appearance so early in the morning it wont permitt every Idle gazer to behold its splendour, a favour it will only grant to such as take pains for it—from hence I conclude if I could have discovered any clothing it would have been the female garb. Besides if it is any mortal transformed to this glorious luminary, why not a woman" (31). The scientific gaze incorporates the fashionable eye as Lucas speculates on the comet's gender. The ease with which Johnson, Laurens, and Lucas engage in these discussions and observations demonstrates their active curiosity about scientific discourse and engagement with the physical world. These writers present a far more active, intelligent woman than the one presented by those who worried about female vulnerability to the passions of novels.

—◦—

Literary allusions enhance women's travel narratives and expand our understanding of women's intellectual lives. And though women were warned to avoid fiction, for fear it would negatively affect their character, their travel narratives challenge such presumptions and indicate that they, indeed, disregarded such warnings. Drawing on literature places their journeys alongside those of more emblematic, symbolic travelers. Their references were not an affectation, but were integrated into their stories, as befit women of their class, who would have also made such references in conversation. Travel and the travel narrative encouraged women's literary expressions, even as women's journals retained their primarily didactic role and thus avoided the dangers of falling through those half-frozen waters described by Anne MacVicar Grant. Such journals are not solely fictions nor completely facts, but the pleasant medium of a journey "happily told." In addition to travel records, women's letters speak to their writing skills and imaginative talents. The next chapter discusses women's epistolary records together with their travel accounts, noting in particular how differently women recorded their impressions from home and on the road, in letter and in journal. This variety and adaptability illustrate women's creativity and demonstrate their astute reading of early American life.

5

Capturing Experience

TRAVEL NARRATIVE AND LETTER, A COMPARATIVE VIEW

*A*s the previous chapters assert, women's travel narratives testify to their active involvement in westward migration and early national settlement and to their extensive literary interests. In tracking women's experiences, travel narratives and letters are indeed valued resources. While there are approximately fifty extant women's travel narratives from early America, letters have been preserved in the thousands, affording a rich complement to the journal and in many cases an extended sample of women's travel experiences. Letters expand the archive of women's writing and reveal what they were thinking and what they deemed important enough to write about. Letters also provide interesting parallels to travel narratives for the ways that they capture experience and mark women's reactions to travel and migration. Women, in turn, used each genre to suit specific purposes. Whereas the travel diary generally addresses a broader audience and sets individual events within a larger, episodic frame determined by the journey itself, the letter reports on a fragment or segment of this larger experience and is addressed to a smaller, more intimate audience. These genres sometimes overlap, as the writer uses the journal as an extended letter directed to a specific recipient, and the letter serves as an abbreviated journal with several installments devoted to a single incident or topic. Travelers who kept a diary and maintained correspondence while traveling, such as Elizabeth House Trist and Susan Edwards Johnson, note similar events differently contingent on audience and scope. Letter writers who corresponded with several recipients, such as Eliza Lucas Pinckney, present similar experiences from various perspectives depending on intention and relationship. Letters and diaries thus complement women's writings as they document early American culture. To extend this examination into the woman's epistolary record, therefore, highlights this participation and further evidences the woman's influence in culture building. Women's letters and diaries clearly insert the female voice into the larger narrative of the early national experience. As the following discussion bears out, women took up the pen from home and from the road with increasing regularity to express their distinctly gendered, cultural visions of the growing republic.

Women's letters and travel diaries find common ground in family concerns and community affairs. Written in installments during convenient breaks from demanding domestic routines or while undertaking rigorous journeys, letters and diaries provided an appropriately convenient venue for women as they noted the sequential rhythms of the passing seasons, provided updates on children's health, jotted daily travel notes, and reported numerous births, marriages, deaths, and celebrations. In this sense, travel diaries and letters offer a measured view of early American life, one that slows down time and counters a more deliberately constructed, nationalistic narrative that depicts migration, in particular, as a sign of inevitable progress and preordained acquisition. For in their immediacy, the diary and letter resist the panoramic view of America found in more proscribed forms of writing and allow the reader to experience an individual's life in "real time," which is perhaps their most compelling quality. This attention to the present moment authenticates the letter's and travel narrative's witnessing component and offers a valuable, refreshing alternative to political pamphlets and promotional rhetoric that were largely male authored and that often neglected the local, regional perspective. In this regard, women's epistolary and travel records not only balance the male point of view but also show the scope of women's interest in matters personal and cultural. Far from being subgenres, letters and travel diaries are central to American literary expression.

For travelers and letter writers alike, home was a touchstone: the traveler wrote from a transient state with home as a key reference, while the letter writer wrote from home with the outside world as an audience.

One writer was in motion, the other in place. Addressed to family and friends, these writings express a voice far more candid than one taken up for a public letter or an official report. As such, letter writers and diarists have less need to contextualize their comments and can potentially indulge in observation and speculation as if in a conversation with a close friend or associate. In each form, a writer may comment on a passing event without being particularly aware of any larger significance or need for elaboration. Susan Johnson's February 13, 1803, letter, for example, that references "the Democratic Thanksgiving" as a gimmick seems almost irreverent to a reader two hundred years hence, but, as she explains, this topic "affords much conversation for both parties & is a good object for Newspapers squabbling, which the Federalists do not neglect."[1] Similarly, Elizabeth House Trist's 1784 speculations on Pittsburgh's future suggest a certain innocence: "[I]f the country which is mountanous was cleared, it wou'd be beyond description beautifull. . . . [A]nd, was there good Society, I shou'd be contented to end my days in the Western country" (213). For Johnson and Trist, such observations took their place among many and were not necessarily singled out or given any particular weight. Any extended explanation was unnecessary, for Johnson, writing a letter to her husband, or Trist, writing in her travel diary, would have expected their audience to attribute appropriate importance to their comments.

Throughout their journeys, women held onto a strong sense of home—what it was and how it could be reconstructed—even though they could not know how it would eventually manifest while caught up in the all-encompassing tasks of travel. From home, the writer reported on household routines and notable events. From the road, the writer drew comparisons to home while describing new surroundings and traveling new routes. Regarding nineteenth-century American women traveling outside of the United States, Mary Suzanne Schriber offers this perspective: "Sometimes writing home from abroad means expanding the definition of home to include communal and municipal spaces, then national boundaries and, finally, the world. And although travel writing by both genders is ostensibly about other lands but paradoxically about home, travel writing by women carries a special relationship to 'home' in a particular way. Whether women's travel writing secures or transforms the definition of 'home,' it writes and rewrites the place and role of women, its rhetorical

ELIZABETH HOUSE TRIST JOURNAL EXCERPT. These entries describe Elizabeth House Trist's impressions of Pittsburgh in April 1784. Partial transcription: "[I]f the country which is mountanous was cleared, it wou'd be beyond description beautifull. . . . [U]pon the whole I like the situation of Pittsburg mightily and was there good Society I shou'd be contented to end my days in the Western country." "Elizabeth House Trist Travel Diary," 1783–84, Papers of the Trist, Randolph and Burke Families (#10487), Special Collections, University of Virginia Library, entries 28 and 29.

center" (9). Women's writings show this center to be quite dynamic and far more fluid than more conventional expressions might allow. For as women ventured into new territory and viewed new sights, they altered notions of self, home, and community, physically and socially. In their willingness to experience change they documented an intersection between gender expectations and individual responses to reveal the tension that results when such cultural assumptions restrict the very women who are shapers of culture.

In this regard, the travel narrative is an especially exciting text, propelled by the energy it took to change and to explore and not yet influenced by the realities of settling in or concerned with the prospect of returning. Thus suspended between home and the frontier or home and a new landscape, women compared and anticipated. How then did movement affect the style and content of the woman's text? As travelers, were women more tentative or speculative than men when separated from familiar surroundings? Did the stationary letter writer express thoughts more confidently? With the domestic arena as common ground, letter writers and travelers captured experience differently; letters demonstrated women's literary versatility, and travel initiated female discourse in the realms of discovery and exploration. Writing from home and on the road, women conscientiously recorded their observations and engaged in lively, critical discourse. Whereas letter writers shifted voice depending on their recipients, the travel diarist maintained a similar tone while addressing different areas of interest. Letters sustained connections with family and friends, and travel diaries focused on the everyday circumstances that the journey entailed.

Women travelers also describe experiences differently depending on the circumstances of writing. The journal reconstructed, for instance, has a very different sense of time and narrative frame than the one written on the road and unedited. The reconstructed or edited account allows its author to consider content and audience more consciously than an account written to the moment. Though both the travel narrative and the letter were often drafted and later copied over or revised, the extent of the editing affects the sense of immediacy. The travel narrative or letter written on the road often adopts less-polished prose, emphasizing the present moment. The deliberate construction of the text brings into consideration matters of the literary self and how women perceived themselves as authors. So often, there is a rush of enthusiasm in these writings, as if they are expressing interests and passions yet unknown to the writer herself. As such, the travel diary strengthens the woman's social voice and encourages participation in the literary realm. These distinctions between the letter and the travel diary are made clearer when an experience is retold after a lapse of time, whereby events recast assume a more deliberately thematic narrative. Elizabeth Van Horne's travel diary, for example, began on October 4, 1807, broke off on October 26, and resumed four months later. The sequence of the journal remains chronological, picking up with details of her father's illness on the twenty-sixth, followed by descriptions of his death on the thirty-first, and ending with the family's arrival at their final destination in Lebanon, Ohio, in mid-December. The shift from a narrative of the moment to a report of the past is highlighted by her lack of specific dates. As a consequence, the second half sounds more like a reminiscence than an eyewitness account. Compare, for example, an entry written on October 25, before the four-month hiatus: "My father has had a very tedious night indeed has slept but very little. . . . This morning he is confined to his bed—this event we have feared and apprehended would be our melancholy situation. We are detained at an indifferent house—far from a home or any friends—not a Dr in 8 miles nor a Town near that we can obtain any thing nessary should it be needed—this trying circumstance we feel severely" (15). Here, Van Horne writes hesitantly, caught in her frustration over inadequate care for her father's failing health: "Unless a very great alteration takes place and I feel very different my journal must be discontinued. Through Attention to my Father, and fatigue I penned a more imperfect journal than I could wish so far but my friends must take the will for the deed. All the Leisure I get to write is after the family are in bed and I owe to you I have sometimes repented my promise" (17). Whereas Van Horne began the journey enthusiastically, she now regrets her promise to keep a record for friends left behind in Scotch Plains. As the narrative resumes in late February or early March, she has taken on a much lighter voice, as she addresses her audience: "Lebanon! Yes my friends I am at Lebanon and until the present could not find leisure, or attain a frame of mind adequate to the task of completing my journal." The subsequent report, while less dramatic, is more reflective: "[October 29] Our wishes all seemed to center in one thing, in one place—that was to be at Pittsburg—when once there we thought my Fathers fatigue would be over. . . . So indeed it proved we reach'd there on thursday morning and satureday night [October 31]—his soul took its flight (we trust) to happier regions" (17). Van Horne waited for the leisure that allowed for a proper "frame of mind" before continuing the story of her father's illness and death. The subsequent narration is indeed more measured and contemplative. In its formality, however, the later record is less compelling, as part summation and part memorial to her father. She concludes with a report on the town's diversity and the many "Young Gentlemen from every part almost—from N York, N. Ark, different parts of Jersey, from Delaware, from different parts of Pennsylvania, from Virginia, Maryland, Kentucky, Cincinati, Franklin, Waynsville Urbana &c &c. The generality of them well educated, genteel, agreeable young men—And we have been happy in finding in the different Towns a small number (in comparison) of hansome, genteel agreeable young Ladies" (22). The summary mode provides a sense of closure to her experiences and, despite her father's death, communicates an overall successful journey. As if to reinforce a positive conclusion, this catalog, with its assurances of gentility, would have comforted the readers back home in Scotch Plains, New Jersey.

As Van Horne's diary suggests, when circumstances allow for retrospection, the traveler might pay more attention to producing a thematically coherent narrative. In this respect, the reconstructed journal is often more compliant with social mores and gender expectations. By contrast, the letter and narrative written "in the moment" have less actual time to invest in framing the situation and thereby capture experience more directly. Less conformist, these spontaneous expressions of actual female responses broaden our understanding of women's experience in important ways. While there is merit to Van Horne's journal regardless of its reconstruction, the content is definitely less exciting as she retells rather than reports her experiences. Unedited communications may seem fragmentary by comparison to a more polished text, but their eyewitness quality documents the complex emotions and issues that travel and migration elicit. As Van Horne and others illustrate, when writing on a daily or periodic basis, the travel diarist is less inclined to place experience within a grander context. Instead, the traveler logs individual events that culminate in an overall tale of travel. In both rough and polished accounts, furthermore, women's writings reflect their social positions. When women write "to the moment," we are more likely to see gaps between expected behaviors and actual responses. In these gaps, women often voice opinions outside of conventional responses. This attention to the woman's experience and her subsequent reaction can most clearly be found in her letters and travel accounts—yet another reason for their study and certainly their preservation.

Letters written from home under less pressing circumstances offered opportunities for lengthy pontification that the demands of travel precluded. Experience could be suspended and thoughts analyzed differently than by the traveler caught up in the movement of travel. Eliza Lucas's letters, for example, with their deliberate, slow pace, model genteel manners and female discourse and resemble conversation, as if she were having a leisurely tea in her sitting room. Olga Kenyon adds to this comparison: "Letters have one considerable advantage over conversation in that they are written with time for reflection, allowing choice of apt wording" (x). A June 1742 letter that Lucas wrote to her brother George in London illustrates this reflective voice: "I have been thinking, My Dear brother, how necessary it is for young people such as we are to lay down betimes a plan for our conduct in life in order to living not only agreeably in this early season of it, but with cheerfulness in maturity, comfort in old age, and with happiness to Eternity." Writing from home, with its comforts and regular rhythms, Lucas anticipated living a good life and imagined meeting lofty goals, as the letter confirms: "To live agreeably to the dictates of reason and religion, to keep a strict guard over not only our actions but our very thoughts before they ripen into action, to be active in every good word and work must produce a peace and calmness of mind beyond expression" (51). Lucas sets up a contemplative basis for her actions, motivated by a desire for peace and calm. Lucas's letters also reflect and document her curiosity and creativity, for she was the first person in colonial America to successfully cultivate indigo. In July 1740, Lucas noted this interest in her letter book: "Wrote my Father a very long letter on his plantation affairs . . . On the pains I had taken to bring the Indigo, Ginger, Cotton, and Lucerne and Casada to perfection" (8). Lucas continues by cataloging various transactions and shipping arrivals and includes an "account of Mr. Whitfield and the Ecclesiastical Court," but does not dwell on these activities or elaborate, for they are only several among many in reports to her father. For Lucas, the letter serves both practical and speculative musings, and when a great distance separates her from her correspondent, as with her brother, it encourages philosophical reflection. And yet, the formality of the letter, as if it were a carefully composed minuet, can appear too practiced when compared to the informality of the travel narrative, which bears similarities more to a folk melody or a spontaneously composed dance tune. There is, of course, value in each form, though the letter may garner more traditional respect.

Although the travel narrative is less prone to extended reflection, given its focus on movement, travelers also sought context for their experiences and used their writing to sort out troubling issues and personal dilemmas, as Margaret Van Horn Dwight did after her encounters with the wagoners. Separated from the familial and civic structures that strengthen identity, some women entertained new perspectives, while others were inclined to reinforce familiar ones, choices that manifest in women's travel journals as either praise or criticism for their new surroundings. That travelers such as Sarah Kemble Knight became social critics bent on imposing certain cultural norms illustrates how seriously women assumed responsibilities as models of genteel behaviors. On the other hand, when women's travel narratives describe the physical challenges of travel and express delight in observation, they present women as active agents of social construction. In this spirit, travel presented opportunity for stimulating change rather than stultifying imposition. The setting thus influenced how women reflected their experiences, and their attitude reveals how they imagined their cultural position.

Letter writing encourages a range of topics from family news, weather conditions, and health concerns to cultural, religious, and social events. Letters serve as important newsletters, ways of keeping track of valuable connections. Elizabeth Hewitt finds that letters "constitute a crucial site by which democratic theory passes into social practice. From the establishment of the Post Office Act of 1792 to southern Succession (and the subsequent establishment of a Confederate postal system) in 1861, we discover an insistent rhetoric that depicts American letter-writing as the means by which both national and familial consensus are to be established"

(6–7). In this regard, letters provide opportunities for communication across class and gender lines. Susan Edwards Johnson, the wife of a public figure and a mother of four, and Eliza Lucas, the single daughter of a wealthy southern planter, for example, both use letter writing to document everyday life with a certain authority that derives from their industry and domestic order. Their attention to such matters reinforced expectations of productivity and female behaviors. When Mary Bartlett asks how Lucas "triffle[s] away" her time in her father's absences, for example, Lucas reports in a letter of April 1742:

> In general then I rise at five o'Clock in the morning, read
> till Seven, then take a walk in the garden or field, see that
> the Servants are at their respective business, then to break-
> fast. The first hour after breakfast is spent at my musick, the
> next is constantly employed in recolecting something I have
> learned least for want of practise it should be quite lost,
> such as French and short hand. After that I devote the rest of
> the time till I dress for dinner to our little Polly and two
> black girls who I teach to read, and if I have my paps's ap-
> probation (my Mamas I have got) I intend [them] for school
> mistres's for the rest of the Negroe children—another scheme
> you see. But to proceed, the first hour after dinner as the
> first after breakfast at musick, the rest of the afternoon in
> Needle work till candle light, and from that time to bed
> time read or write. (34)

Lucas maps out her daily schedule with a keen sense of purposefulness and managerial expertise. The interjection to describe teaching "little Polly" and the "two black girls," specifically illustrates Lucas's interest in education. She had been teaching her charges for over a year, as indicated in a February 6, 1741, letter to the "Honble. Crs. Pinckney, Esqr.," noting she had a "Sister to instruct and a parcel of little Negroes whom I have undertaken to teach to read" (12). By charting her schedule and tracking her industry, she compartmentalizes time and experience.

For Susan Johnson, the letter not only affirms her productive domestic-ity but also provides an opportunity to exert control over the representation of her life. For example, in letters to her husband and friends, she asserts order, as on February 1, 1803: "I suffer nothing to interrupt the studies of my girls, for the last two months they have not lost a day. . . . [E]very morning is devoted to study & every afternoon to work"; and on January 18, 1803, in "addition to the daily studies, every evening is devoted to reading some book of instruction & amusement which we perform alternately." By properly instructing her daughters, in this case by reading Goldson's *History of Rome*, which they were "much pleased with," Johnson modeled virtuous behaviors and promoted female education. Johnson also notes the dependable rhythms of domesticity with a sense of accomplishment, as in a letter to her close friend Faith Wadsworth on March 9, 1803: "My life has been as uniform as yours can possibly have been. There has been little variation, from rising in the morning, eating three meals & going to bed again. I have had no company & made as few visits as yourself—have attended strictly to my family economy, taught my Children, & rejoiced at the close of each day, that we were all in health." In each letter, Johnson takes pleasure in well-ordered domesticity. In letters to family and friends, Lucas and Johnson demonstrate their versatility by shifting voices from formal to candid and covering a range of topics, as they discuss everyday events, mark daily schedules, and offer thoughtful pronouncements.

Letters as Private Conveyance, Public Forum, and Literary Device

Far from marginalizing women and excluding them from the "literary world," letters cultivated intellectual exchange. David S. Shields elaborates: "These networks were amorphous, much as the readerships for women's novels in the early Republic were. Nevertheless, they constituted a fundamental part of the republic of letters. Most importantly, they supplied the filaments of affection that bound the nation together" (Civil, 319). As noted in the previous chapter, and as Shields confirms, epistolary relationships created a virtual salon in which women expressed opinions, shared ideas, and discussed literature. In doing so, women could step beyond gender expectations that might confine them to "genteel" subjects in order to entertain topics public and private, thus challenging essentialist notions of the "feminine letter." Terry Eagleton, for one, eschews "any simple opposition between masculine and feminine, 'work' and 'text,' the possessed and the protean self," and notes, instead, the incorporation of difference. Citing Richardson's novel, Eagleton elaborates: "The letter in *Clarissa* is masculine and feminine together. I have suggested that it lies on some troubled frontier between private and public worlds, symbol at once of the self and of its violent appropriation" (54). Clarissa's letters, thus suspended between private and public, and more specifically virtue and sacrifice, provide an interesting metaphor for the traveler straddling the worlds of the genteel and the rustic.

Letters were also important sources of information and, as previously noted, were read aloud as a newsletter or a broadside would be. The acts of reading and writing encouraged interaction with an audience. The novel written in letters was naturally appealing, as it capitalized on this desire for collective reading and on the popularity of letter writing itself. Thomas O. Beebee elaborates on these developments: "Epistolary form became important to fiction in the early modern period because of the discursive power it possessed due to the letter's heterogeneous social uses" (6). The performance aspect of letters was thus showcased in the eighteenth-century epistolary novel, in which letters present a character's voice and perspective and model various styles of writing. Letters, in turn, could be quite imaginative. Amanda Gilroy and W. H. Verhoeven accurately assess the letter as "a cultural institution with multiple histories" (4). Bruce Redford observes that the familiar letter "turns on the complex interplay between the natural and the fictive—between reflection and creation, history 'outside' and artifice 'within.' The peculiar richness of the genre results from this very ambiguity of status" (13). In Mary Favret's evaluation of the history of the letter, she reminds us that the letter as literary device may be traced to Horace and Seneca, and that Pope's "Epistle to Dr. Arbuthnot" (1735) revived the popularity of the familiar letter as social forum. Redford identifies the familiar letter "as intimate conversation" and "a performance" that builds on its function as public forum: "Through a variety of techniques, such as masking and impersonation, the letter writer devises substitutes for gesture, vocal inflection, and physical context" (1–2). By adapting these techniques and shifting narrative voice, letter writers could be both informative and creative. In framing a domestic moment, for example, the writer could choose which parts to emphasize and what mood to convey. Rosemarie Bodenheimer affirms these conventions and finds "letters are fictions of a sort, self-presentations addressed to a particular reader under very specific conditions of time and place and relationship" (7). The relationship between letters and novels speaks to these choices. For Terry Castle, the "actual letter" in an epistolary novel, such as *Clarissa*, "is a reading taken of one's experience. Individuals confront and interpret events; the letter registers, or recapitulates this initial hermeneutic process. The letter is the visible trace left by a prior apprehension of the world; it is an attempt to preserve meaning" (50). As Castle affirms, the letter captures experience and encourages a subjective reading of events. The recipient, or novel reader, as the case may be, interacts with these presentations via response or critical interpretation. The letter thus parallels and invites conversation. The various perspectives and shifts in voice so evident in the novel resonated with women's own depictions of various scenes from differing viewpoints.

Shifts of voices correspond in fiction to characterizations themselves. And though men wrote many of the early novels, their letter-writing characters are predominantly women. The male author constructs the female character along traditional gender conventions, and, as seen in the previous chapter, early American women variously responded to the authenticity of these representations. Barbara Maria Zaczek remarks on this gender imbalance: "In creating a letter of passion as a feminine domain, the law of the genre wanted to restrict and to exclude women from the literary territory. However, it proved to be a blessing in disguise [and] opened the public sphere for women writers and allowed them to contest openly the restrictions imposed on them by social conventions" (64). Samuel Richardson's *Pamela* thus elicited heated debates among women that invited them into the critical realm. Similarly, Nicola J. Watson finds that in the British novel from 1790 to 1825, the letter serves as "double agent" that is "accordingly unmasked by its subjection to a process of re-circulation, surveillance, edition, censorship, and commentary" (70). The subsequent "public scrutiny of the letter," as Watson notes, places it at the center of the novel, wherein we learn about characters from their reactions and interpretations. Correspondence turned novel was therefore a natural extension and an appropriate entrée for women into the literary world. Women may not have been equally represented as authors, but their discursive outlet is clearly evident in their epistolary exchanges. It would follow then that from reading these novels, women ascertained the letter's power as a notable source of information and modeled their analysis accordingly. Significantly, the epistolary novel reinforced the letter's influence, and letters provided an "acceptable" realm for women's writing. Though the travel narrative was fundamentally grounded in reality and was not a fictional text, the traveler's composition of setting, representation of character, and description of events all exercised talents similar to those employed in novel writing. Women were, therefore, participating in the literary arena without a formal invitation through their letters and in their travel narratives.

Novels may have been questionable as moral guides, as per Mrs. Grant's concerns about "walking on a river half frozen," but their influence on social discourse was undeniable. For Terry Eagleton, the act of writing a letter in the epistolary novel takes on particularly political meaning: "If letter-writing is in one sense free subjectivity, it is also the function of an ineluctable power system. Certainly no activity could be more minutely regulated. To 'correspond' is to implicate a set of political questions: Who may write to whom, under what conditions? Which parts may be cited to another, and which must be suppressed? Who has the authority to edit, censor, mediate, commentate?" (50). The dramatic tension in *Clarissa* depends on these conditions. And while most women corresponded under far less dramatic circumstances, the novel illustrated the range of the letter in terms of audience and content. In response to these epistolary moments and various directives, the letter writer adapted a "multilingual" voice and directed her discourse accordingly. Lucas Pinckney, for example, wrote on different topics and adapted different voices for various correspondents, male and female, peers and elders. Janet Gurkin Altman adds a spatial element to this epistolary diversity: "An entire plot tradition, the novel of seduction through letters, is built around the letter's power to suggest both presence and absence, to decrease and increase distance" (15). The letter as centerpiece encouraged women to record their opinions and thereby emphasize their presence, and letters written from the road drew attention to their absence. Even as some cast aspersions on the novel, others recognized its value as a guide for letter composition. Letter writing thus encouraged women to engage in social discourse and to participate in literary conversation.

Letter Writing Culture: Style and Content

Women's engagement in epistolary exchanges was part of a larger interest in letter writing and in public forms of communication. Robert Adams Day charts the popularity of the familiar letter in seventeenth-century England as it "began to appeal to a large and enthusiastic public, as distinguished from a choice audience of scholars, and to develop the quality of negligent charm which culminated in the famous correspondence of such men as Pope, Walpole, Gray, and Cowper. People apparently became genuinely hungry to read other people's letters" (48). This appeal legitimized letter writing, for those engaged in elevated discourse and those employed in everyday communication. David S. Shields notes a subsequent broadening of the letter's scope: "While courtship was the central transaction demanding polite and personal communication, it did not monopolize the posts. Every social interaction in which trust, personal connection, and privacy were crucial made use of the manuscript letter. . . . Commercial negotiation, motherly advice, friendly admonition, and commiseration all used private letter" (Civil, 317). The assumption that letters would not be published, moreover, gave writers license to express opinions without undue self-consciousness and further encouraged accounting of one's experiences. Shields describes how these changes evolved: "As the public prints burgeoned during the 1780s and 1790s, a powerful reactive expansion of epistolary writing and communication took place. With this expansion came a shift of emphasis away from the individual letter as an event of communication to the idea of correspondence in which an enduring relationship grounded in feeling might be cultivated" (318). These developments encouraged women to entertain topics domestic and social and to embrace the letter as an extended conversation, philosophical platform, or intellectual forum. Patricia Meyer Spacks adds this historical context: "The eighteenth-century flurry of published letters coincides chronologically with a proliferation of secular autobiography and with philosophic preoccupations about questions of identity" (69). Rosemarie Zagarri marks yet another trend from 1780 to 1830, during which time "women shifted from writing primarily for private audiences to writing for a broader public" due in part to the "expansion of the print culture" ("Postcolonial Culture," 19). With such support, women were less delegated to event-oriented material. These larger trends supported women's epistolary output by encouraging discussions domestic, philosophical, and literary.

Letters, like travel narratives, were variously directed to either single individuals or an extended family circle, which influenced how they described circumstances and relayed experiences. Mary A. Favret identifies a key romantic view of the private letter: "An emphasis upon the 'private moment' expressed in letters tends to erase the outside world and ignore the structures of time and distance which, in fact, dictate the letter's form" (19). Significantly, this emphasis coincides with growing westward migration and increased leisure travel, both key occasions for writing. Although the letter from home could more readily "erase the outside world," an increased attention to the "private moment" influenced how travelers wrote about their experiences and how letter writers wrote about their daily lives. Such developments explain why women's travel accounts from early America and the New Republic are different historically from earlier explorer's accounts. They also suggest one reason why women kept travel diaries in the first place—as part of an increased interest in personal records—and why keeping a record of travel was deemed important—it marked an exceptional moment in one's life. The letter also granted women, as Favret notes, permission to gather their thoughts on paper amidst the demands of domestic activities. For Patricia Meyer Spacks, letters are interesting because they "affirm the timeless possibility of communication. A self keeps asserting itself by words on a page intended for another; the reader finds sustenance in that capacity of selves and in the demonstrated will to establish and preserve human contact" (89). In this manner, letters provide a historical record, and, when correspondence spanned years, serve as family gazettes and histories with their detailed portraits of daily life.

Susan Johnson, for example, wrote at the end of long days, often nearing midnight in the summer, or on winter evenings surrounded by her children Ann Frances (1792–1839), William Samuel Johnson (1795–1883), and Sarah Elizabeth Johnson or Betsey (1797–1867). On January 4, 1800, for instance, in a letter to her husband, Johnson wrote: "[B]ehold <u>me</u> now seated before my bed roome fire Betsey in my bed, the two children in the little bed, all fast asleep, if you were but at my side I think I should not have a <u>care</u>." Johnson frames this intimate portrait as an expression of familial harmony. Save for her husband's absence, it is a satisfying moment. The letter allows the necessary privacy for this personal missive. Johnson's scene of peaceful domesticity anticipates what Suzanne Bunkers identifies in nineteenth-century diaries, wherein midwestern woman found "a safe place where she could generate a sense of self, share thoughts and feelings, contemplate her relationships with others, and comment on institutions and events" (15). Bunkers's description is also consistent with contemporary expectations for journal keeping and, as the previous chapters demonstrate, represents a change from how travelers initially perceived their journals. For, as Margo Culley explains, "It is only relatively recently (roughly in the last one hundred years) that the content of the diary has been a record of private thoughts and feelings to be kept hidden from others' eyes. . . . Diaries were semi-public documents intended to be read by an audience" (3). These are important distinctions for understanding voice and intention in early American letters and diaries, in that the confessional, private expression was not yet synonymous with letter writing or diary keeping. Instead, appreciation for the personal voice developed gradually, allowing for even more distinctive narrations of early America.

The popularity of the familial and private letter was buoyed by an increase in literacy rates and the lowering of postage rates, which gave rise to letter-writing manuals. In 1680, as Robert Adams Day explains, the London penny post allowed people to "correspond on matters of no particular importance and to send and receive letters quickly and often"; to meet these needs, letter-writing manuals "adapted to the tastes of all social levels" (49). In this context, letters codified relationships and strengthened networks, and letter-writing manuals addressed style and etiquette. Ruth Perry discusses the social context of letters: "Educated people were expected to know how to write graceful letters, how to compose their thoughts on paper. Schools trained this skill—letter-writing was a standard composition assignment, and students read and copied from classical examples" (64). Bodenheimer cites Richardson as the "acknowledged 'father' of the English form" whose letter manual was published anonymously in 1741 and then "brought to light under Richardson's name in 1928 as *Familiar Letters on Important Occasions*" (8). She also finds that social concerns turned "the letter-manual into a conduct book that works by example to instruct parents on the diction and tone of advice to their children or servants, children and servants on the epistolary formulas of deference and request, lovers on discreet rituals of courtship, and so forth" (9). By assuming distinct differences in address, letters marked and reinforced social structures. Women instructed in the art of letter writing understood the conventions and expectations that directed their topics and influenced their style.

In addition to letter manuals, the letter book facilitated style by providing a space for drafting and composing. As Elise Pinckney, editor of *The Letterbook of Eliza Lucas Pinckney, 1739–1762*, notes, the letter book served its author "as a place to draft outgoing communications and to record memoranda or to copy a finished letter" (xxvii). Bodenheimer adds to this description: "The most popular form of the letter book in seventeenth- and eighteenth-century England was the 'letter-writer'—a manual that combined advice on letter form and language with an anthology of fictional letters intended to serve as models for a 'complete' range of common epistolary situations" (9). Marjorie McNinch notes the "custom for girls away at school to practice good writing style in their letters home. They often turned to textbooks for improvement in epistolary style. Moral tales such as those of Maria Edgeworth or Samuel Richardson, or the poetry of Anne MacVicar Grant, were also models for developing a good writing style" (228). Susan M. Stabile explains how specific instruction in handwriting and writing desks designed especially for women further encouraged women's epistolary and literary efforts: "Forwarding the etiquette propounded by professional penmen, such a design authorized a woman's ability to pen manuscripts at a time when writing was still considered a masculine pursuit" (90). Letter books, novels, and public letters thus encouraged diverse styles, inspired production, and validated voice; and manuals reinforced and facilitated social order.

Glancing through women's correspondence, such standardization is evident, as one notes that women not only write on common topics but also use similar phrasing and standard salutations and closings. William

Merrill Decker elucidates this conformity: "Such resemblances may be attributed to the fact that writers modeled the letters they wrote on those they received; the authority of letter-writing manuals and conduct books would have played a secondary role in encouraging an unquestioning acceptance of certain structures and phrasings" (95). Epistolary conventions evolved somewhat organically, according to Decker, and the manuals provided a starting point or template. Repetitive or standard phrases were also practical, as they referenced distance between correspondents, lapses of time, and means of conveyance. This regularity can be seen in Susan Johnson's letters, which begin consistently with the salutation "My dearest friend" and close with such phrases as "be ever assured I am with unremitting sincerity Yours," "Believe me my dearest, best of friends, with unceasing affection always tenderly yours," and "Adieu my dearest friend & know that I am always your tenderly affectionate wife, Susan Johnson." In the letters themselves, there are stylistic and practical reasons for Johnson to repeat information. She sometimes sent six letters from Stratford, Connecticut, to her husband's one from Milton, North Carolina, and she worried about these gaps in their communication. In a letter dated January 18, 1803, that includes passages from several subsequent days, Johnson notes on January 20, "I am sorry to hear you do not get my letters more regularly: this is the fifth I have written, in all of which I have endeavored to be very minute in every thing interesting or amusing to you." On January 4, 1800, upon finally receiving one of his letters, she wrote: "I am out of all patience, that the communication is so seldom between us; I used to get Stark's letters from Pittsburgh in nine day, & yours are twenty one days coming to me." Anticipating these lapses, Johnson not only wrote in great detail but often repeated information in case a letter went missing. On December 20, 1803, when the last letter she had received from her husband was dated five weeks earlier, she had quite had it: "I assure you the post-masters throughout the continent have not escaped, an abundance of abuse from me." Johnson's repetitions not only served a purpose—in the case of missing letters, for example—but also suggest a need to maintain order, if not equilibrium.

Repetitions and narrative breaks are more than lapses or quirks. They served practical purposes by assuring that ideas were communicated, and they reflect reality in that women wrote when time allowed. Narrative structure and composition take on gendered implications whereby authority is associated with linearity. Although episodic style may be less valued, such assumptions warrant reconsideration. In Susan S. Kissel's discussion of letter writing and anxiety, she notes: "We read again and again of the daily wants and needs, of the same hardships and frustrations, as we move from one letter to another. The very repetition—itself a seeming weakness—becomes a unifying factor, an emotional refrain that charges the collection" (55). Sharon M. Harris, in turn, understands the repetitions and jumps from topic to topic found in letters and diaries as an "associativeness born of interruptibility" that allows the woman writer in particular "to rove through multiple associations" (*American Women*, 21). Harris elaborates on this narrative style: "Associativeness inherent in a poetics of interruptibility is a kind of intellectual looping, episodic and disjunctive in form" (*American Women*, 28). It follows then that early American letters covered several topics and, like Johnson's, were written sporadically over the course of a day or sometimes several days. Given the relationship between writer and recipient such "interruptibility" did not necessarily undermine coherence; rather, this flexibility proved an asset.

As letter writers and travel diarists move from one topic to another, they catalog information and elaborate on how a certain event affected them and their immediate community. Rebecca Hogan finds this reporting style an "open, elastic form," in that "no particular moment of time, event, reflection, feeling, state of mind, or voice is privileged over any other in the diary" ("Engendered Autobiographies," 103). Rosemarie Bodenheimer, in turn, distinguishes between autobiography, letter, and diary, and notes: "The autobiographical 'I' looks back in retrospection to create a continuous narration; the diarist and the letter writer write relatively noncontinuous fragments from a dated point of the present with no knowledge of what is to happen next. Dating proclaims diaries and letters to be works composed at a particular moment of time—although they may not in every case have been—and make it possible to place the writing in relation to a historical day" (17). The episodic quality of letters and diaries, therefore, creates a focus on experience and actions. The degree to which the writer elaborates on a subject depends on situation and intention. As Susan M. Stabile reminds us, writing also aids women's memories: "Initiating a stream of associations, commonplace books re-produce memories, compensating for the cumulative losses that accom-pany aging" (133). Larger eighteenth-century interest in epistemology and self-improvement thus contributed to a cataloging of daily schedules and the sharing of such agendas in letters.

This structuring of discourse, however, represents a marked contrast to the actual mixing of social classes on the frontiers of early America. Women trained by manuals to direct correspondence, and by extension social exchange, were at a loss to respond in environments less beholden to these codes. This difference explains why Sarah Kemble Knight and Margaret Van Horn Dwight, for example, set many of their encounters with locals in dialogue rather than prose. The more theatrical format ac-centuates the conflict between a desire to act according to proper etiquette and the frustration when such codes were irrelevant. Women trained to delineate class differences were momentarily displaced in social environ-ments uninterested in sustaining such distinctions. This contrast between social models and actual events sheds light on the female traveler's ad-justment in mind and spirit as she moved from one culture to another. Faced with the opportunity to evaluate natural resources or scout new lo-cations, women trained to catalog social interactions and to weigh class differences had to reposition themselves in this new discourse. Clearly, the experience of travel needed a different language than one endorsed in any letter manual. For though a discursive form may advocate a dis-tinct cultural order, it does not dictate stratification.

Writing from the Road: Elizabeth House Trist's Narrative and Letters

In both letters and travel diary, Elizabeth House Trist reflected on the chal-lenges of travel differently dependent on circumstance and mood.[2] On December 8, 1783, two weeks before departing Philadelphia, Trist de-scribed her approaching journey: "It is a very great undertaking for me who has never experienced any hardships to ride over the Mountains this season of the year. I expect to suffer a little but this I am certain the fa-tigues of the Body can not be worse than that of the mind which I have experienced in the extreem" (Jefferson, 6:376).[3] The letter, to her friend Thomas Jefferson, addresses the journey in the abstract and imagines the difficulties rationally, as inevitable "fatigues" of the body and mind. Over-all, she perceived the anticipated journey as a sacrifice, one with the even-tual rewards of reunion with her husband, Nicholas Trist, and establishing a home. Given the proposed December departure, Jefferson thought it prudent to wait until spring and for milder weather, but Trist was deter-mined to leave as scheduled. Jefferson apparently understood, for in a letter on December 11, 1783, from Annapolis, he was clearly supportive: "I think you will be a distinguished creditor if you pursue your wild Mississippi scheme. . . . I hope the day is near when Mr. Trist's return will make amends for the crosses and disappointments you complain of, and render the current of life as smooth and placid as you can wish" (Jeffer-son, 6:383). Though there were financial and personal risks to this "wild" plan, Jefferson acknowledged the journey as the fulfillment of a larger domestic dream; and if successful, the Trists would indeed be financially sound as "distinguished creditors." This exchange of letters imagines a successful journey and provides an interesting prelude to Trist's travel diary. The measured tone of this exchange, moreover, belies the drama ahead, which she could never have imagined, and the rational underpin-nings do not consider the emotional impact of separation or the dangers of travel. The genteel is preserved in the calm demeanor of logical assess-ment. Indeed, these letters provide telling contrast to the journey itself and reinforce the difference between letter and travel narrative as a differ-ence between perceiving experience as a stationary event or as a series of individual acts within a larger context.

Once underway, travel absorbed Trist's attention, and the record was attentive to daily progress. On December 23, 1783, her style shifted, and she was all reporter: "dinner and at 6 O Clock PM arrived at Lancaster. Put up at *Steel's* tavern, a very good house" (201). The notations are con-cise and uncomplicated. Trist did not muse here on the overall precari-ousness of her journey, but she focused, instead, on the details of travel. Seventy miles from Philadelphia, the scene had not altered dramatically, and Trist was quite comfortable as she proceeded to have tea with an "old friend" and retired early for the morning departure. On January 9, 1784, Trist noted the land's potential with an eye for settlement and crop yields while writing about "Cole Hill" across the "Monongahala" river: "It is equeal in quallity to the N'castle or any other I ever saw. The Hill is seven

Hundred feet perpendicular, and on the top is a settlement. The land is fertile and capable of raising all kinds of grain. The timber is very large, and the shrubbery pretty much the same as is produced in the bottoms" (212–13). Again, the syntax is simpler and the tone more declarative as motion emphasizes observations of the physical world more than it encourages internal contemplations.

With less time spent on matters of polite society and decorum, the traveler in motion focuses on observation and survival. For example, on June 10, 1784, Trist described a visit to the Big Cave, "which appears to be about forty feet high and sixty in width and resembles an old castle. . . . The driping of water form'd some petrefactions that resembled columns." The specifics then lead to an overall assessment, "Upon the whole, I think it one of the most grand and beautifull natural structures and the greatest curiossity I ever beheld" (223). With perspective gained from six months of travel, Trist's pronouncement is notably enthusiastic as she reflects a newfound authority. She only regrets not having more daylight for exploration. Again, on June 14, she showed increased knowledge of the land and speculated on future development: "At dawn of day we left the shore and soon came in sight of the Iron bank; a great quantity of ore may be picked up on the surface of the earth. It is 16 miles from the Ohio, a fine high situation. And I am told there is to be a town laid out here very soon" (225). Caught in the rhythms of travel, Trist confidently declares her progress, assesses the mineral resources, and anticipates future settlement. Whereas the more formal setting or more contemplative pose might reinforce genteel ways, the changing scenes of travel inspire bolder expressions and active exploration. And as wilderness may soon become homestead, it promises to become a "pastoral dream of harmony," as Leo Marx describes it, by striking a balance between "decadence and wildness, too much and too little civilization" ("Pastoralism," 38). In her own attempt to strike such a balance, Trist looks down from her saddle as she rides along new roads or out from her boat, which glides down unfamiliar rivers, with an inquisitive, critical eye. In this pose, Trist embodies the American as transforming agent who is no longer a stranger in a strange land but in the process of speculating on future properties.

The thirty-year correspondence between Elizabeth House Trist and Thomas Jefferson from 1783 to 1814 not only is a rich study in itself but also offers valuable comparisons between letters and travel diaries. Trist and Jefferson had met in Philadelphia around 1775, during the convening of the Second Continental Congress, when Jefferson lodged at Mary House's boardinghouse, located on the corner of Fifth and Market Streets, and Trist worked in her mother's establishment. In the December 8, 1783, letter, Trist gives a sense of their friendship: "I can and will say that you are incapable of esteeming me more than I do you. I cou'd give as many reasons were I to enumerate your Virtues as wou'd fill a Volume folio. Your caracter was great in my estamation long before I had the pleasure of your acquaintance personally for I allways understood your Country was greatly benefited by your councels; and I value you now because I know you are good" (Jefferson, 6: 375). Along with Abigail Adams and Maria Cosway, Trist was one of many female correspondents to whom Jefferson wrote, as Andrew Burstein conjectures, to share his "fanciful notions"; being female, they might best "understand outpourings of emotion" (Inner, 65–66). Burstein identifies Trist as Jefferson's "sensitive, good-hearted Philadelphia friend." Jefferson's interest in the frontier may have further inspired Trist to speculate on resources and potential for community; though, as Annette Kolodny has suggested, it is not certain if he "directly asked his friend to gather information for him" (Introduction, 187). Trist did mention her travel diary to Jefferson in a letter from the Acadian Coast on March 12, 1785: "Shall I ever have the pleasure of seeing you again I mean to give you an account of my peregranation. I fancy your travils will afford much greater entertainment than mine" (Jefferson, 8:25). The shared interest in the frontier and subsequent family connections sustained friendship and correspondence. As noted, their friendship endured for two decades after Trist's frontier journey, and their mutual appreciation is evident in this letter from Jefferson, written from Paris on August 18, 1785: "I pray you to write to me often. Do not you turn politician too; but write me all the small news; the news about persons and not about states. Tell me who die, that I may meet these disagreeable events in detail, and not all at once when I return: who marry, who hang themselves because they cannot marry &c. &c" (8:404).

Jefferson's letters to Trist illustrate the outsider's assessment of frontier travel. For though he had Trist's safety in mind and had warned about the dangers of winter travel, Jefferson did not fully know her state of mind.

When the previously noted December letter eventually reached Trist in Pittsburgh, where her party had wintered and waited for the rivers to thaw, she replied on April 8, 1784: "I had the pleasing satisfaction to receive a letter of yours dated 22nd of Dec. which was the day after I set out on my journey. Had I received it in time I do not think it wou'd have prevented my undertaking the journey tho no ones advise wou'd have had greater weight" (Jefferson, 7:86). From his stationary home base, Jefferson offered his kind, logical advice, and yet when Trist eventually read this letter from the road, such warnings had become not only irrelevant but inappropriate to her sense of purpose. The four-month gap provided Trist new perspectives, and the hiatus allowed her to process the experience. She appreciated the journey and Thomas Jefferson in new ways, as evidenced on April 13, 1784: "Cou'd I possibly be so happy as to have your company, my jaunt down the River might be enviable but in the present situation of affairs I dont expect much satisfaction till I arrive at my place of destination" (Jefferson, 7:97). Describing her trip as a "jaunt down the River" frames her frontier experience as quite genteel, and the polite discourse of the letter reflects an altered sense of time, unlike the faster pace of the journal entries. Brevity exerts a certain control, while elaboration entertains possibilities. Imagining Jefferson as her companion somehow validated her journey, perhaps for the benefit of companionship, if not his status, and for the scientific investigations that they may have initiated, albeit twenty years before the Lewis and Clark Expedition.

The extended time away from home also altered Trist's immediate response to class differences and to frontier poverty more specifically. After six months of travel, for example, her empathy for other travelers deepened, as in her entry from June 15, 1784, in which she remarks on "a poor family encamp'd" at "Loncela Greece," later called "Lance la Greece," located, according to Trist, "80 miles from the Ohio," near present day Memphis. This "Man and his Wife" with five children had "left the Natchez seven months ago . . . and had not a morsel of bread for the last three months," and had recently "buried one of the oldest of their sons." Upon seeing Trist's party, the children "cry'd for some bread" and the "Gent. gave some flour," while Trist gave the woman "some tea and sugar, which was more acceptable to them than diamonds or pearls." Trist prefaces the scene with this reflection: "Every one thinks our troubles the greatest, but I have seen so many poor creatures since I left home who's situation has been so wretched, that I shall begin to consider my self as a favored child of fortune" (226). Blending the thoughtful quality of a letter with the unique perspective of travel, Trist momentarily forgot her own troubles as she recorded this impoverished frontier scene. Reflection requires stationary moments and distance from familiar surroundings, whereby the traveler has moved beyond the initial reactive excitement of comparison and stimulation and has settled into new rhythms and acclimated to difference. Trist still viewed the frontier according to standards of propriety and social order, yet here she withheld judgment and refrained from asserting a superior attitude. In this regard, class distinctions are fluid as people are more subject to misfortune on the frontier. Trist's letters and travel narrative express a range of reactions, from confidence to uncertainty, that in many ways blends these two genres. In each form, she distinguishes her accounts from the explorer's straightforward record of progress by including personal responses and genteel assessments that will in many ways anticipate the pioneer's journal, with its more thematic style and pronounced individual voice.

Letters also help the traveler ascertain his or her place within the larger journey. For in writing a letter from the road, the traveler pauses to take stock of the journey and in doing so might create a narrative or cast a theme about the journey. In this regard, Trist's letters to Jefferson are multivoiced. At times, she speaks assertively as a potential landowner whose high standards will bring order to the wilderness. In other moments, she expresses uncertainty and vulnerability and wonders how she will adjust, if at all. From Pittsburgh on April 8, 1784, Trist was ultimately optimistic in her role as traveler-scout: "I have seen many delightfull prospects from the Hills that surround the Town." At times, though, she was quite critical: "Next Week I am to take a ride to the country for a few days. I shall then be able to judge what sort of farmers inhabit this in its self a good country. I am apprehensive very slovenly ones, if the inhabitants of this Town are a specimen" (Jefferson, 7:87). Poised on the western edge of Pennsylvania, Trist takes seriously her role as guardian of the genteel and promoter of the gentleman farmer. Upholding certain standards, she writes with benevolent authority: "I grieve to see the poor starved cattle crawling and dieing in the streets. I have no patience where there is so much good land, that they raise so little fodder. Half the Winter the poor beasts have only two or three ears of corn a day which bearly prolongs their miserable existance. I have frequently seen the horses eating wood, the cleanings of a well provided stable wou'd be a great repast." Her patience tested, Trist speaks to the sensibility of the cultivator who values well-managed fields and well-tended horses. Not only does local husbandry receive poor marks, but farming techniques are also subject to scrutiny: "[Y]esterday I cross'd the river to the Indian side, as its call'd, to see them making sugar which is all the use except Hunting. They seem to have far the most delightfull soil I ever saw. How I lament their Idleness and inattention to agriculture. I cou'd allmost banish them of the earth if it was only for their method of living, so uncomfortable and beastly" (Jefferson, 7:87). Trist again privileges eastern notions of order and bemoans that such a promising landscape should be so poorly managed. This authoritative tone is also found in the later stages of her journal. Whereas observations are tentative and sketchy in the beginning, Trist reasserts her genteel view as her confidence increases. Trist noted similar judgments in her journal on June 10, 1784, after visiting the "Indian side"; she condemned the Indians for their "beastly" lifestyle and disdained what she perceived as their "[i]dleness and inattention." And when she met members of the Delaware tribe and their chief, James Dickison, she described him as a "sensible fierce looking fellow, but his character is very bad. They say he has plundered several boats and murdered many people that have been going down this river" (222). Despite her preconceptions, she adds, "[M]y curiossity led me to visit them, as they had all the appearance of friendship. . . . As it is good to have friends at court, I carried the Squaw some bread; and as her Infant was exposed to the sun, I gave her my Hankerchief to shade it, for which she was very thankfull" (222). As she had with her gestures of kindness to the impoverished family on "Loncela Greece," Trist acted according to her genteel sensibilities. In these entries, she departs from straight reporting mode to include "fixed portraits," as Joyce E. Chaplin identifies them, in this case of poverty on the frontier and "benevolence extended." These shifts in voice from tentative to confident, speculative to assertive reflect Trist's various moods and the states of travel she experiences. For

Trist, journal and letter clearly provided platforms for social assessment, while marking personal experience.

Trist's letters from the road were also occasions for contemplation. On April 8, 1784, for example, Trist wrote to Jefferson from Pittsburgh and admitted that although she was "not naturally gloomy minded," her present situation rendered her incapable of "tranquillity": "[T]here is a something which I can not express that hangs about me to embitter the sweets of my life. But why shou'd I trouble my friends with my complainings. I can only plead in excuse that it [is] the greatest consolation I have and I am convinced your goodness will not suffer you to ridicule female nature. Tho the imbecility of mind is not altogether confined to our sex I must acknowledge they have less firmness than yours. If I cou'd possess a little of your Philosophy my happiness wou'd be within my reach, my mind wou'd be exalted above those trifles that at present is the sourse of my disquiets. Dash—I am done, I will change the subject" (Jefferson, 7:86). Whereas movement and anticipation had lightened her mood and attitude, the late-spring layover had dampened her enthusiasm, as evidenced in her self-conscious remarks about her "imbecility of mind" and concern for a more philosophic mind that could presumably transcend the experience. Why, then, does Trist write more self-consciously in her letters about her travel experiences than in her journal? Perhaps the letter's specific audience encourages the more reflective tone. To some extent, she follows the expectations of the genres, using the travel narrative for more general observations. Notably, as she travels further into the Ohio frontier, the blending of the genres parallels her integration of experience. Initially, Trist focuses on day-to-day events, reflecting the process of orientation. As she grows more comfortable with travel, she expands the scope of her writings.

The Pittsburgh interlude offered Trist valuable perspective and a more realistic understanding of her journey. Separated from family, friends, and home and headed toward unfamiliar landscapes, she constantly needed to adjust. Writing to Jefferson allowed Trist to maintain valued connections that reassured her of her identity. At times, though, she seems overwhelmed by the immensity of her situation, as on April 13, 1784: "Whatever observations I am capabl of making I shall not fail to communicate to you but when ever I see any thing out of the common way if they are beautifull prospects my sensations are very singular I believe for I can hardly suppress the tears starting from my eyes and I am lost in wonder but a Philosophical mind like yours can gather information from all you see, account for many that appear misterious to vulgar minds and make observations as will benefit Mandkind in general" (Jefferson, 7:97). Her sense of wonder at the "beautifull prospects" overwhelmed her, a sensation that she then qualified as somehow less sophisticated than that of a "Philosophical mind." This new territory took on a mysterious quality marked by her emotional response. As her moods shifted from excitement to contemplation, her sentences lengthened and the prose expanded. Movement provided stimulus and kept Trist in a more present state of mind, with less time to reflect and grow melancholic. The letter contextualizes experience, with a greater sense of her past, while the travel narrative keeps her focused on the present and at times has her projecting into the future.

While audience was an influential factor in letter writing, the uncertainty of mail delivery also influenced the traveler's state of mind. Travel into the frontier presented obvious communication gaps between a traveler and home, which contributed to isolation and intensified the separation. One indication of this heightened sense of distance is a shift in tone and subject matter whereby the traveler provides a simple listing of places and noting of climate and geography without extensive commentary. To some extent a traveler does not fully understand what he or she is experiencing, and so the descriptions are generally concise. Travelers also presume that the conditions they left behind and that supply a certain context for the journey itself will stay relatively unchanged, but instead these conditions may have altered or may no longer exist once travelers reach their destination or return home. A traveler confidently imagines establishing a home, discovering a water route, or finding valuable resources with some authority, however unfounded. In Trist's case, her main reason for the journey was undermined without her knowledge. For, even as Elizabeth Trist pursued a journey toward reunion with her husband, Nicholas Trist had died from illness months before. The news had reached the East, but not Trist. For her friends in Philadelphia, this was a difficult, frustrating situation as they debated how to reach her. Jefferson, for example, wrote to James Madison on May 25, 1784: "Poor

Mrs. Trist is in a situation which gives us much pain. Her husband is dead, and she without knowing it proceeding down the Ohio and Mississippi in hopes of joining him. There is a possibility only that letters sent from hence may overtake her at the Falls of Ohio and recall her to this place" (Jefferson, 7:289). While these exchanges illustrate an interesting example of lapses in communication, they also draw attention to the degree of isolation of the frontier traveler. To venture beyond Pittsburgh placed Trist out of touch, even by eighteenth-century standards. Madison expressed similar concerns to Jefferson from Philadelphia on September 7, 1784, regarding the difficulties of Trist's passage homeward: "We hear nothing of Mrs. Trist, since her arrival at the Falls of the Ohio, on her way to N. Orleans. There is no doubt that she proceeded down the river thence, unapprized of her loss. When & how she will be able to get back since the Spaniards have shut all their ports against the U. S., is uncertain & gives much anxiety to her friends" (2:79). One month later, on October 17, Madison wrote again from Philadelphia and gave Jefferson this update: "[Mrs. House] has lately received a letter from poor Mrs. Trist, every syllable of which is the language of affection itself. [In *The Papers of Thomas Jefferson*, edited by Julian P. Boyd, this letter reads "affliction itself."] She had arrived safe at the habitation of her deceased Husband, but will not be able to leave that Country till the Spring at the nearest. The only happiness she says she is capable of there, is to receive proofs that her friends have not forgotten her" (2:86). This emotional situation illustrates how states of mind can motivate travelers and affect their accounts, even though the circumstances that propelled them to travel can radically change.

Curiously, even though Trist had no knowledge of either her husband's death or her friends' concerns, her mood had darkened and infringed on her sightseeing, as on May 27, when she described Fort Nelson in Louisville, Kentucky: "The situation of this place is very pretty: the bank high and commands a view of the falls and Islands. At any other time, I shou'd take much more satisfaction in examining the beauties of this place, but my mind is at present not in a very tranquil state" (219). Trist then explains troubles with low river levels that impeded the boat's progress. Although she located this anxiety in the physical aspects of travel, Trist's sense of foreboding was identified as an uneasy state of mind, preventing her from enjoying the beauty as she might have "[a]t any other time." Travel was thus propelled by the possibility of reunion, which generated the stamina and optimism to continue the journey. The tragedy caught up to Trist on July 1, 1784: "My journey is most compleated. Three days more I shall be happy in sight of the Natchez. Will write to Mr. Trist. Perhaps a boat may be just setting of, and he will be glad to see me, I know. As our boat is to be detain'd to unload some flour . . ." (232). However she had imagined the frontier experience, its reality could not be fully comprehended. These circumstances dramatically illustrate the components of intention, pose, voice, and genre, wherein travel challenges presumptions of authorial control and possibly undermines the genteel prerogative.

Where the travel diary breaks off in midsentence, the letters complete her record. Trist's letters post-Natchez encapsulate the westward traveler's experience and name a key challenge: how to sustain optimism and hope amidst limited resources, inclement weather, and social isolation. While Trist awaited passage from the Acadian Coast in Spanish Louisiana to Cuba and then eventually to Philadelphia, she wrote long letters to Jefferson about the value of family and community, placing them more central to her happiness than settling on the frontier. On December 25, 1784, six months after reaching Natchez, Trist referred to one of Jefferson's previous letters about his wife's death: "I was at that time sensible of justness of your observation and forgot my own troubles in commiserating the pang your heart must have felt when you suggested that thought to me by way of consolation. I did sincerely Sympathize with you and since I have experienced the like calamity I have thought of your sufferings when I was allmost sinking under my own" (Jefferson, 7:583). These letters cast her journey in a very different perspective than the diary, as she tells Jefferson: "I have been severely afflicted, and my situation peculiarly unfortunate. I received the cruel stab when I least expected it. My mind was prepared for happiness, my tedious journey allmost compleated, two days more I was certain wou'd reunite me with my Dear Mr. Trist, when I received the dreadfull account of his being no more. Tho in a strange country I experienced great kindness but I wanted the consolation of my friends, and that has been denied me. . . . For however strong the mind may be fortified, few are proof against the shock attending such a seperation" (Jefferson, 7:583). Whereas her travel diary anticipates discovery and emphasizes movement, these letters appraise emotions and express uncertainty.

The letter allows for personal assessment and confession. As with her letters from Pittsburgh, Trist turns to the epistolary mode for solace and reflection. In her most perspective-making moment yet, Trist fills these last letters from the Acadian Coast with meditations on family, westward travel, and personal loss. On March 12, 1785, Trist explained to Jefferson: "I have experienced too much pain and anxiety allready in this country and every hour presents something that reminds me of my misfortune" (Jefferson, 8:24). As the letter continues, it underscores the importance of social contacts, for place without community is "most miserable," and she tells Jefferson: "I have no other expectation of happiness but the company and conversation of my friends. Here I am shut out from all intercourse with them. I was so long deprived of the pleasure of hearing from them that I began to think myself the most miserable of all human beings, forgot by them all at a time when my wounded mind required the aid of friendship to sooth and allay its painful perturbation. As gloomy Ideas are ever attendant on the wretched my real troubles were constantly augmenting by antisipating other Calamities" (Jefferson, 8:24–25). Frontier travel and its subsequent isolation were tolerable when an end was in sight. The diary could only hint at disappointment with day-to-day issues; it could not convey a sense of the overall value or success of a journey. In both letter and diary, Trist thus describes the optimism necessary to even commence a journey and shows how style and voice significantly alter when the outcome was unfavorable.

For Trist, the journey was not successful, not for any of the reasons that she may have imagined to begin with—such as problems with working the land, building a home, planting crops—but for the very essential loss of her social and family network. Without familial connections, Trist admits little attraction to the frontier, as she concludes: "I can not give you a very flattering discription of this country. It has been a bubble from the beginning. The poor can live in it, but there are few rich and I fancy tis the policy of the spanish goverment to keep people poor. The climate is not disagreeable. I have seen full as good land in my own country as any on this river but I must conclude for I have not time to enter into a regular detail. You can easily find out that I am not partial to It, but no country wou'd be agreeable to me under the same circumstances that I have labourd under" (Jefferson, 8:26). Social ties have taken precedence over fulfilling frontier dreams. Though she was clearly in mourning, Trist was able to separate her emotions from her assessments, as if recalling earlier conversations with Jefferson and his requests for a report.

With her departure pending, Trist seemed more conciliatory about her overall frontier experience. Though she saw the Ohio frontier as less than hospitable, she preserved her initial explorer's interest in discovery and resources. On May 4, 1785, Trist explained to Jefferson: "I have no fault to find with the country or climate or inhabitants under any other government, tho it has been the source of much sorrow to me. But a Paradise wou'd not tempt me to be seperated any longer from my Dear Mother and child, since I am deprived of what cou'd only make me amends for the loss of their society" (Jefferson, 8:136). Trist may have considered the Natchez venture as a paradise at one time, but paradise has been refigured, not just as a fertile homestead but as a community of family and society. In the Trist narrative, confidence comes from familiarity, and even when she was on the road, a certain predictability in the patterns of travel brought her comfort. She was most disturbed by the unknown and the lack of family and community, which provided a context for her identity. Still, even as she prepared to set sail, Trist reflected kindly on Jefferson's friendship: "I did myself the pleasure to write you some time ago . . . returning you my sincere acknowledgments for your goodness towards me, the remembrance of which will never be eras'd from my heart. May you my worthy friend ever experience that felicity which your benevolent mind is intitled to. May health and prosperity attend you, and your children live to call you blessed" (Jefferson, 8:136). Her mood lightened, Trist uses prayerlike prose to acknowledge friendship and express gratitude. And in a letter from Paris on August 18, 1785, Jefferson seems to understand Trist's ordeal: "By this time I hope your mind has felt the good effects of time and occupation. They are slow physicians indeed, but they are the only ones. Their opiate influence lessens our sensibility tho their power does not extend to dry up the sources of sorrow" (Jefferson, 8:403). Trist returned to Philadelphia and eventually settled in Virginia. Forty years later, in 1824, she and Jefferson celebrated the marriage of their grandchildren Nicholas Philip Trist and Virginia Randolph at Monticello. Jefferson and Trist thus remained life-long friends.[4] Unlike the travel narrative, in which Trist could only speculate on the eventual success of her journey, her letters provide closure and a convincing example of the tenuousness of relocation itself. The framing of her experience, from December 1783 to May 1785, tells a tale of both hope and despair, not unlike the stories of other westward travelers. Thus, this one, significant journey proves unique in Trist's overall biography and also emblematic of the hardships and discoveries of westward travelers to follow.

Writing from Home and on the Road: Susan Edwards Johnson's Letters and Journal

The Susan Johnson correspondence addresses class and gender issues, while illustrating her particular views of genteel society. The 178 letters that make up the Johnson correspondence (1792–1850) offer a rich portrait of a New England family and its community. In letters to her primary correspondents—her husband, Samuel William Johnson, and her friend Mrs. Faith Wadsworth (nee Trumbull)—Johnson affirms her appreciation for good health, close friendships, and amiable marriage. As previously noted, Susan Edwards Johnson hailed from a distinguished lineage, as the daughter of Pierpoint Edwards and Frances Ogden Edwards and granddaughter of Rev. Jonathan Edwards. Her aunt Mary Edwards Dwight was, by the way, the grandmother of Margaret Van Horn Dwight. Her father-in-law was William Samuel Johnson, a senator from Connecticut and a president of Columbia College of New York (now Columbia University). The Johnsons' social circles included the Verplanck, Trumbull, Wadsworth, and Devereux families,[5] connections that were intertwined quite naturally in her letters, lending Johnson a certain weight, or what James Daybell refers to as a "degree of confidence and authority." In his study "Women's Letters and Letter Writing in England, 1540–1603," Daybell also notes "women's persuasive and rhetorical skills, the degree of confidence and authority that they displayed, self-fashioning and the creation of personas, empowerment and female agency, as well as the intimacy and emotional content of social and family relationships" (162). Similarly, Johnson's letters were not filled with equivocation and rarely contained self-doubt. Worries were well grounded in the frequency of sickness and the real concern that if her husband had met with misfortune she would have been faced with uncertain financial circumstances.

Susan Johnson's correspondence covers various time frames, from the immediate to the long term, and reflects both calm contemplation and sporadic activity. With her focus on home, she preserves a cohesiveness while documenting a demanding schedule. Letters to her husband, for example, could be both businesslike and intimate, and, given the couple's frequent separations, provided an important domestic link. The Johnsons were separated because Samuel Johnson was either working in Hartford on state business, traveling the lawyer circuit, or establishing a lumber mill in North Carolina. In general, Susan Johnson accepted the periodic absences caused by the political life—when her husband was merely sixty miles away in Hartford—better than his lengthy stays fourteen hundred miles away in Milton, near Fayetteville. Before what was to be her husband's last term, after six sessions as representative in the General Assembly, Johnson wrote from Stratford on May 14, 1797, "I rejoic'd for you on Election day, you had such Charming weather—I have not yet heard who is elected to the Offices, excepting the Speaker, but hope your are not <u>honored</u>." On May 24, 1797, writing from Stratford, she again expressed mixed emotions: "I earnestly hope nothing will happen in the Assembly to prevent your joining us again the beginning of the next week. . . . I will confess myself a selfish mortal in wishing forever to retain you to myself but we are all unwilling to part with what is our greatest happiness as your society is certainly mine." Her devotions divided, Johnson was ultimately supportive of her husband's civic duties. Her letters are filled with the concerns and complications of any long-distance relationship.

During those three- to six-month intervals, Johnson wrote consistently, every other week, timed with the post deliveries from Carolina so that she could respond to his letters, should they arrive. These were difficult separations, as they left her to manage the household and to care for the couple's small children. At times, she expressed frustration: "New Haven, November 21, 1792, without you I concider every thing as indifferent, and pass every thing in which you are not concerned as a blank in my life." Nevertheless, Johnson maintained her social calendar and recounted her activities, including visits to "Mr. Hubbard's church, that he might not think himself neglected, on Monday we had Mrs. Nicoll and Mrs. Platt to drink tea, and were engaged to spend the evening with Mr. Hey-begar, who gave an elegant supper, . . . a day at Mrs. Broomer and this afternoon at Mrs. George Browns." It is clear that she missed her husband, as in an April 1796 letter in which she explains: "[I]ndeed I had enjoyed but little peace of mind since you left me, my mind constantly suggested a thousand dangers to which you must be exposed. . . . Every moment I am anxiously wishing your return, I do not know when I have felt so lonesome, every thing in the house wears such a gloomy aspect that I can scarcely bear to stay in it." By contrast, upon receipt of a letter on April 4, 1797, she adds this note: "Evening). Since writing the above, I have received yours—to express the happiness, I derive from your letters would indeed require some new language—something which I cannot command, to express my present feelings." In one sense, his absences curtailed participation in the very social circles with which she most identified. Still, she sent along her support, as on June 4, 1799, from Stratford: "I begin to count the weeks untill you return, four have already past, & in four more you will certainly be here; I think you will by that time be as weary of seeing great trees, and your own company, as I am of wandering about my house, whitewashing, painting & c." The letter functioned as family memo, whereby Johnson updated her husband on household activities and communicated practical concerns.

For their details of domestic life and her adjustments to the separations, Susan Johnson's letters are interesting in themselves, and for the purpose of this larger discussion of capturing experience and class construction, they demonstrate the capacity of the letter to express emotion and to reinforce social order. On January 1, 1804, she wrote candidly about the stress of separation: "I was not sensible that my disposition was intirely owing to the state of my mind untill I found myself well, as soon as the letters came. . . . I am not very polite in giving you such a miserable account of myself—it cannot afford an additional reason for you to hurry home to see such a miserable decrepit old woman as I am—but I trust you have long since given up all hopes of perfection in a wife & estimate this mortal part according to its real merit." Johnson thus catalogs marital relations disrupted by long distance and competing

agendas, financial gain versus domestic harmony. Her repeated wishes
for her husband's return combine with requests for his comments on
household decisions—difficult at best considering the distance and unreliable mail. On February 11, 1798, from Stratford, Johnson turned
mock confessional in a letter to her husband: "I shall remember the advice about gambling; & suppose if [I] give up that, and only keep to
drinking (which I have long been in the habit of) you will not think my
situation disparate." On December 11, 1803, she reported her speculation
in stocks: "I feel a little strange as this is my first embarkation on the sea
of speculation but hope not to be so far intoxicated with it as to require
the <u>indorsements</u> of all my family to keep me from <u>ruin</u>—if you should
not be pleased with the arrangement pray write me, & if the plan is carried into effect, the share can be disposed of directly." Her need for con-
sultation, if not conversation, drove such moments, and Johnson reveals,
albeit reluctantly, her financial competency.

   In Johnson's letters to Faith Wadsworth, she reinforces her own gentility and social position within their elite circles. For example, on February 4, 1799, she wrote: "My dear Faithy, I am really mortified that I
have been obliged, to delay, writing you so long. . . . I shou'd not have
neglected, to express to you my gratitude for the very friendly, & flattering, attention, which I received from yourself, and good Husband while
at Hartford; I am certain no person derives more sensible pleasure from
such friendly communications than myself I really feel as if my visit to
H— had made me of more consequence, in the world than I ever considered myself before; to find yourself & Cathy, established in life, &
myself received, as one of your most intimate friends, and rank'd among
those, whome if [it] will ever give <u>you</u> pleasure to welcome, under your
hospitable roof, are circumstances of no small moment in my list of enjoyments." Pleased with these reminders of an ordered, social world, she
is keen to acknowledge Faith Wadsworth's social connections and yet
maintains her own authority by positioning them as among a "list of enjoyments." Johnson reiterated her sentiments on November 2, 1803, describing for her husband a recent visit from Faith and her sister Maria
Trumbull: "[T]he more I see this excellant woman, the more I respect &
love her; she has made this journey on <u>purpose</u> to visit me." These connections reinforced what she called "that pure friendship which is the

very balm of our existence" (November 24, 1803). Johnson valued the sphere of female friendship as much for her own emotional gratification as for its reassurance of social status. Here the letter allows Johnson to retain and promote genteel relations.

When Susan Johnson's letters focus on domestic details, she asserts her authority within the home. Clearly, she managed quite adeptly in her husband's absence, as on March 22, 1799, when she reported: "Major Dagget has paid me $114. on Milton's account $80 of which I have let Whitman have & taken his receipt for it and kept 34 for my own use— you did not give me any order to send money to your Father as you mentioned I shall therefore not send it untill I get his or your orders." "Milton's account" probably refers to Samuel Johnson's lumber mill in North Carolina, which would indicate her involvement in family business. On June 4, 1799, she wrote this note:

> A few days since, I had a letter from your good father with the note for the Bank, which I got Pappa to indorse & have given to Judson—he likewise sent Ives's deed; which I have left with Dagget, with the other papers as Ives is to pay all the money—I have received of Daniel Nettleton $190—& from Johnson $63—so that I am quite in Cash, & am notwithstanding economising very closely—A letter from Rhineland acknowledges the receipt of the money—& one from William Ogden that he has received the Certificate & say he expected a mortgage from you, as collateral security; & begs you to forward it as soon as may be; this letter was dated the 7th of May, but did not come untill some days after you went away.

Johnson thus demonstrates her financial aptitude and her accurate record keeping. On January 18, 1803, Johnson sent another financial summary: "I trust you will find my family economy conducted in such a way as to convince you I have not been unmindful of the exertions & sacrifices you are making." With careful wording, Johnson extends her compassion for her husband's hard work while justifying her management of the "family economy." In an earlier letter from New York on April 4, 1797, she includes these notes on their finances: "Mr. Euen accepted the order, & I shall now, have plenty of Money. I am very economical, but my <u>expenditures exceed</u> my expectations—a white Lutestring gown, a muslin gown, a black bevor hat; with a gold band, a fashionable bonnet, are very costly things." Having acknowledged exceeding her budget, Johnson does not apologize for her need to dress according to their social position—thus a lutestring gown made of flossy fabric, 10–20 shillings, and a gold-banded beaver hat, 8–20 dollars.

To explore yet another angle, whereas the traveler observes a town and its community in passing, the letter writer from home brings detail to a familiar scene enlivened by the occasional celebration or unusual event. In this capacity, the letter served as local gazette, with news and neighborhood gossip. Susan Johnson, for example, recounted a quarrel between Abigail Brooks and E. Hawes on February 13, 1803: "B[rooks] struck H[awes] with an ax in the head which has such a serius effect that H—s life is dispared of." Johnson then followed up on March 13, 1803: "A. Brooks will not be <u>hung</u> as many people hoped." Johnson also reported on engagements and flirtations on November 22, 1799: "I must tell you something of Polly Ogden—she has had an offer from a <u>Widower</u>, 4th— with eight children, his wife has not been dead quite five months—it is no less a person, than Jonathan Mia. I assure you it affords us small degree of mirth—as it has circulated all over New Haven that she had accepted the offer. He sent three <u>envoys</u> before he wou'd be satisfied with her denial which she gave to each, in the most preemptory manner. Our Neighbour Mrs. Pessit gave her <u>heart</u> & hand to Mr. Leffingwell, last Saturday <u>night</u> & left us on Monday." Interesting distinctions are implied, with Polly Ogden's possible marriage discussed in terms of status and Mrs. Pessit's engagement portrayed as the more emotional attachment. Sad news is included as well: "You will sincerely Lament with his many friends when I tell you of the death of Mr. Gillian Verplank. President of the New York Bank—he died of a fit on Wednesday last, very suddenly— These melancholy events cannot but leave an impression upon my spirits—that God wou'd preserve you from <u>every</u> evil is my constant prayer, & let me have the certainty of knowing that you pay the greatest attention to your health & that you are happy in pursuing your duty—& rest assured that my exertions to preserve honorable spirits are not fruitless." Verplank's death reminded Johnson of her own husband's absence, and so the tone of her letter turns somber. As Johnson passes along daily affairs, she preserves continuity with her recipients while marking key moments in her New Haven life. One is reminded here of Samuel Sewall's extensive, fifty-six-year diary, kept from 1674 to 1729. Including details on family, politics, religion, social events, weather, and trade in the diary, Sewall monitors colonial Boston behaviors and provides an eyewitness perspective. Susan Johnson's newsy letters, in particular, serve a similar purpose, and women's letters, in general, show their intense involvement in domestic and civic affairs.

Johnson's letters also exemplify "multiple associations," which Sharon M. Harris notes are characteristic of women's letters, without losing their coherence. For as previously noted, such letters depend on a shared history with their readers that makes such jumps in topic understandable. Johnson could thus relay concerns for her husband's safety, provide an update on her health, and discuss meal preparation in the same letter, as on February 11, 1798: "My dear Johnson, I was truly happy to hear of your safe arrival in New York, notwithstanding the severity of the season—I assure you I had many anxieties for your safety—My own health I find daily mending; but unfortunately I caught a little cold yesterday, but it was lucky for me, it settled in my <u>limbs</u> & has only made me a little <u>lame</u>; I was obliged to go frequently to the kitchen, to attend to the Sausage making, and putting up the pork—& as I have not been much used to the cold, this winter, I cou'd not but <u>imbibe</u> a little of it." In another letter, written from New York on April 4, 1797, she combines health issues with a report of her social activities: "My own health is better than it has been for some time—except the pain in my head, which still torments me—as soon as you come down I shall get you to ask Dr. Clarke, to bleed me,—When I last wrote you I felt myself so ill, that I was scarcely able to sit up, it was from the fatague of my journey." This litany of complaints is immediately followed by this report: "Tomorrow we dine with your father—several of Catherine's acquaintance have visited me—& I really find a great deal of business upon my hands—& that the <u>money goes very</u> fast[.] I have not yet chosen my Carpet I wait for you to assist me. Yesterday we dined at Mrs. Verplancks, & in the evening went to the play, where I was well entertained." Susan Johnson thus describes the compromises inherent in marriage and other relationships, particularly those compounded by long distance. Here, she balances the practical with the pleasant, deferring a purchase until her husband's return and reporting on an enjoyable evening. Johnson's letters are characteristically detailed and distinctly conversational. With Samuel William Johnson frequently away from home, Susan Johnson's long, chatty letters reflect the style of linked associations. On, June 4, 1799, for example, she addressed domestic and political issues: "I promised to write my letters journalwise if I was to give you an account of one day, it woud be of each, I have passed since you left me, you know I rise about six, eat the lime, & go to bed again, sometimes enliven'd by a little scholding or schooling, but never <u>interrupted</u> by the entrance of a friend. . . . Our dear little ones are very hearty, Betsy has a troublesome turn with her teeth, but hope it is almost over now. You beg'd me to write you polatics, I do not find anything in the papers of any consequences they generally speak of France discovering a more pasific disposition towards this Country." Acknowledging the blending of letter and journal, Johnson makes certain to include the many dimensions of family life while maintaining her personal connections with her husband.

While Susan Johnson's correspondence marks her life in predictable rhythms and cycles, her "Journal of a Trip" presents a more adventurous side. In each form, Johnson remains strong-minded and forthright and maintains her pose as a social superior. In general, Johnson writes much more optimistically while traveling or when reporting on a visit to friends and family, and health complaints are minimal, confined mostly to the fatigues of travel itself. For example, on December 23, 1801, during her six-month journey from Stratford to Fayetteville, Johnson recorded: "[T]his day it rained in the morning, so that we did not set out untill ten oclock; & travel'd but 32 miles—to Fishers 22 miles to Fayetteville—24th arose at six this morning, & breakfasted and set out just at day light & arrived here (Fayette-ville) at one oclock, was received very politely by Mr & Mrs Mallette—I found myself very much fateagued with so long a journey; and was obliged to go to bed after dinner from which I did not arise untill the next morning—25th Christmas day a delightful day; took a walk after breakfast to see the town" (37–38). Unlike the malaise expressed in the April 1796 letter, in which she confesses having "little peace of mind," the exhaustion here is primarily physical.

Johnson did not dwell on her fatigue but rebounded the next day for yet another visit.

Throughout her travels, Johnson maintained her identity as a genteel northerner and, in keeping with the traveler's comparative mode, often criticized her surroundings. In a letter on March 12, 1802, from New Bern, North Carolina, for example, she wrote to Samuel Johnson with this mixed review: "much pleased with the appearance without & within" of a "house kept by one Davis. . . . [B]ut what was our horror, when we were shown our bed and our dirty sheets, & they had no others, mine were left! & we had no alternative but to make use of our cloaks, for this situation, & were terrably bitten with bed bugs untill light." On the journey outbound in November, Johnson had alleviated this problem by producing her own pair of sheets when she and her husband stayed at "an ill looking house kept by Macky" and "requested to have clean sheets; which I presume, they had not but having a pair with me I was independent of her frowns." She had no such luck this time, though, and the dreaded dirty sheets remained a plague for all genteel travelers. Johnson also included this interesting comment: "I fear all the money you are going to make will scarcely be a compensation for the sacrifices of domestic life." Even on the road, she continued to address domestic and familial concerns. On December 2, 1801, Johnson wrote to her husband, who was in Fayetteville working on the mill while she remained in New Bern with the Devereux, with concerns about the financial soundness of the mill venture: "I am anxious to hear in what state you have found your affairs, on Black river; I hope prosperous—I want to join you, & witness your great schemes." Her support was equivocal, for she wished him success so that he might finally return home. She adds, "We have matters in train for obtaining a black boy," but as she mentions in the travel diary, she and her husband did not "obtain" anyone. The letter does not elaborate; instead, she moves from one topic to the other as if writing a newsletter from home.

In the March 12, 1802, letter, Johnson relates a dream in which she was helping her husband in his log cabin at Milton and woke up tired, perhaps reflecting her impatience with his logging endeavors. Her own travels and time spent away from home may have contributed to her reservations about this venture, for three weeks later, on March 20, 1802, she wrote: "You certainly know that the acquisition of property will be no gratification to me if you are obliged to make so great sacrifices, on the contrary a source of the keenest misery." When she was home, her concerns centered on keeping the household and supporting his enterprise, but now that she too had experienced the inconveniences of travel and a lengthy separation from her children, she cast her husband's time away from home, and his business, in doubt. As Johnson was less prone to self-analysis while traveling, she reported instead on various entertainments and occasional sightseeing. In her December 6, 1801 letter from New Bern, she mentions her great interest in a popular novel, as previously discussed in her journal: "We ride walk & read novels; last night we sat up until near one oclock & were then quite unwilling to leave the interesting history of the beggar Girl." Similarly, she makes this entry in her travel diary for December 2, 1801: [D]ress't myself & paid all my visit—the remainder of the week; passed our time principally in reading the beggar Girl; we got so much interested, that we sat up untill near one oclock, (reading) saturday night." The repetitions in both letter and journal suggest the novel's importance. Although travel provided Johnson a chance to break from domestic routines, she maintained some semblance of a schedule, which included walking, socializing, and reading. This frame of reference persisted in both letter and journal. By contrast to westward travelers, such as Sarah Beavis and Elizabeth House Trist, Johnson had the leisure for genteel activities and consequently asserted herself as a "cultural guide." It is hard to say whether Johnson felt burdened by this role, but she played it so emphatically that one might suspect some anxiety in her position as a northerner and an outsider.

While on the road, Johnson also maintained connections with the women in her epistolary community, writing to Faith Wadsworth from Wilmington, for example, on January 26, 1802: "As we all travel for improvement, I flatter myself you will confess that all my labour is not lost by answering your letter so promptly, (which came in hand the 22nd) you will be convinced I have improved, in one respect, if no other; whether it is self-love, or a more generous sentiment, that activates me, in writing you so soon, I shall not attempt to define." Johnson offers this apology for writing a letter while traveling and draws on assumptions that one travels for self-improvement, a distinctly leisured point of view.

Johnson's letter turns all travelogue as she recounts her journey from New Bern: "then went to Fayetteville where I was a fortnight then came here, where I have been three weeks." No further descriptions enhance these explanations other than a note on the mild weather that seemed more like "a fine June day than mid Winter." She then focuses on more pressing matters—her social calendar and her many invitations and amusements—and concludes with a comparison between New Bern and New Haven society: "[T]he more I see the more I am convinced that our mode of living in Connecticut is far preferable to what I have seen here. They appear to live at a great expense without comfort or convenience, & in general there is a great want of neatness." The last remark is most telling with regard to her genteel sensibilities. On March 25, 1802, Johnson expressed her homesickness to Faith: "[M]y impatience to get home is so great, as to almost deprive me of the enjoyments within my reach." The appeal of travel apparently had its limits. Johnson's letters give full expression to doubts and complaints that her travel diary only touches on. Given that the travel diary was intended for a larger audience, such ruminations may not have been appropriate. For Susan Edwards Johnson, the letter as journal documented daily life, allowing her to maintain domestic order and conjugal harmony. In travel narratives and letters, Trist and Johnson mark moments both contemplative and dramatic. From the road and from home, they capture experiences from various points of view, in voices both direct and unassuming, a blend that can occur only when an author presumes to be marginalized and yet is actually documenting experiences in an authentic, viable manner.

—⌒

To study women's letters alongside their travel journals expands our sample of women's writings and exemplifies their participation in the cultural construction of early America; they documented their lives in a uniquely personal manner even when all was in flux. The letter provides a chance to create a "set piece" to frame the experience of travel and to reflect on its significance relative to home. The journal records daily movements and events, with less attention devoted to philosophical musings. In each instance, women demonstrate a keen sense of marking experience within a specific frame of reference, directing their accounts to a particular audience. Eliza Lucas Pinckney, Susan Edwards Johnson, and Elizabeth House Trist all address personal, familial, and social concerns, focusing alternately on the immediate moment and the larger context. In the travel diary, coherence and style are sometimes sacrificed for information and expedience, and in letters a particular moment sometimes eclipses the larger context. Occasionally, these intentions merge, and the letter tells of adventures and the travel diary waxes philosophical. Adapting different styles for different media, these women offer compelling visions. At times, their letters resemble a diary, which in Suzanne Bunkers's explanation is a safe, private space, while also demonstrating David S. Shields's assessment of the letter's versatility in addressing audiences public and private. In each form, early American women offer their experiences as fragments and as cohesive narratives, with the travel diary at a slight disadvantage as the ultimate work in progress. Women may not have been invited formally to share the arena of social and literary discourse with men, but as their letters and diaries attest, they were obviously participating—quite energetically in fact—in these discussions. In doing so, women significantly contributed to the cultural construction of early America and the New Republic.

Conclusion

Women's travel narratives express genuine engagement in westward settlement and the cultural development of early America. From the woman's travel narrative, we understand early American life as a constant exchange of information that required adaptation and innovation. Travel appears exciting and frustrating on levels both simple and grand; startling vistas, rugged mountains, crude accommodations, and stunning beauty are all depicted. The woman's voice articulates relocation and travel as events with profound psychological and social implications. Travel was adventurous, no doubt, but also a serious matter that the woman's travel narrative accurately and astutely documents. Expressing both delight and discomfort, these narratives leave a record of individual experience and personal reaction unique to the woman traveler. For even though women had been instructed to conduct themselves as compliant and dutiful, their narratives belie such directives. Whereas the larger cultural message was to remain close to home, women were in fact traversing the roads, crossing the mountain ranges, and exploring the great falls of early America and the New Republic. They were mobile, curious, and opinionated. With some irony, they admired the heroines of popular novels, all the while embarking on far more interesting adventures and authoring their own texts. For an appreciation of the woman's active role in shaping cultural taste and transferring social mores, the woman's travel narrative is simply a key source.

In marking confrontations with the new and the unknown, women's travel narratives teach us about the women and the frontier in refreshing ways. Neither was static; each was a complex, constantly changing phenomenon of early America. Not only do women's narratives provide interesting travel stories, but their attention to detail brings early American life into sharper focus and illustrates underlying political and social currents. Unlike today's travelers, who have access to a visual image of a destination to prepare them for adjustment or acclimation, these women journeyed forth with partial, often unreliable, information about what lay ahead. The experience of travel, past and present, refines preconceptions by providing a more realistic understanding of a given locale. For many women, the journey westward presented an increasingly altered social landscape that proved invigorating and challenging. As we discover how they traveled, what they observed, and what they experienced, we also learn how roles defined by gender and class influenced social interactions.

The women's candor, in turn, marks an intriguing moment of contact between genteel expectations and rustic conditions that challenged notions of an egalitarian society while documenting an evolving class structure in early America and the New Republic. At times emboldened, at other times burdened, by this role of cultural emissary, women modeled genteel behaviors as they engaged in cultural commerce. The anxiety and discomfort that arose when genteel met rustic speak to the clash between a democratic future and an autocratic past. Clinging to the familiar may be natural, but to insist on antiquated, irrelevant models signals insecurity. The woman's travel narrative marks these tensions and the energy they generated.

Why did women keep journals? Perhaps the woman writer wanted to record what would be her only significant journey. Or perhaps, participating in a later fashion, she wanted to record her journey over the Alleghenies and her crossing of the Ohio. However, fashion alone never overwhelmed these women. They complained, but as they settled into the rhythms of travel and survived the pains of leaving loved ones behind, many of these women expressed enthusiasm for exploration itself, for the break in routines, and for the chance to be the authors of their own narratives. Travel elicited variable and enriching observations. That travel was a unique opportunity did not escape these women, and their letters and travel diaries mark a clear commitment to succeed. The frustrations were manifold, their hardships hardly fully anticipated, and yet there was a definite conviction that their struggles were valid. Elizabeth House Trist shows us Pittsburgh as a fledgling town, Lydia B. Bacon marvels at the Niagara Falls, and Margaret Van Horn Dwight offers warnings about uneven roads and rowdy travelers. Travel north and south along the eastern seaboard codified social class and identified regional differences. Eliza Bridgham delights in the diverse visitors to Saratoga Springs, Susan Edwards Johnson reports on poverty in the south, and Sarah Kemble Knight documents accommodations along the Boston Post Road. Travel west suggested new social structures and the beginnings of a far different class structure. The story of expansion may be told with a certain thematic intention, and yet the organic unfolding of the tale leaves these reports largely unfettered. This unassuming quality is their strength. Their vulnerability exists in the attitudes and assumptions that the women brought with them about social class and gender roles. Thus, Dwight complains of rude behaviors, Beavis of the lack of food, and Trist of unpleasant sleeping conditions. As their genteel expectations and presumptions were so challenged by rustic conditions, many of these women reacted with frustration. Amidst their complaints and their discomfort, though, they left a valuable record of early American life. They show us what it was like to travel and how very different this country was becoming. Ultimately, the journey westward proved invigorating and challenging, as women describe the quality of their accommodations, the potential for community, and the opportunity for sociability. As these accounts verify, travel inevitably evokes mixed emotional responses. New landscapes are constantly compared to familiar ones left behind, while the prospect of a new home inspires the imagination. Out of the discomfort of separation come curiosity and even enthusiasm. These tensions are all too evident in the women's travel narratives of early America, which provide a history of settlement unlike any of the official reports or histories.

Travel inevitably invites commentary, for the traveler is constantly measuring the present locale against former ones and often anticipating the future. This mobility elicits questions of identity: Just who is this person traveling and how, if at all, will he or she be affected by the new environs? Given the essential flux of travel, the records are unique and fascinating for the moment of time they capture and for the cultural readings they produce. From these accounts, it is clear that early American women viewed their surroundings differently than men. With an eye for sociability and productivity, they were invested in perpetuating genteel social codes and interested in social integration; they were generally less concerned with wholesale alteration of their new locations. Instead they carried a different mission; charged by their milieu to model cultural values, women negotiated between expectations and realities, which often manifested in judgmental pronouncements. Women attempted to model virtuous behaviors, while they risked alienating the locals with their criticisms, an interesting tension. The woman's travel narrative reveals significant gaps between how women were expected to act and how they chose to act given the sense of movement and change indelibly connected to travel. In these tense moments, we learn how women actually experienced their journeys and faced their uncertainties, as they candidly express their disappointments and their pleasures, thus laying aside the genteel mask for the more unscripted response. Women's travel narratives are also geared to be instructional and entertaining. The desire to frame the travel experience as a presentation, however, is often overwhelmed by the circumstances of travel itself, which results in a less polished, though dynamic, record of the moment.

Ultimately, these texts show us what women were doing and what they were thinking in ways that complement and even contradict the historical record. For though women were largely absorbed in domestic activities, family, community, home, they were also active in the business of nation building. As these accounts attest, women were astute observers passionately connected to their world as consumers and shapers of culture. Women's travel narratives, moreover, complement other early American women's writings, such as poetry, letters, plays, and novels. And yet, they remain an understudied genre. One aim of this book is to offer these accounts of early American life in a prerailroad, prephotographic age to a larger audience. Before one could traverse the country with relative speed, these women followed the routes and roads of early America at a moderate pace of five to six miles per hour, which allowed for careful observation, as illustrated in their detailed records. Prior to the portable camera, their word sketches recreated images and encounters with an accuracy mindful of those left behind. Women's travel narratives thus significantly contribute to our cultural history, as they tell us about the actual experience of moving through and interacting in a diverse, mobile society. From these accounts, we can better understand and imagine the material and social worlds of early America and the New Republic.

NOTES

Introduction

1. The Susan Edwards Johnson, Sarah Beavis, and Lucy Newton narratives appear here for the first time in print and are used by permission. In addition, selected letters from Susan Edwards Johnson are also printed here for the first time and used by permission. Please see individual citations below.

Susan Edwards Johnson's letters have been transcribed from manuscript on microfilm from the Connecticut Historical Society. Her travel narrative, "Journal of a Trip from Stratford, Connecticut to Fayetteville, North Carolina (1801–1802)," in a typescript transcription by Max Farrand, is located at the Huntington Library, San Marino, California, Ms. FAR, box 20 (10). The manuscript is housed at the Connecticut Historical Society, Hartford, Susan Edwards Johnson Papers, 1792–1851, 2 boxes. The letters and the journal are used here by permission of the Connecticut Historical Society. The Sarah Beavis journal has been transcribed from the 1783 manuscript "Sarah Beavis: Her Pamphlet," Edward E. Ayer Manuscript Collection, Ayer MS 691, Newberry Library, Chicago, and is used here by permission. The Lucy Newton narrative, "Memorandum, December 1817, of a Trip from Union, Ohio, to Mechanicksburg, Ohio, and to Anderson Township," has been transcribed from manuscript from the Ohio Historical Society, Columbus, VFM 1010, and is used here by permission of the Ohio Historical Society.

2. Sarah Kemble Knight was born on April 19, 1666, the first daughter of Boston merchant Thomas Kemble and his wife, Elizabeth Terice Kemble. In 1689, at the age of twenty-three, Sarah Kemble married Richard Knight, "a shipmaster and London agent for an American company," according to Wendy Martin, who provides biographical details in her introduction to *The Journal of Madam Knight* (1704), in *Colonial American Travel Narratives*, edited by Wendy Martin (New York: Penguin, 1994), 51–52. Their only child, Elizabeth, was born in Boston on May 8, 1689. During her husband's frequent absences from home, Sarah Knight successfully managed both domestic and business affairs, taught handwriting, copied legal manuscripts, and kept a shop on Moon Street in Boston. Richard Knight died in 1706, and Sarah Knight never remarried. When her daughter married in 1712, Knight moved to New London, Connecticut, where she "kept

a shop and an inn, pursued farming and Indian trading." Sarah Kemble Knight died in 1727, leaving "a sizeable estate of eighteen hundred pounds."

3. Elizabeth House, the first child of Samuel and Mary House, was born in Philadelphia at the end of 1751. Samuel House was a merchant, and Mary House ran a popular boardinghouse, located on the corner of Fifth and Market streets in downtown Philadelphia. Elizabeth House met Nicholas Trist, a young British officer from Devonshire, England, who had been stationed in the colonies. They married in 1774. Shortly after the birth of their child, Hore Browse Trist Jr., in 1775, Nicholas Trist set off on the first of many journeys down the Mississippi River to find a settlement near Natchez where the new family could establish a home. Trist died on December 9, 1828. See Annette Kolodny, introduction to *The Travel Diary of Elizabeth House Trist: Philadelphia to Natchez, 1783–84,* in *Journeys in New Worlds: Early American Women's Narratives,* edited by William L. Andrews (Madison: University of Wisconsin Press, 1990), 183–85.

4. According to Samuel P. Cochran, Mary Coburn Dewees (fl. 1780–89) "was the wife of Samuel Dewees. Her maiden name was Mary Coburn, and she was a sister of John Coburn, the first I believe, Federal Judge for the district of Kentucky." Publisher's note, Mary Coburn Dewees, *Journal of a Trip from Philadelphia to Lexington in Kentucky, 1787,* edited by R. E. Banta (Crawfordsville, IN: R. E. Banta, 1936). As a correction to the Banta edition, according to the handwritten journal, Dewees began her journey September 27, 1788; the journey ended February 11, 1789.

5. Susan Edwards Johnson (1771–1856) of New Haven, Connecticut, was connected to several prominent New England families. She was the daughter of Pierpoint Edwards (1750–1826) and Frances Ogden Edwards (1750–1800). Her paternal grandfather was Rev. Jonathan Edwards (1703–58), and her aunt, Mary Edwards Dwight (1732–58), was the grandmother of Margaret Van Horn Dwight. Susan Edwards Johnson's first cousins (all children of Mary Edwards Dwight) included Yale president Timothy Dwight, Dr. Maurice William Dwight (d. 1796), and their sister, Elizabeth Dwight Woolsey, who married William Walton Woolsey, the guardian of Margaret Van Horn Dwight after Mary Edwards Dwight's death in 1807. Another of Johnson's first cousins was Aaron Burr (1756–1836). Susan Edwards married Samuel William Johnson in 1791. Her father-in-law was William Samuel Johnson, a senator from Connecticut and a president of Columbia College of New York (now Columbia University). (This information was obtained with assistance from Susan Schoelwer of the Connecticut Historical Society, Hartford.)

6. Margaret Van Horn Dwight was born on December 29, 1790. Her father, Dr. Maurice William Dwight, was a brother of Timothy Dwight, president of Yale, and her mother was Margaret (DeWitt) Dwight. When her father died in 1796 and her mother remarried shortly thereafter, Margaret Dwight was taken to Northampton to live with her grandmother, Mary Edwards Dwight, a daughter of Jonathan Edwards. Upon her grandmother's death in 1807, Margaret went to New Haven to live with her aunt and uncle Elizabeth Dwight and William

Walton Woolsey. Margaret Dwight married William Bell Jr. on December 17, 1811, a year after she arrived in Warren, Ohio. Margaret Dwight Bell became mother of thirteen children and was known as a hospitable and active member of the community. She died on October 9, 1834. Biographical and family connections suggest possible literary links between the Margaret Van Horn Dwight, Sarah Kemble Knight, and Susan Edwards Johnson narratives, though such links are purely speculative. The three narratives share a humorous, sometimes satirical, critical vein when sketching the distinctions between social classes. Parallels in tone and content suggest that Johnson and Dwight may have known about Knight's journey, particularly since Theodore Dwight was the first to publish Sarah Knight's 1704 narrative, in 1825.

7. Lydia B. Bacon was born in Boston on May 13, 1786, oldest child of Levi and Mary Stetson, and died in Brookline, Massachusetts, in 1853. "Mrs. Lydia B. Bacon's Journal, 1811–12," edited by Mary M. Crawford, *Indiana Magazine of History* 40 (1944): 367–68.

8. Quotations from the Elizabeth House Trist narrative are taken from *The Travel Diary of Elizabeth House Trist: Philadelphia to Natchez, 1783–84*, edited by Annette Kolodny, in Andrews, *Journeys*, 201–32. The Trist manuscript is housed with the Papers of Trist, Randolph and Burke Families (#10487), Special Collections, University of Virginia Library.

9. Elizabeth Gilpin (1804–92) was a native Philadelphian from a prominent Quaker family of papermakers and printers. Quotations from the narrative are taken from Gilpin's "Journal from W[ilming]ton to Johnstown, New York and back again," 1830, The Historical Society of Delaware, Wilmington, Delaware, and used here by permission. The journal appears in print as "Elizabeth Gilpin's Journal of 1830," edited by Margorie McNinch, *Delaware History* 20 (1983): 223–55.

10. Quotations from Margaret Van Horn Dwight are taken from *A Journey to Ohio in 1810*, edited by Max Farrand (New Haven, CT: Yale University Press, 1912). The Dwight manuscript is housed with the Dwight Family Papers, box 5, folder 30, Manuscripts and Archives, Yale University Library.

11. As Margorie McNinch explains, "noted female educator Emma Willard established the New York Female Seminary in Troy, N.Y. in 1821"; see "Elizabeth Gilpin's Journal of 1830," *Delaware History* 20 (1983): 250.

Chapter 1: The Language of Travel

1. Quotations from Mary Bishop Cushman's diary are taken from "A Propper Yankee in Central New York: The Diary of Mary Bishop Cushman, 1795–1797," edited with introduction and afterword by Jamie O. Shafer, *New York History* 79 (July 1998): 255–312, and used here by permission of the *Quarterly Journal of the New York State Historical Association*.

2. Quotations from the Elizabeth Van Horne journal narrative are taken from *Journey to the Promised Land: Journal of Elizabeth Van Horne 1807*, edited by Elizabeth Collette, (Pittsburgh: Historical Society of Western Pennsylvania, 1939). According to Collette, Elizabeth Van Horne was born on December 14, 1776, in South Hampton, Bucks County, Pennsylvania. In 1808, she married Joshua Collette, "a lawyer of French Huguenot stock, five years her junior, who had come to Ohio from Virginia in 1802." They had six children, "only two of whom lived to maturity." Elizabeth Van Horne Collette died on February 19, 1846. Collette includes these notes on the text: "The journal itself is written in a remarkably clear and legible hand in the latter half of a small note-book, which has been sewed and re-sewed. It was returned to the writer by the Jersey friends for whom it was written. The first page and about one-third of the final page, which have been lost, are supplied from a copy made soon after the Civil War. The original text, with these brief additions, is here reproduced" (8). In addition, Collette notes, "The spelling and punctuation of the original and of the passages supplied by the copy, have been followed as closely as possible, but to facilitate reading, minor liberties have been taken with the form, principally in the way of paragraphing" (9n2).

3. Quotations from Eliza Williams Bridgham's diary are taken from the "Diary of a Journey through New England and New York 1818," housed at the Historical Society of Delaware, Wilmington, Misc. Mss 9001-B, box 11, and used here by permission. Bridgham's diary appears in print as "A Journey through New England and New York in 1818," in the *Magazine of History* 2 (1905): 14–27, 90–95.

4. Quotations from the Susan Johnson narrative are taken from her journal, which is untitled, but in *The Connecticut Historical Society Annual Report, 1914*, compiled by Max Farrand, it is listed under "Susan Johnson Papers," as "Journal of a journey from Stratford to Fayetteville, N.C., and other places 1801–1802." The manuscript is housed in the Susan Edwards Johnson Papers 1792–1851, 2 boxes, the Connecticut Historical Society Museum, Hartford, Connecticut and is used here by permission. A typescript of Johnson's journal edited by Max Farrand, entitled "Journal of a trip from Stratford, Connecticut to Fayetteville, North Carolina (1801–1802)," is housed at the Huntington Library, San Marino, California, Ms. FAR, box 20 (10).

5. Other accessible publications by foreign travelers include Frances Trollope's *Domestic Manners of the Americans* (1832) and the *Journal* by Frances Anne Butler (1835), better known as Fanny Kemble. Alexis de Tocqueville's *Journey to America*, based on his fourteen notebooks, was published in English for the first time in 1959.

6. Quotations are from "Mary Coburn Dewees Journal," University of Chicago Library Special Collections, Durrett Manuscripts, Ms. 58, and used by permission. A printed version appears as *Journal of a Trip from Philadelphia to Lexington in Kentucky* (1787), edited by R. E. Banta (Crawfordsville, IN: R. E. Banta, 1936).

7. Mary Mason Lyon (1797–1849) was born in Buckland, Massachusetts, on February 28, 1797. Lyon opened the Buckland Female School in 1824. From 1828 to 1834, she taught at the Ipswich Female Seminary. In 1837, Lyon founded Mount Holyoke Female Seminary in South Hadley, Massachusetts, where she remained principal until her death on March 5, 1849. *Mary Lyon through Her Letters*, edited by Marion Lansing (Boston: Books, 1937).

8. Quotations from the Sophia Maria Quincy Journal are taken from Maria Sophia Quincy, Journal, 3 August–5 September, 1829." Quincy family papers, 1639–1930. Massachusetts Historical Society, Boston, and used here by permission.

9. Harry Parker Ward's genealogy *The Follett-Dewey, Fassett-Safford Ancestry* (1896) contains this listing: "Elizabeth Dewey, born in Westfield, Massachusetts, July 12, 1743; died in Cambridge, Vermont about 1832. Married to Eliphalet Follett March 8, 1764. Eliphalet Follett was born in Windham, Connecticut, January 16, 1741, and died in the Wyoming Massacre July 3, 1778"; see, "A Few Pages from My Great Grandmother's Diary," transcribed by Jane Elizabeth Parker Ward, 1880, edited by Annette Persis Ward, 1931. Ohio Historical Society. PA Box 25, 1, iii.

10. Quotations from Elizabeth Dewey Follett are taken from "A Few Pages from My Great Grandmother's Diary," 1. See note 9 above.

Chapter 2: Ordinary Travel

1. Portions of this chapter have been adapted from Susan Clair Imbarrato, "Ordinary Travel: Tavern Life and Female Accommodation in Early America and the New Republic," *Women's Studies: An Interdisciplinary Journal* 28 (1998): 29–57. They are used here by permission. I thank *Women's Studies: An Interdisciplinary Journal* for permission to adapt these materials.

2. In addition to court records and newspapers, see Kym S. Rice, *Early American Taverns: For the Entertainment of Friends and Strangers* (Chicago: University of Chicago Press, 1983), 49–52.

3. Elizabeth Anthony Dexter cites the entries for Elizabeth Pike in Portsmouth and Mrs. Abigail Jarvice in Roxbury as having appeared in the *Boston Evening Post* on April 15, 1742, and April 8, 1751, respectively, but rechecking has shown that the notices appeared in the April 5, 1742, and April 15, 1751, issues, respectively. All other dates have been verified and appear in the *Boston Evening Post* as noted. See Elizabeth Anthony Dexter, *Colonial Women of Affairs: Women in Business and the Professions in America before 1776* (Boston: Houghton Mifflin, 1924), 12.

4. The French War, or King George's War (1744–48), was part of a larger series of territorial conflicts between France and England over land in Europe, Canada, and the western territories.

5. Quotations from Knight are taken from *The Journal of Madam Knight*, in *Colonial American Travel Narratives*, edited by Wendy Martin (New York: Penguin, 1994), 51–75. The Knight text is based on Theodore Dwight's 1825 edition of the handwritten

journal, "a faithful copy from a diary in the author's own hand-writing, compiled soon after her return home, as it appears, from notes recorded daily, while
on the road" (85). As Sargent Bush Jr. explains, the original manuscript has
been "inadvertently destroyed." See *Journeys in New Worlds: Early American Women's
Narratives*, edited by William L. Andrews (Madison: University of Wisconsin Press,
1990), 80.

6. Although Polly's identity is not made more explicit in the diary, Trist offers
a clue in a letter to Jefferson from "[o]n board the Ship Matilda, Balize Mississippi," written on May 4, 1785: "Poly [sic] joins me in affectionate love to Patsy
who I suppose by this time is quite a french woman." Boyd, 8:136. Polly has
thus accompanied Trist since December 1783 and had known Patsy before their
departure. Kolodny speculates that, as Trist's traveling companion, Polly may
have been a "younger relative or family friend"; see Kolodny, introduction, 198.

7. Quotations from Lucy Newton are transcribed from "Memorandum, December 1817, of a Trip from Union, Ohio, to Mechanicksburg, Ohio, and to Anderson Township," Ohio Historical Society, Columbus, VFM 1010, Lucy Newton
Papers, 1817 Dec., and are used here by permission.

Chapter 3: Writing into the Ohio Frontier

1. *Miss Leslie's Complete Cookery*, 1839 contains this recipe: "Cherry Bounce: Mix
together six pounds of ripe morellas and six pounds of large black heart cherries. Put them into a wooden bowl or tub, and with a pestle or mallet mash them
so as to crack all the stones. Mix with the cherries three pounds of loaf-sugar,
or of sugar candy broken up, and put them into a demijohn, or into a large
stone jar. Pour on two gallons of the best double rectified whiskey. Stop the ves-
sel closely, and let it stand three months, shaking it every day during the first
month. At the end of the three months you may strain the liquor and bottle it
off. It improves with age." See John Hull Brown, *Early American Beverages* (Rutland,
VT: Charles E. Tuttle, 1966), 54.

2. Quotations from the Sarah Beavis Journal have been transcribed from her
manuscript, "Sarah Beavis her pamphlet." (1783), housed with the Edward E.
Ayer Manuscript Collection, Ayer MS 691, Newberry Library, Chicago, and are
used here by permission.

3. The Johnsons' children included Ann Frances (1792–1839); William
Samuel Johnson (1794–95); William Samuel Johnson (1795–1883); Sarah Elizabeth Johnson (1797–1867); Edwards (1804–73); and Robert Charles (1807–66).
In 1791, Susan Edwards married Samuel William Johnson (1761–1846), a prominent lawyer who served as representative in the general assembly in seven sessions between 1790 and 1797. In 1815, he was elected an assistant, and he held
that office for three years. In 1807, he became the presiding judge of the Fairfield County Court. In 1811, he was elected judge of the probate court for Strat-

ford District, but he was superceded in this office due to the political revolution in 1818. "He was a gentleman of the old school, and was distinguished for the frankness and urbanity of his manners, as well as for the kindness and generosity of his feelings." See *Biographical Sketches of the Graduates of Yale College with Annals of the College History*, vol. 4, July 1778–June 1792 (New York: Holt, 1907), 118.

According to Max Farrand, Susan Edwards Johnson's father-in-law, William Samuel Johnson, was "rightly regarded as one of the most learned men of his time in this country. A lawyer of ability and reputation he became a member of the colonial legislature, he was a delegate to the Stamp Act Congress, and a special agent of Connecticut in London in 1766–71. He could not bring himself to take an active part against England and after the Declaration of Independence he withdrew from public life. He was one of the delegates from Connecticut at the convention that framed the Constitution of the United States, and he was elected the first United States senator from Connecticut." At the same time he was "elected president of the college over which his father has presided, and he resigned his United States senatorship that he might devote his time to the presidency of Columbia, which he did until his retirement in 1800." See Max Farrand, American Antiquarian Society, Worcester, Massachusetts, October 1913, "Papers of the Johnson Family of Connecticut," 238.

4. According to the journal's editor, Jamie O. Shafer, "Gimp was a flat braid or trimming or cord of silk, wool, or, linen." See "A Propper Yankee in Central New York," 269.

5. From editor Elizabeth Collette's note: "This and other bracketed portions following are taken from the above-mentioned copy of the journal, because a third of the last page of the original is missing." Elizabeth Van Horne, *Journey to the Promised Land: Journal of Elizabeth Van Horne 1807*, edited by Elizabeth (Van Horne) Collette, *Historical Society of Western Pennsylvania*, December 1939, notes 9, 22.

6. In fact, "James the Farmer," in letter 9 of his *Letters from an American Farmer*, provides a more impassioned response to his encounter with slavery: "I perceived a Negro, suspended in the cage and left there to expire! I shudder when I recollect that the birds had already picked out his eyes; his cheek-bones were bare; his arms had been attacked in several places; and his body seemed covered with a multitude of wounds. . . . I found myself suddenly arrested by the power of affright and terror; my nerves were convulsed; I trembled; I stood motionless, involuntarily contemplating the fate of this Negro in all its dismal latitude." James's impassioned, empathetic, graphic description may indeed be as much antislavery as antisouthern. See J. Hector St. John de Crèvecoeur, *Letters from an American Farmer*, 1782 (New York: Penguin, 1986), 178. Moreover, in Joseph Fichtelberg's extensive analysis of Crèvecoeur's *Letters*, he notes this particular moment as pivotal, in that "slavery reveals to [James] the irresistible drive toward accumulation, toward excess." See *Critical Fictions: Sentiment and the American Market, 1780–1870* (Athens: University of Georgia Press, 2003), 45–47. Although

Crèvecoeur's *Letters* stands outside of the travel narrative genre proper in its semi-historical, quasi-fictional mode, it serves here to dramatize the northern antislavery voice.

7. Mrs. Devereux is a friend and relative. Susan Edwards Johnson's aunt, Eunice Edwards (1743–1822), had married Thomas Pollock. His daughter, Frances Pollock, married John Devereux of New Bern, North Carolina, in 1793. Mrs. Frances Pollock Devereux is thus a distant cousin to Susan Johnson, later related by marriage when, in 1827, Susan Edwards Johnson's daughter Sarah Elizabeth Johnson (1797–1867) married George Pollock Devereux of North Carolina, son of Frances Pollock and John Devereux.

Chapter 4: Literary Crossroads

1. In *Letters for Literary Ladies* (1795), Maria Edgeworth (1767–1849) argues for the education of women. In addition to *Patronage* (1814), Edgeworth is known for her novels of Irish life: *Castle Rackrent* (1800), *Belinda* (1801), and *The Absentee* (1812).

2. Thomas Moore (1779–1852) wrote *Sacred Songs* (1816, 1824).

3. John Griscom (1774–1852), in *A Year in Europe* (1819), offers observations on European culture.

4. Sicherman elaborates: "One of the city's most prominent families, Hamiltons of three generations were distinguished by their literary interests. The oldest members of the third generation, seven women and one man all born between 1862 and 1873, belonged to three nuclear families. . . . Two of them attained international renown: Edith Hamilton as a popular interpreter of classical civilizations, her younger sister Alice Hamilton as a pioneer in industrial medicine and Harvard's first woman professor." See "Sense and Sensibility: A Case Study of Women's Reading in Later-Victorian America," in *Reading in America: Literature and Social History*, edited by Cathy N. Davidson (Baltimore: Johns Hopkins University Press, 1989), 203.

5. Eliza Lucas Pinckney (1722–93) was born on December 28, 1722, in the West Indies, to George and Anne Lucas. Her father served as lieutenant governor on the British island colony of Antigua. In 1738, her family moved to a plantation on Wappoo Creek, in South Carolina. Pinckney was also the mother of Thomas and Charles Cotesworth Pinckney, who became prominent political and diplomatic figures after the American Revolution. Eighteen-year-old Eliza Lucas was appointed manager of her father's six-hundred-acre plantation in South Carolina when Lt. Col. George Lucas was ordered to return to duty by the British Army.

6. Elizabeth Lamb Pinckney was born in London circa 1702 and moved to South Carolina upon marriage to Charles Pinckney (c. 1699–1758). She died January 23, 1744. Eliza Lucas married Charles Pinckney on May 27, 1744.

7. All quotations from Eliza Lucas Pinckney are taken from *The Letterbook of Eliza Lucas Pinckney*, 1739–1762, edited by Elise Pinckney (Chapel Hill: University of North Carolina Press, 1972). They are used here by permission. The Eliza Lucas Pinckney letters are housed in the South Carolina Historical Society, Charleston, Pinckney Family, Pinckney Family Papers, 1708–1878, 37/38.

8. This discussion of Elizabeth Ashbridge's *Some Account of the Fore Part of the Life of Elizabeth Ashbridge* appeared in a different form in Susan Clair Imbarrato, *Declarations of Independency in Eighteenth-Century American Autobiography*. Copyright © 1998 University of Tennessee Press. It is reproduced by permission. I thank the University of Tennessee Press for permission to adapt these materials.

9. All quotations from Ashbridge are from *Some Account of the Fore Part of the Life of Elizabeth Ashbridge*, edited with an introduction by Daniel B. Shea, in Andrews, *Journeys*, 117–80.

10. Virgil's *Eclogues*, or *Bucolics*, completed in 37 BC, idealize rural life in the manner of his Greek predecessor Theocritus.

Samuel Richardson (1689–1761), author of *Pamela; or, Virtue Rewarded* (1740); *Clarissa; or, The History of a Young Lady* (1747–48); and *In The History of Sir Charles Grandison* (1753–54).

Joseph Addison (1672–1719), English essayist, poet, and statesman, was a regular contributor to Richard Steele's publications, *The Tatler* (1709–11) and *The Spectator* (1711–12), which he also copublished.

Plutarch (46–c. 122), biographer and author whose works strongly influenced the evolution of the essay, the biography, and historical writing in Europe from the sixteenth to the nineteenth century.

Edward Young (1683–1765), English poet, dramatist, and critic; see note 12 below.

Thomas Parnell (1679–1718), Irish poet, essayist, and friend of Alexander Pope, who relied on Parnell's scholarship in his translation of the *Iliad*.

Francis Thompson (1859–1907), British poet. "The Hound of Heaven": "All which I took from thee I did but take, / Not for thy harms, / But just that thou might'st seek it in My arms" (lines 171–73).

11. I would like to thank Timothy Steele for his helpful and thorough explanation of "stichic" verse and other matters metrical regarding Knight's verse. Please see Timothy Steele, *All the Fun's in How You Say a Thing: An Explanation of Meter and Versification* (Athens: Ohio University Press, 1999).

12. In November 1759, the recently widowed Eliza Lucas Pinckney again turned to poetry as she shared her grief in a letter to a family friend, Mr. George Keate, and quoted Edward Young's *The Complaint; or, Night Thoughts* (1742–45), a blank-verse dramatic monologue of nearly 10,000 lines, divided into nine parts, or "Nights." Lucas Pinckney begins with a reminiscence over the "the happy hours when we used to read together entertaining letters in your own agreeable

manner from deferent parts of Europe to your friends at Riply, and made me then make, as I often do the melancholy applica[tion] of those lines in Dr. Young to my self, He says, speaking of Thoughts: 'I tremble at the blessings once so dear / And every pleasure pains me to the heart'" (130). Pinckney then quotes a long passage:

> Strays Wretched Rover! o're the pleasing past
> In quest of wretchedness perversely strays;
> And finds all desart now; and meets the Ghost
> Of my departed joys, a Numerous train!
> I rue the riches of my former fate;
> Sweet comfort's blasted clusters make me sigh.
> I tremble at the blessings once so dear
> And every pleasure pains me to the heart.
> (1:237–34)

For Pinckney, literature was not ornamental but provided her with a means for coping with loss.

13. Written by James Hogg (1770–1835), the verse-tales of *The Queen's Wake* (1813) assume various styles: martial, comic, horrible, and mystical.

14. *L'histoire de Gil Blas de Santillane* was written in French between 1715 and 1735 by Alain-René Lesage (1668–1747). Its picaresque adventures are set in Spain.

Chapter 5: Capturing Experience

1. Quotations from Susan Edwards Johnson's letters have been transcribed from manuscript copies on microfilm. The letters are part of the Susan Edwards Johnson papers 1792–1851, 2 boxes, housed at the Connecticut Historical Society Museum, Hartford, Connecticut and are used here by permission. There are 178 letters, including 56 to her husband, Samuel William Johnson, and 87 letters written to Mrs. Faith Wadsworth.

2. This discussion of the Elizabeth House Trist correspondence with Thomas Jefferson appears in a different form in Susan Clair Imbarrato, *Declarations of Independency in Eighteenth-Century American Autobiography*. Copyright © 1998 University of Tennessee Press. Reproduced by permission. I thank the University of Tennessee Press for permission to adapt these materials.

3. Quotations from Jefferson's correspondence, unless otherwise noted, are taken from Thomas Jefferson, *The Papers of Thomas Jefferson*, edited by Julian P. Boyd et al., 26 vols. to date (Princeton: Princeton University Press, 1950–).

4. As Annette Kolodny explains, Trist returned to Philadelphia and remained there until her mother's death, in 1793. When her son, Hore Browse Trist, pur-

chased Birdwood Plantation, located next to Monticello, in 1798, Trist moved to Virginia to stay with her son and his wife, Mary. Trist briefly relocated to New Orleans, where her son had been appointed by Jefferson as port collector for the lower Mississippi River. He died of yellow fever in 1804, and Elizabeth Trist returned to Virginia. From 1808 to 1823, Trist traveled from friend to friend as "a welcome if perpetual houseguest," until she settled as a permanent guest at Monticello in 1823. Jefferson and Trist celebrated the marriage of their grandchildren at Monticello, and they remained friends until Jefferson's death in 1826. Trist died on December 9, 1828. Kolodny, introduction, 196–97.

5. Gulian Verplanck (1751–99) was the youngest brother of Samuel Verplanck. After graduating from King's College (now Columbia University) in 1768, he went to Holland to acquire practical experience in mercantile and banking procedures by working at his uncle's firm, Daniel Crommelin and Sons. Returning to America, Gulian pursued a brief but successful career combining business and politics. In 1788 he was elected to the state assembly, serving twice as speaker. He became president of the Bank of New York and in 1792 helped found the Tontine Association, a precursor of the New York Stock Exchange. In 1784 he married Cornelia Johnston. They lived in New York with their seven children in the vicinity of Riverside Drive and 123rd Street.

According to Judith Ellen Johnson, of the Connecticut Historical Society, Hartford, Mrs. Faith Wadsworth is Faith Trumbull, oldest daughter of (second) Governor Jonathan and Eunice (Backus) Trumbull, and granddaughter of (first) Governor Jonathan and Faith (Robinson) Trumbull. Faith Trumbull was born February 1, 1769, in Lebanon, Connecticut, and was baptized May 7, 1769, in the First Congregational Church of Lebanon. In the same church, on June 26, 1794, she married Daniel Wadsworth, Esq., of Hartford. She died on October 19, 1846, in Hartford, and is buried with her husband and several children in that city's Old North Cemetery.

BIBLIOGRAPHY

Adams, Abigail. *Letters of Mrs. Adams, the Wife of John Adams.* 3rd ed., vol. 2. Edited by Charles Francis Adams. Boston: Little, Brown, 1841.

————. *New Letters of Abigail Adams: 1788–1801.* Edited by Stewart Mitchell. Boston: Houghton Mifflin, 1947.

Adams, Abigail, and John Adams. *The Adams Papers, Series II: Correspondence; Adams Family Correspondence.* 4 vols. Edited by L. H. Butterfield. Cambridge, MA: Harvard University Press, 1963.

————. *The Book of Abigail and John: Selected Letters of the Adams Family, 1762–1784.* Edited by L. H. Butterfield. Cambridge, MA: Harvard University Press, 1975.

Adams, Hannah. *A Memoir of Miss Hannah Adams, Written by Herself: With Additional Notices, by a Friend.* Boston: Gray and Bowen, 1832.

Adams, John. *The Adams Papers, Series I: Diaries; Diary and Autobiography of John Adams.* 4 vols. Edited by L. H. Butterfield. Cambridge, MA: Harvard University Press, 1961.

Aldridge, Alfred Owen. "Enlightenment and Awakening in Edwards and Franklin." In *Benjamin Franklin, Jonathan Edwards, and the Representation of American Culture,* edited by Barbara B. Oberg and Harry S. Stout, 27–41. New York: Oxford University Press, 1993.

Altman, Janet Gurkin. *Epistolarity: Approaches to Form.* Columbus: Ohio State University Press, 1982.

American Weekly Mercury, October 25, 1722.

Andrews, William L. Introduction to *Journeys in New Worlds: Early American Women's Narratives,* edited by William L. Andrews, 3–10. Madison: University of Wisconsin Press, 1990.

Appleby, Joyce. *Liberalism and Republicanism in the Historical Imagination.* Cambridge, MA: Harvard University Press, 1992.

Armstrong, Nancy. *Desire and Domestic Fiction: A Political History of the Novel.* New York: Oxford University Press, 1987.

Armstrong, Nancy, and Leonard Tennenhouse. *The Imaginary Puritan: Literature, Intellectual Labor, and the Origins of Personal Life.* Berkeley and Los Angeles: University of California Press, 1992.

Ashbridge, Elizabeth. *Some Account of the Fore Part of the Life of Elizabeth Ashbridge* (1755). Edited by Daniel B. Shea. In *Journeys in New Worlds: Early American Women's Narratives,* edited by William L. Andrews, 117–80. Madison: University of Wisconsin Press, 1990.

Ayer, Sarah Newman (Connell). *Diary of Sarah Connell Ayer: Andover and Newburyport, Massachusetts; Concord and Bow, New Hampshire; Portland and Eastport, Maine.* Portland, ME: Lefavor-Tower, 1910.

Backscheider, Paula R. "The Novel's Gendered Space." In *Revising Women: Eighteenth-Century "Women's Fiction" and Social Engagement*, edited by Paula R Backscheider, 1–30. Baltimore: Johns Hopkins University Press, 2000.

Bacon, Lydia B. "Mrs. Lydia B. Bacon's Journal, 1811–12." Edited by Mary M. Crawford. *Indiana Magazine of History* 40 (1944): 367–86; 41 (1945): 59–79.

Balkun, Mary McAleer. "Sarah Kemble Knight and the Construction of the American Self." *Women's Studies: An Interdisciplinary Journal* 28 (1998): 7–27.

Banta, R. E. Publisher's Note to *Journal of a Trip from Philadelphia to Lexington in Kentucky* (1787), by Mary Cobern Dewees. Edited by R. E. Banta. Crawfordsville, IN: R. E. Banta, 1936.

Barnes, Elizabeth. *States of Sympathy: Seduction and Democracy in the American Novel.* New York: Columbia University Press, 1997.

Bartram, William. *Travels through North and South Carolina, Georgia, East and West Florida, the Cherokee Country, the Extensive Territories of the Muscogulges or Creek Confederacy, and the Country of the Chactaws* (1791). In *William Bartram: Travels and Other Writings*, 3–425. New York: Library of Congress, 1996.

Baym, Nina. "Between Enlightenment and Victorian: Toward a Narrative of American Women Writers Writing History." *Critical Inquiry* 18, no. 3 (1991): 22–41.

Beasley, Faith E. "The Voices of Shadows: Lafayette's *Zaïde*." In *Going Public: Women and Publishing in Early Modern France*, edited by Elizabeth C. Goldsmith and Dena Goodman, 146–60. Ithaca, NY: Cornell University Press, 1995.

Beavis, Sarah. "Sarah Beavis: Her Pamphlet" (1783). Edward E. Ayer Manuscript Collection, Ayer MS 691, Newberry Library, Chicago.

Beebee, Thomas O. *Epistolary Fiction in Europe, 1500–1850.* New York: Cambridge University Press, 1999.

Bennett, Mrs. *The Beggar Girl and Her Benefactors in Three Volumes.* 1797. Reprint, Philadelphia: printed for John Conrad and Company by William W. Woodward, 1801.

Berry, Brain J. L. *America's Utopian Experiments: Communal Havens from Long-Wave Crises.* Dartmouth, NH: University Press of New England, 1992.

Blecki, Catherine La Courreye. "Introduction: Reading Moore's Book: Manuscripts vs. Print Culture, and the Development of Early American Literature." In *Milcah Martha Moore's Book: A Commonplace Book from Revolutionary America*, edited by Catherine La Courreye Blecki and Karin A. Wulf, 59–106. University Park: Pennsylvania State University Press, 1997.

Blecki, Catherine La Courreye, and Karin A. Wulf, eds. *Milcah Martha Moore's Book: A Commonplace Book from Revolutionary America.* University Park: Pennsylvania State University Press, 1997.

Bodenheimer, Rosemarie. *The Real Life of Mary Ann Evans: George Eliot, Her Letters and Fiction.* Ithaca: Cornell University Press, 1994.

Bohls, Elizabeth A. *Women Travel Writers and the Language of Aesthetics, 1716–1818.* New York: Cambridge University Press, 1995.

Booth, Stephane Elise. *Buckeye Women: The History of Ohio's Daughters.* Athens, OH: Ohio University Press, 2001.

Boston Evening Post, April 8–22, 1751.

Brereton, Virginia Lieson. *From Sin to Salvation: Stories of Women's Conversions, 1800 to the Present.* Bloomington: Indiana University Press, 1991.

Bridenbaugh, Carl. *Cities in the Wilderness: The First Century of Urban Life in America.* New York: Ronald, 1938.

Bridgham, Eliza Williams. "Diary of a Journey through New England and New York 1818," The Historical Society of Delaware, Misc. Mss, 9001-B Box 11.

———. "A Journey through New England and New York in 1818." *Magazine of History with Notes and Queries* 2 (1905): 14–27, 90–95.

Brown, Dona. *Inventing New England: Regional Tourism in the Nineteenth Century.* Washington DC: Smithsonian Institution Press, 1995.

Brown, John Hull. *Early American Beverages.* Rutland, VT: Charles E. Tuttle, 1966.

Brown, Richard D. *Knowledge Is Power: The Diffusion of Information in Early America, 1700–1865.* New York: Oxford University Press, 1989.

Bunkers, Suzanne. "Reading and Interpreting Unpublished Diaries by Nineteenth-Century Women." *a/b: Auto-Biography Studies* 2, no. 2 (1986): 15–17.

Burke, Edmund. *A Philosophical Inquiry into the Origin of Our Ideas of the Sublime and Beautiful* (1757). 1812. Reprint, Charlottesville, VA: Ibis Publishing, n.d.

Burnaby, Andrew. *Travels through the Middle Settlements in North America: In the Years 1759 and 1760 with Observations upon the State of the Colonies.* 1798. Reprint, New York: Sentry, 1970.

Burr, Esther Edwards. *The Journal of Esther Edwards Burr, 1754–1757.* New Haven, CT: Yale University Press, 1984.

Burstein, Andrew. *The Inner Jefferson: Portrait of a Grieving Optimist.* Charlottesville: University Press of Virginia, 1995.

———. *Sentimental Democracy: The Evolution of America's Romantic Self-Image.* New York: Hill and Wang, 1999.

Bush, Sargent, Jr. Introduction to *The Journal of Madam Knight.* In *Journeys in New Worlds: Early American Women's Narratives,* edited by William L. Andrews, 69–83. Madison: University of Wisconsin Press, 1990.

Bushman, Richard L. "American High-Style and Vernacular Cultures." In *Colonial British American Essays in the New History of the Early Modern Era,* edited by Jack P. Greene and J. R. Pole, 345–83. Baltimore: Johns Hopkins University Press, 1984.

———. *The Refinement of America: Persons, Houses, Cities.* New York: Knopf, 1992.

Butler, Jon. *Becoming America: The Revolution before 1776.* Cambridge, MA: Harvard University Press, 2000.

Buzard, James. "The Grand Tour and After (1660–1840)." In *The Cambridge Companion to Travel Writing,* edited by Peter Hulme and Tim Youngs, 37–52. New York: Cambridge University Press, 2002.

Carson, Barbara G. "Early American Tourists and the Commercialization of Leisure." In *Of Consuming Interest: The Style of Life in the Eighteenth Century*, edited by Gary Carson, Ronald Hoffman, and Peter J. Albert, 373–405. Charlottesville: University of Virginia Press, 1994.

Castle, Terry. *Clarissa's Ciphers: Meaning and Disruption in Richardson's "Clarissa."* Ithaca, NY: Cornell University Press, 1982.

Chaplin, Joyce E. *An Anxious Pursuit: Agricultural Innovation and Modernity in the Lower South, 1730–1815.* Chapel Hill: University of North Carolina Press, 1993.

Chastellux, Marquis de. *Travels in North America in the Years 1780, 1781, and 1782.* 1788. Reprint, New York: Arno Press, 1968.

Cohen, Lester H., "Mercy Otis Warren: The Politics of Language and the Aesthetics of Self." *American Quarterly* 35 (1983): 481–98.

Collette, Elizabeth (Van Horne). Preface to *Journey to the Promised Land: Journal of Elizabeth Van Horne 1807*, by Elizabeth Van Horne, edited by Elizabeth Collette. Pittsburgh: Historical Society of Western Pennsylvania, December 1939.

Conroy, David W. *In Public Houses: Drink and the Revolution of Authority in Colonial Massachusetts.* Chapel Hill: University of North Carolina Press, 1995.

Cook, Elizabeth Heckendorn. *Epistolary Bodies: Gender and Genre in the Eighteenth-Century Republic of Letters.* Stanford: Stanford University Press, 1996.

Cott, Nancy F. *The Bonds of Womanhood: "Woman's Sphere" in New England, 1780–1835.* New Haven, CT: Yale University Press, 1977.

Crawford, Mary Caroline. *Little Pilgrimages among Old New England Inns: Being an Account of Little Journeys to Various Quaint Inns and Hostelries of Colonial New England.* 1907. Reprint, Detroit: Singing Tree Press, 1970.

Crawford, Mary M., ed. "Mrs. Lydia B. Bacon's Journal, 1811–12." *Indiana Magazine of History* 40 (1944): 367–86; 41 (1945): 59–79.

Crèvecoeur, J. Hector St. John de. *Letters from an American Farmer.* 1782. Reprint, New York: Penguin, 1986.

Culley, Margo, ed. *A Day at a Time: The Diary Literature of American Women from 1764 to the Present.* New York: Feminist Press, 1985.

Cuming, Fortescue. *Tour to the Western Country* (1807–1809). 1810. In *Early Western Travels 1748–1846*, edited by Reuben Gold Thwaites, 4:17–377. New York: AMS Press, 1966. Reprint of 1901 ed. of 1810 original, which was titled *Sketches of a Tour to the Western Country*.

Cushman, Mary Bishop. *The Diary of Mary Bishop Cushman, 1795–1797.* In "A Proper Yankee in Central New York: The Diary of Mary Bishop Cushman, 1795–1797," edited by Jamie O. Shafer. *New York History* 79 (July 1998): 255–312.

Danckaerts, Jasper. *Journal of Jasper Danckaerts, 1679–80.* Edited by Bartlett Burleigh James and J. Franklin Jameson. New York: Scribner's, 1913.

Davidson, Cathy N. Introduction to *Revolution and The Word: The Rise of the Novel in America.* Expanded ed. New York: Oxford University Press, 2004.

———. "Introduction: Toward a History of Books and Readers." In *Reading in America: Literature and Social History*, edited by Cathy N. Davidson, 1–26. Baltimore: Johns Hopkins University Press, 1989.

———. "The Life and Times of Charlotte Temple: The Biography of a Book." In *Reading in America: Literature and Social History*, edited by Cathy N. Davidson, 157–79. Baltimore: Johns Hopkins University Press, 1989.

———. *Revolution and The Word: The Rise of the Novel in America*. New York: Oxford University Press, 1986.

Davis, Richard Beale. *A Colonial Southern Bookshelf: Reading in the Eighteenth Century*. Athens: University of Georgia Press, 1979.

———. *Intellectual Life in the Colonial South, 1585–1763*. 3 vols. Knoxville: University of Tennessee Press, 1978.

Day, Robert Adams. *Told in Letters: Epistolary Fiction before Richardson*. Ann Arbor: University of Michigan Press, 1966.

Daybell, James. "Women's Letters and Letter Writing in England, 1540–1603: An Introduction to the Issues of Authorship and Construction." *Shakespeare Studies Annual* (1999): 161–86.

Decker, William Merrill. *Epistolary Practices: Letter Writing in America before Telecommunications*. Chapel Hill: University of North Carolina Press, 1998.

DeJean, Joan. *Ancients against Moderns: Culture Wars and the Making of a Fin de Siecle*. Chicago: University of Chicago Press, 1996.

———. "The (Literary) World at War, or What Can Happen When Women Go Public." In *Going Public: Women and Publishing in Early Modern France*, edited by Elizabeth C. Goldsmith and Dena Goodman, 116–28. Ithaca, NY: Cornell University Press, 1995.

Dewees, Mary Coburn. *Journal of a Trip from Philadelphia to Lexington in Kentucky* (1787). Edited by R. E. Banta. Crawfordsville, IN: R. E. Banta, 1936.

———. "Mary Coburn Dewees Journal." University of Chicago Library, Special Collections, Durrett Manuscripts, Ms. 58.

Dexter, Elizabeth Anthony. *Colonial Women of Affairs: Women in Business and the Professions in America before 1776*. Boston: Houghton Mifflin, 1924.

Dillon, Elizabeth Maddock. *The Gender of Freedom: Fictions of Liberalism and the Literary Public Sphere*. Stanford: Stanford University Press, 2004.

Dollarhide, William. *Map Guide to American Migration Routes*. Bountiful, UT: AGLL Genealogical Services, 1997.

Douglass, Frederick. *Narrative of the Life of Frederick Douglass, an American Slave*. 1845. Edited by William L. Andrews. New York: Norton, 1997.

Drake, Samuel Adams. *Old Boston Taverns and Tavern Clubs*. Boston: Butterfield, 1917.

Dwight, Margaret Van Horn. *A Journey to Ohio in 1810*. Edited by Max Farrand. New Haven, CT: Yale University Press, 1912.

Dwight, Theodore. *The Northern Traveller and Northern Tour, with the Routes to the Springs, Niagara, and Quebec, and the Coal Mines of Pennsylvania, also Tour of New England*. 4th ed. New York: Goodrich and Wiley, 1834.

Eagan, Jim. *Authorizing Experience: Refigurations of the Body Politic in Seventeenth-Century New England Writing*. Princeton, NJ: Princeton University Press, 1999.

Eagleton, Terry. *The Rape of Clarissa*. Minneapolis: University of Minneapolis Press, 1982.

Earle, Alice Morse. *Stage-Coach and Tavern Days.* 1900. New York: Blom, 1969.

Earle, Rebecca, ed. *Epistolary Selves: Letters and Letter-Writers, 1600–1945.* Aldershot, England: Ashgate, 1999.

Elliott, Emory, general ed. *The Columbia History of the American Novel.* New York: Columbia University Press, 1991.

Elliott, Emory. "New England Puritan Literature." In *The Cambridge History of American Literature: Volume I 1590–1820*, edited by Sacvan Bercovitch, 169–306. New York: Cambridge University Press, 1994.

———. *Revolutionary Writers: Literature and Authority in the New Republic, 1725–1810.* New York: Oxford University Press, 1982.

Evans, Sara M. *Born for Liberty: A History of Women in America.* New York: Free Press, 1989.

Farrand, Max. Introduction to *A Journey to Ohio in 1810*, by Margaret Van Horn Dwight, edited by Max Farrand. New Haven, CT: Yale University Press, 1912.

———. "Papers of the Johnson Family of Connecticut." *American Antiquarian Society*, October 1913, 237–46.

Favret, Mary A. *Romantic Correspondence: Women, Politics, and the Fictions of Letters.* New York: Cambridge University Press, 1993.

Ferguson, Robert A. "The American Enlightenment." In *The Cambridge History of American Literature: Volume I, 1590–1820*, edited by Sacvan Bercovitch, 345–537. New York: Cambridge University Press, 1994.

———. "'We Hold These Truths': Strategies of Control in the Literature of the Founders." In *Reconstructing American Literary History*, edited by Sacvan Bercovitch, 1–28. Cambridge: Harvard University Press, 1986.

Fichtelberg, Joseph. *Critical Fictions: Sentiment and the American Market, 1780–1870.* Athens: University of Georgia Press, 2003.

Field, Edward. *The Colonial Tavern: A Glimpse of New England Town Life in the Seventeenth and Eighteenth Centuries.* Providence, RI: Preston and Rounds, 1897.

Fish, Cheryl J. *Black and White Women's Travel Narratives: Antebellum Explorations.* Gainesville: University Press of Florida, 2004.

Fisher, Sydney Geo. *Men, Women and Manners in Colonial Times.* Vol. 1. 1897. Philadelphia: Lippincott, 1900.

Flaherty, David H. *Privacy in Colonial New England.* Charlottesville: University of Virginia Press, 1972.

Fliegelman, Jay. *Prodigal and Pilgrims: The American Revolution against Patriarchal Authority.* New York: Cambridge University Press, 1982.

Follett, Elizabeth Dewey. "A Few Pages from My Great Grandmother's Diary." Transcribed by Jane Elizabeth Parker Ward, 1880. Edited by Annette Persis Ward, 1931. Ohio Historical Society, Columbus, PA box 25, 1.

Forbes, Allan. *Taverns and Stagecoaches of New England: Anecdotes and Tales.* 2 vols. Boston: State Street Trust, 1953–54.

Foster, Emily. Introduction to *The Ohio Frontier: An Anthology of Early Writings*, edited by Emily Foster. Lexington: University of Kentucky Press, 1996.

Foster, Hannah Webster. "The Power of Sympathy" by William Hill Brown and "The Coquette" by Hannah Webster Foster, edited by Carla Mulford. New York: Penguin, 1996.

Foster, Shirley, and Sara Mills. Introduction to An Anthology of Women's Travel Writing, edited by Shirley Foster and Sara Mills. New York: Manchester University Press, 2002.

Franks, Abigail. The Lee Max Friedman Collection of American Jewish Colonial Correspondences: Letters of the Franks Family (1733–1748). Edited by Leo Hershkowitz and Isidore S. Meyer. Waltham, MA: American Jewish Historical Society, 1968.

Georgi-Findlay, Brigitte. The Frontiers of Women's Writing: Women's Narratives and the Rhetoric of Westward Expansion. Tucson: University of Arizona Press, 1996.

Gilmore, Michael T. The Middle Way: Puritanism and Ideology in American Romantic Fiction. New Brunswick, NJ: Rutgers University Press, 1977.

Gilpin, Elizabeth. "Elizabeth Gilpin's Journal of 1830." Edited by Margourie Mc-Ninch. Delaware History 20 (1938): 223–55.

———. "Journal from W[ilming]ton to Johnstown, New York and back again," 1830. The Historical Society of Delaware, Wilmington, Delaware.

Gilpin, Henry Dilworth. A Northern Tour: Being a guide to Saratoga, Lake George, Niagara, Canada, Boston, &c. &c. through the States of Pennsylvania, New-Jersey, New-York, Vermont, New-Hampshire, Massachusetts, Rhode-Island, and Connecticut; Embracing an Account of the Canals, Colleges, Public Institutions, Natural Curiosities, and Interesting Objects Therein. Philadelphia: H. C. Carey and I. Lea., 1825.

Gilpin, William. Three Essays: On Picturesque Beauty; On Picturesque Travel; and On Sketching Landscape: To Which Is Added a Poem, On Landscape Painting. 2nd ed. 1794. Westmead, England: Gregg, 1972.

Gilroy, Amanda. Introduction to Romantic Geographies: Discourses of Travel, 1775–1844, edited by Amanda Gilroy, 1–15. New York: Manchester University Press, 2000.

Gilroy, Amanda, and W. M. Verhoeven. Introduction to Epistolary Histories: Letters, Fiction, Culture, edited by Amanda Gilroy and W. M. Verhoeven, 1–25. Charlottesville: University Press of Virginia, 2000.

Godbeer, Richard. Sexual Revolution in Early America. Baltimore: Johns Hopkins University Press, 2002.

Goldsmith, Elizabeth C., ed. Writing the Female Voice: Essays on Epistolary Literature. Boston: Northeastern University Press, 1989.

Goldsmith, Elizabeth C., and Dena Goodman, eds. Going Public: Women and Publishing in Early Modern France. Ithaca, NY: Cornell University Press, 1995.

Gould, Philip. "The African Slave Trade and Abolitionism: Rereading Antislavery Literature, 1776–1800." In Periodical Literature in Eighteenth-Century America, edited by Mark L. Kamrath and Sharon M. Harris, 201–19. Knoxville: University of Tennessee Press, 2005.

———. Covenant and Republic: Historical Romance and the Politics of Puritanism. New York: Cambridge University Press, 1996.

Grant, Anne MacVicar. Memoirs of an American Lady: With Sketches of Manners and Scenes in America, as They Existed Prior to the Revolution. 2nd ed. 2 vols. London: Longman, 1809.

Greenfield, Bruce. *Narrating Discovery: The Romantic Explorer in American Literature, 1790–1855.* New York: Columbia University Press, 1992.

Hall, Basil. *Travels in North America in the Years 1827 and 1828.* Edinburgh: Cadell, 1829.

Hall, David D. *Cultures of Print: Essays in the History of the Book.* Amherst: University of Massachusetts Press, 1996.

———. *Worlds of Wonder, Days of Judgment: Popular Belief in Early New England.* Cambridge, MA: Harvard University Press, 1989.

Hamilton, Alexander. *The Itinerarium of Dr. Alexander Hamilton.* In *Colonial American Travel Narratives,* edited by Wendy Martin, 173–327. New York: Penguin, 1994.

Harris, Sharon M., ed. *American Women Writers to 1800.* New York: Oxford University Press, 1996.

———. "Early American Women's Self-Creating Acts." *Resources for American Literary Study* 19, no. 2 (1993): 223–45.

———. "The New-York Magazine: Cultural Repository." In *Periodical Literature in Eighteenth-Century America,* edited by Mark L. Kamrath and Sharon M. Harris, 339–64. Knoxville: University of Tennessee Press, 2005.

Harris, Thaddeus Mason. *Journal of a Tour . . . Northwest of the Alleghany Mountains, 1803. 1805.* In *Early Western Travels 1748–1846,* edited by Reuben Gold Thwaites, 3:307–82. New York, AMS Press, 1966.

Hayes, Kevin J. *A Colonial Woman's Bookshelf.* Knoxville: University of Tennessee Press, 1996.

Hewitt, Elizabeth. *Correspondence and American Literature, 1770–1865.* New York: Cambridge University Press, 2004.

Hogan, Rebecca. "Diarists on Diaries." *a/b: Auto/Biography Studies* 2, no. 2 (1986): 9–14.

———. "Engendered Autobiographies: The Diary as a Feminine Form." In *Autobiography and Questions of Gender,* edited by Shirley Neuman, 95–107. London: Frank Cass, 1991.

Howe, M. A. De Wolfe, ed. *The Articulate Sisters: Passages from Journals and Letters of the Daughters of President Josiah Quincy of Harvard University.* Cambridge, MA: Harvard University Press, 1946.

Hulme, Peter, and Tim Youngs, eds. *The Cambridge Companion to Travel Writing.* New York: Cambridge University Press, 2002.

Hunt, Douglas R. *The Ohio Frontier: Crucible of the Old Northwest, 1720–1830.* Bloomington: Indiana University Press, 1996.

Imbarrato, Susan Clair. *Declarations of Independency in Eighteenth-Century American Autobiography.* Knoxville: University of Tennessee Press, 1998.

———. "Ordinary Travel: Tavern Life and Female Accommodation in Early America and the New Republic." *Women's Studies: An Interdisciplinary Journal* 28 (1998): 29–57.

Irving, Washington. *The Salmagundi Papers* (1801), vol. 18. In *The Works of Washington Irving,* edited by Pierre Monroe Irving. Philadelphia: University Library Association, 1860.

————. *A Tour on the Prairies*. 1835. Norman: University of Oklahoma Press, 1959.

Jefferson, Thomas. *The Papers of Thomas Jefferson*. Edited by Julian P. Boyd et al. 26 vols. to date. Princeton, NJ: Princeton University Press, 1950–.

Johnson, Susan Edwards. "Journal of a journey from Stratford, [Connecticut,] to Fayetteville, N.C., and other places, 1801–1802." Susan Edwards Johnson Papers 1792–1851. 2 boxes. The Connecticut Historical Society Museum, Hartford.

————. "Journal of a trip from Stratford, Connecticut to Fayetteville, North Carolina (1808–1802)." Typescript. Mss. FAR Box 20 (10). Huntington Library, San Marino, California.

————. Letters. 2 boxes. Susan Edwards Johnson Papers, 1792–1851. Connecticut Historical Society, Hartford.

Juster, Susan. "'In a Different Voice': Male and Female Narratives of Religious Conversion in Post-Revolutionary America." *American Quarterly* 41, no. 1 (1989): 34–62.

Kamuf, Peggy. *Fictions of Feminine Desire: Disclosures of Heloise*. Lincoln: University of Nebraska Press, 1982.

Kauffman, Linda S. *Discourses of Desire: Gender, Genre, and Epistolary Fictions*. Ithaca, NY: Cornell University Press, 1986.

Kelley, Mary. *Private Woman, Public Stage: Literary Domesticity in Nineteenth-Century America*. New York: Oxford University Press, 1984.

Kenyon, Olga, ed. *800 Years of Women's Letters*. New York: Penguin, 1992.

Kerber, Linda. *Toward an Intellectual History of Women: Essays by Linda Kerber*. Chapel Hill: University of North Carolina Press, 1997.

————. *Women of the Republic: Intellect and Ideology in Revolutionary America*. Chapel Hill: University of North Carolina Press, 1980.

Kierner, Cynthia A. "Eliza Lucas Pickney." In *Dictionary of Literary Biography: American Women Prose Writers to 1820*, vol. 200, edited by Carla Mulford with Angela Vietto and Amy E. Winans, 278–86. Detroit: Gale Research, 1999.

Kissel, Susan K. "Writer Anxiety versus the Need for Community in the Bottts Family Letters." In *Women's Personal Narratives: Essays in Criticism and Pedagogy*, edited by Leonore Hoffmann and Margo Culley, 48–56. New York: Modern Language Association, 1985.

Knight, Sarah Kemble. *The Journal of Madam Knight* (1704). In *Colonial American Travel Narratives*, edited by Wendy Martin, 51–75. New York: Penguin, 1994.

Kolodny, Annette. Introduction to *The Travel Diary of Elizabeth House Trist: Philadelphia to Natchez, 1783–84*, by Elizabeth House Trist. In *Journeys in New Worlds: Early American Women's Narratives*, edited by William L. Andrews, 183–200. Madison: University of Wisconsin Press, 1990.

————. *The Land Before Her: Fantasy and Experience of the American Frontiers, 1630–1860*. Chapel Hill: University of North Carolina Press, 1984.

————. *The Lay of the Land: Metaphor as Experience and History in American Life and Letters*. Chapel Hill: University of North Carolina Press, 1975.

————. "Letting Go Our Grand Obsessions: Notes toward a New Literary History of the American Frontiers." *American Literature* 64 (1992): 1–18.

Lathrop, Elsie L. *Early American Inns and Taverns.* New York: Blom, 1968.

La Tour du Pin Gouvernet, Herriette Lucie (Dillon). *Memoirs of Madame de La Tour du Pin* (1794). New York: McCall, 1971.

Laurens, Caroline Olivia. "Journal of a Visit to Greenville from Charleston in the Summer of 1825." Annotated by Mrs. Louise C. King. *South Carolina Historical Magazine* 72 (1971): 164–73, 220–33.

Lawrence, Karen R. *Penelope Voyages: Women and Travel in the British Literary Tradition.* Ithaca, NY: Cornell University Press, 1994.

Lewis, Meriwether, and William Clark. *The Journals of Lewis and Clark.* 1904. Edited by John Bakeless. New York: Signet, 2002.

Logan, Lisa M. "'The Ladies in Particular': Constructions of Femininity in the *Gentlemen and Ladies Town and Country Magazine* and the *Lady's Magazine; and Repository of Entertaining Knowledge.*" In *Periodical Literature in Eighteenth-Century America,* edited by Mark L. Kamrath and Sharon M. Harris, 277–306. Knoxville: University of Tennessee Press, 2005.

Lueck, Beth L. *American Writers and the Picturesque Tour: The Search for National Identity.* New York: Garland Press, 1997.

Lyon, Mary. *Mary Lyon through Her Letters.* Edited by Marion Lansing. Boston: Books, Inc., 1937.

Madison, James. *The Writings of James Madison: Comprising His Public Papers and His Private Correspondence, Including Numerous Letters and Documents; Now for the First Time Printed.* Vol. 3, 1783–87. Edited by Gaillard Hunt. New York: G. P. Putnam's, 1900–10.

Marshall, David. "The Problem of the Picturesque." *Eighteenth-Century Studies* 35 (2002): 413–37.

Martin, Wendy. *An American Triptych: Anne Bradstreet, Emily Dickinson, Adrienne Rich.* Chapel Hill: University of North Carolina Press, 1984.

———. Introduction to *The Journal of Madam Knight* (1704). In *Colonial American Travel Narratives,* edited by Wendy Martin, 51–52. New York: Penguin, 1994.

Marx, Leo. *The Machine in the Garden: Technology and the Pastoral Ideal in America.* New York: Oxford University Press, 1964.

———. "Pastoralism in America." In *Ideology and Classic American Literature,* edited by Sacvan Bercovitch and Myra Jehlen, 36–69. Cambridge: Cambridge University Press, 1986.

McNinch, Margorie. Introduction to "Elizabeth Gilpin's Journal of 1830," edited by Margorie McNinch. *Delaware History* 20 (1983): 223–55.

Melton, Jeffrey Alan. *Mark Twain, Travel Books, and Tourism.* Tuscaloosa: University of Alabama Press, 2002.

Michaux, François André. *Travels to the West of the Alleghany Mountains. . . . 1801–1803.* 1805. In *Early Western Travels 1748–1846,* edited by Reuben Gold Thwaites, 3:105–306. New York: AMS Press, 1966.

Micklus, Robert. *The Comic Genius of Dr. Alexander Hamilton.* Knoxville: University of Tennessee Press, 1990.

Mills, Sara. "Written on the Landscape: Mary Wollstonecraft's *Letters Written* during *a Short Residence in Sweden, Norway, and Denmark.*" In *Romantic Geographies: Discourses of Travel,* 1775–1844, edited by Amanda Gilroy, 19–34. New York: Manchester University Press, 2000.

Mulford, Carla, general ed., with Angela Vietto and Amy E. Winans. *Dictionary of Literary Biography: American Women Prose Writers to* 1820. Vol. 200. Detroit: Gale Research, 1999.

————. Introduction to *"The Power of Sympathy" by William Hill Brown and "The Coquette"* by Hannah Webster Foster, edited by Carla Mulford. New York: Penguin, 1996.

Mullan, John, and Christopher Reid, eds. *Eighteenth-Century Popular Culture: A Selection.* New York: Oxford University Press, 2000.

Newton, Lucy. "Memorandum, December 1817, of a Trip from Union, Ohio, to Mechanicksburg, Ohio, and to Anderson Township." Ohio Historical Society, Columbus, VFM 1010.

Norton, Mary Beth. *Liberty's Daughters: The Revolutionary Experiences of American Women,* 1750–1800. Boston: Little, 1980.

Nussbaum, Felicity. "Heteroclites: The Gender of Character in the Scandalous Memoirs." In *The New Eighteenth Century: Theory, Politics, English Literature,* edited by Felicity Nussbaum and Laura Brown, 144–67. New York: Methuen, 1987.

Oberholtzer, Ellis Paxson. *The Literary History of Philadelphia.* 1906. Reprint, Detroit: Gale, 1969.

Parrish, Susan Scott. "Women's Nature: Curiosity, Pastoral, and the New Science in British America." *Early American Literature* 37 (2002): 195–246.

Pennsylvania Gazette, June 5, 1755.

Philadelphia Chronicle, February 9, 1767; August 31–September 7, 1767.

Philyaw, L. Scott. *Virginia's Western Visions: Political and Cultural Expansion on an Early American Frontier.* Knoxville: University of Tennessee Press, 2004.

Pike, Zebulon Montgomery. *Exploratory Travels through the Western Territories of North America . . .* 1805–1807. 1811. Reprint, Denver: W. H. Lawrence, 1889.

Pinckney, Eliza Lucas. *The Letterbook of Eliza Lucas Pinckney,* 1739–1762. Edited by Elise Pinckney. Chapel Hill: University of North Carolina Press, 1972.

Perry, Ruth. *Women, Letters, and the Novel.* New York: AMS Press, 1980.

Pratt, Mary Louise. *Imperial Eyes: Travel Writing and Transculturation.* New York: Routledge, 1992.

Prince, Thomas. *The Vade Mecum for America; or, A Companion for Traders and Travellers.* Boston: N.E. printed by S. Kneeland and T. Green for D. Henchman & T. Hancock, 1732.

Quincy, Maria Sophia. Journal, 3 August–5 September, 1829. Quincy family papers, 1639–1930. Massachusetts Historical Society, Boston.

————. "Sister Sophia: From a Journal of Maria Sophia Quincy, 1829." In *The Articulate Sisters: Passages from Journals and Letters of the Daughters of President Josiah Quincy of Harvard University,* edited by M. A. De Wolfe Howe, 149–89. Cambridge, MA: Harvard University Press, 1946.

Redford, Bruce. *The Converse of the Pen: Acts of Intimacy in the Eighteenth-Century Familiar Letter.* Chicago: University of Chicago Press, 1986.

Rice, Kym S. Early American Taverns: For the Entertainment of Friends and Strangers. Chicago: University of Chicago Press, 1983.

Riley, Glenda. Women and Nature: Saving the "Wild" West. Lincoln: University of Nebraska Press, 1999.

Robinson, Sidney K. Inquiry into the Picturesque. Chicago: University of Chicago Press, 1991.

Robinson, W. Stitt. The Southern Colonial Frontier, 1607–1763. Albuquerque: University of New Mexico Press, 1979.

Rorabaugh, W. J. The Alcoholic Republic: An American Tradition. New York: Oxford University Press, 1979.

Salem Gazette, April 16, 1784; June 15, 1784.

Salinger, Sharon V. Taverns and Drinking in Early America. Baltimore: Johns Hopkins University Press, 2002.

Samuels, Shirley. Romances of the Republic: Women, the Family, and Violence in the Literature of the Early American Nation. New York: Oxford University Press, 1996.

Schaw, Janet. Journal of a Lady of Quality: Being the Narrative of a Journey from Scotland to the West Indies, North Carolina, and Portugal, in the Years 1774 to 1776. Edited by Evangeline Walker Andrews, in collaboration with Charles McLean Andrews. New Haven, CT: Yale University Press, 1923.

Schlissel, Lillian. Women's Diaries of the Westward Journey. New York: Schocken, 1982.

Schoelwer, Susan P., ed. Lions and Eagles and Bulls: Early American Tavern and Inn Signs from the Connecticut Historical Society. Princeton, NJ: Princeton University Press, 2000.

Schriber, Mary Suzanne. Writing Home: American Women Abroad, 1830–1920. Charlottesville: University of Virginia Press, 1997.

Schultz, Christian. Travels on an Inland Voyage through the States of New-York, Pennsylvania, Virginia, Ohio, Kentucky and Tennessee, and through the Territories of Indiana, Louisiana, Mississippi, and New-Orleans; Performed in the Years 1807 and 1808; Including a Tour of nearly Six Thousand Miles. New-York: Isaac Riley, 1810.

Schweitzer, Ivy. The Work of Self-Representation: Lyric Poetry in Colonial New England. Chapel Hill: University North Carolina Press, 1991.

Sears, John F. Sacred Places: American Tourist Attractions in the Nineteenth Century. New York: Oxford University Press, 1989.

Seelye, John. Prophetic Waters: The River in Early American Life and Literature. New York: Oxford University Press, 1977.

Shea, Daniel B., Jr. Introduction to Some Account of the Fore Part of the Life of Elizabeth Ashbridge: Journeys in New Worlds; Early American Women's Narratives, edited by William L. Andrews, 119–46. Madison: University of Wisconsin Press, 1990.

———. Spiritual Autobiography in Early America. Princeton, NJ: Princeton University Press, 1968.

Shields, David S. "British-American Belles Lettres." In The Cambridge History of American Literature: Volume I, 1590–1820, edited by Sacvan Bercovitch, 307–43. New York: Cambridge University Press, 1994.

———. Civil Tongues and Polite Letters in British America. Chapel Hill: University of North Carolina Press, 1997.

Shuffleton, Frank. "The Round Table: Power, Desire, and American Cultural Studies." *Early American Literature* 34 (1999): 94–103.

Sicherman, Barbara. "Sense and Sensibility: A Case Study of Women's Reading in
Later-Victorian America." In *Reading in America: Literature and Social History*, edited
by Cathy N. Davidson, 201–25. Baltimore: Johns Hopkins University Press,
1989.

Slotkin, Richard. *Regeneration through Violence: The Mythology of the American Frontier*,
1600–1860. Middleton, CT: Wesleyan University Press, 1973.

Smith, Sidonie. "The Autobiographical Manifesto: Identities, Temporalities, Politics." In *Autobiography and Questions of Gender*, edited by Shirley Neuman,
186–212. London: Frank Cass, 1991.

———. "Performativity, Autobiographical Practice, Resistance." *a/b: Auto/Biogra-
phy Studies* 10 (1995): 17–33.

Spacks, Patricia Meyer. *Gossip*. New York: Knopf, 1985.

Spengemann, William C. *The Adventurous Muse: The Poetics of American Fiction, 1789–1900*.
New Haven, CT: Yale University Press, 1977.

Stabile, Susan M. *Memory's Daughters: The Material Culture of Remembrance in Eighteenth-
Century America*. Ithaca, NY: Cornell University Press, 2004.

Steele, Timothy. *All the Fun's in How You Say a Thing: An Explanation of Meter and Versification*. Athens: Ohio University Press, 1999.

Stern, Julia A. *The Plight of Feeling: Sympathy and Dissent in the Early American Novel*.
Chicago: University of Chicago Press, 1997.

———. "To Relish and to Spew: Disgust as Cultural Critique in *The Journal of
Madam Knight*." *Legacy* 14, no. 1 (1997): 1–12.

Stockdale, John. *Part of the United States of North America*. London: J. Stockdale, ca.
1798. Harvard College Library, Map Coll (Pusey) MAP-LC, G3700 1798 .S7.

Stout, Janis P. *Through the Window and Out the Door: Women's Narratives of Departure, from
Austen and Cather to Tyler, Morrison, and Didion*. Tuscaloosa: University of Alabama
Press, 1998.

Sumter, Nathalie de Lage. *Fifteen Letters of Nathalie Sumter* (1809). Introduction and
notations by Mary Virginia Saunders White. Columbia, SC: printed for
Gittman's Book Shop by the R. L. Bryan Company, 1942.

Taylor, Alan. *American Colonies*. New York: Viking Press, 2001.

Thompson, Peter. *Rum Punch and Revolution: Taverngoing and Public Life in Eighteenth-
Century Philadelphia*. Philadelphia: University of Pennsylvania Press, 1999.

Thorp, Daniel B. "Taverns and Tavern Culture on the Southern Colonial Frontier:
Rowan County, North Carolina, 1753–1776." *Journal of Southern History* 42
(1996): 661–88.

Thurman, Suzanne. "*O Sisters Ain't You Happy?*": Gender, Family, and Community among the
Harvard and Shirley Shakers, 1781–1918. New York: Syracuse University Press, 2002.

Thwaites, Reuben Gold, ed. *Early Western Travels, 1748–1846*. 32 vols. New York: AMS
Press, 1966.

Tlusty, B. Ann. *Bacchus and Civic Order: The Culture of Drink in Early Modern Germany*. Charlottesville: University Press of Virginia, 2001.

Towner, John. *An Historical Geography of Recreation and Tourism in the Western World, 1540–1940*. New York: John Wiley and Sons, 1996.

Trist, Elizabeth House. *The Travel Diary of Elizabeth House Trist: Philadelphia to Natchez, 1783–84*. Edited by Annette Kolodny. In *Journeys in New Worlds: Early American Women's Narratives*, edited by William L. Andrews, 201–32. Madison: University of Wisconsin Press, 1990.

Ulrich, Laurel Thatcher. *Good Wives: Image and Reality in the Lives of Women in Northern New England, 1650–1750*. New York: Oxford University Press, 1980.

———. *A Midwife's Tale: The Life of Martha Ballard, Based on Her Diary, 1785–1812*. New York: Vintage Press, 1991.

Van Horne, Elizabeth. *Journey to the Promised Land: Journal of Elizabeth Van Horne 1807*. Edited by Elizabeth (Van Horne) Collette. Historical Society of Western Pennsylvania, December 1939.

Verhoeven, W. M. "Land-Jobbing in the Western Territories: Radicalism, Transatlantic Emigration, and the 1790s American Travel Narrative." In *Romantic Geographies: Discourses of Travel, 1775–1844*, edited by Amanda Gilroy, 185–203. New York: Manchester University Press, 2000.

Wall, Helena M. *Fierce Communion*. Cambridge, MA: Harvard University Press, 1990.

Warner, Michael. *The Letters of the New Republic: Publication and the Public Sphere in Eighteenth-Century America*. Cambridge, MA: Harvard University Press, 1990.

Warner, William B. *Licensing Entertainment: The Elevation of Novel Reading in Britain, 1684–1750*. Berkeley and Los Angeles: University of California Press, 1998.

Warren, Mercy Otis. *History of the Rise, Progress and Termination of the American Revolution Interspersed with Biographical, Political and Moral Observations*. 2 vols. Edited and annotated by Lester H. Cohen. 1805. Reprint, Indianapolis: Liberty Fund, 1989.

Watkins, Owen C. *The Puritan Experience: Studies in Spiritual Autobiography*. New York: Schocken, 1972.

Watson, Nicola J. *Revolution and the Form of the British Novel, 1790–1825: Intercepted Letters, Interrupted Seductions*. New York: Oxford University Press, 1994.

Watts, Edward. *An American Colony: Regionalism and the Roots of Midwestern Culture*. Athens: Ohio University Press, 2002.

Welby, Adlard. *A Visit to North America and the English Settlements in Illinois, with a Winter Residence at Philadelphia: Solely to Ascertain the Actual Prospects of the Emigrating Agriculturalist, Mechanic, and Commercial Speculator*. London: Printed for J. Drury, Baldwin, Cradock, and Joy, 1821.

Weld, Isaac. *Travels through the States of North America, and the provinces of Upper and Lower Canada, during the years 1795, 1796 and 1797*. London: Printed for J. Stockdale, 1807.

Wesley, Marilyn C. *Secret Journeys: The Trope of Women's Travel in American Literature*. Albany: SUNY Press, 1999.

Whale, John. "Romantics, Explorers and Picturesque Travelers." In *The Politics of the Picturesque: Literature, Landscape and Aesthetics since 1770*, edited by Stephen Copley and Peter Garside, 175–95. Cambridge: Cambridge University Press, 1994.

Whitehall, Walter Muir. Introduction to *The Letterbook of Eliza Lucas Pinckney, 1739–1762*, edited by Elise Pickney, ix–xiii. Chapel Hill: University of North Carolina Press, 1972.

Wilson, Mona. *These Were Muses*. 1924. Reprint, Port Washington, NY: Kennikat, 1970.

Winans, Robert B. "Bibliography and the Cultural Historian: Notes on the Eighteenth-Century Novel." *Printing and Society in Early America*, edited by William L. Joyce, David D. Hall, Richard D. Brown, and John B. Hench, 174–85. Worchester, MA: American Antiquarian Society, 1983.

Winthrop, John. *The Journal of John Winthrop, 1630–1649*. 2 vols. Edited by Richard S. Dunn, James Savage, and Laetitia Yeandle. Cambridge, MA: Belknap Press, 1996.

Wolf, Edwin, II. *The Book Culture of a Colonial American City: Philadelphia Books, Bookmen, and Booksellers*. New York: Clarendon, 1988.

Wulf, Karin A. "Introduction: Milcah Martha Moore's Book: Documenting Culture and Connection in the Revolutionary Era." In *Milcah Martha Moore's Book: A Commonplace Book from Revolutionary America*, edited by Catherine La Courreye Blecki and Karin A Wulf, 1–57. University Park: Pennsylvania State University Press, 1997.

Zaczek, Barbara Maria. *Censored Sentiments: Letters and Censorship in Epistolary Novels and Conduct Material*. Newark: University of Delaware Press, 1997.

Zagarri, Rosemarie. "The Postcolonial Culture of Early American Women's Writing." In *The Cambridge Companion to Nineteenth-Century American Women's Writing*, edited by Dale M. Bauer and Philip Gould, 19–37. New York: Cambridge University Press, 2001.

———. *A Woman's Dilemma: Mercy Otis Warren and the American Revolution*. Wheeling, IL: Harlan Davidson, 1995.

Ziff, Larzer. *Writing in the New Nation: Prose, Print, and Politics in the Early United States*. New York: Yale University Press, 1991.

Zimmerman, Philip D. "Reading the Signs: An Object History of Tavern Signs from Connecticut, 1750–1850." In *Lions and Eagles and Bulls: Early American Tavern and Inn Signs from the Connecticut Historical Society*, edited by Susan Shoelwer, 22–35. Princeton, NJ: Princeton University Press, 2000.

Zuk, Rhoda, ed. *Catherine Talbot and Hester Chapone*. In *Bluestocking Feminism: Writings of the Bluestocking Circle, 1738–85*, edited by Rhoda Zuk, vol 3. London: Pickering and Chatto, 1999.

INDEX